NUTS AND BOLTS

NUTS AND BOLTS
A Practical Guide to Teaching College Composition

Edited by Thomas Newkirk
UNIVERSITY OF NEW HAMPSHIRE

with contributions by

Patricia A. Sullivan
Rebecca Rule
Susan Wheeler
Donna Qualley
Bruce Ballenger
Jane Harrigan
Elizabeth Chiseri-Strater

Boynton/Cook Publishers, Inc.
Heinemann
Portsmouth, New Hampshire

Boynton/Cook Publishers, Inc.

361 Hanover Street
Portsmouth, NH 03801-3912
Offices and agents throughout the world

We gratefully acknowledge the people who have given their permission to include in this book material written for classes they attended while students at the University of New Hampshire. Every effort has been made to contact copyright holders for permission to reprint borrowed material where necessary, but if any oversights have occurred, we would be happy to rectify them in future printings of this work.

Thanks to the following for permission to include previously printed material:

Page 40: From "Photograph of the Girl." In *The Dead and the Living* by Sharon Olds. Copyright © 1984. Published by Alfred A. Knopf, Inc. Reprinted by permission.

Page 181, Figure 7–1: From *A Community of Writers: Teaching Writing in the Junior and Senior High School* by Steven Zemelman and Harvey Daniels (Heinemann Educational Books, Inc., Portsmouth, NH, 1988). Reprinted by permission.

Library of Congress Cataloging-in-Publication Data
Nuts and bolts : a practical guide to teaching college composition /
   edited by Thomas Newkirk, with contributions by Patricia A. Sullivan
   . . . [et al.].
      ISBN 0–86709–321–8
      1. English language — Rhetoric — Study and teaching.   I. Newkirk,
   Thomas.   II. Sullivan, Patricia A., 1956–
   PE1404.N87   1993
   808'.042'07 — dc20   92–42069
                                                                              CIP

Cover designed by Wladislaw Finne
Printed in the United States of America on acid-free paper
09 10 11 12   EB   17 16 15 14

Contents

Contents

Introduction

Locating Freshman English

Thomas Newkirk

To understand Freshman English[1] at the University of New Hampshire, you need to picture the third floor of Hamilton Smith Hall. It's not easy to get to. The main stairway at the front of the building stops at the second floor. At the beginning of each semester, students mill around the corridors looking for the one poorly marked stairway that reaches the third floor. At the landing of the third floor students for two years had to avoid drip buckets that caught leaks from the roof, repaired only after staff members sent color photos to campus maintenance.

The third floor is a world apart. Most faculty members have never been on it. The offices are a beehive of tiny cubicles occupied by two, sometimes three, instructors or teaching assistants. At about any time of the week students will be sitting outside these offices, stoically waiting for their writing conferences, while the hum of counsel fills the corridors ("I really like the way...." "What point are you making here when you...?" "Sorry, I'm running a little behind....") Between conferences, teachers will walk to

---

[1] The terminology used to describe beginning writing courses is currently in a state of transition. "Freshman English," "Freshman Composition," and "First-Year English" are now used for the course described in this book. We have made no effort to standardize terminology.

the water cooler to joke, commiserate ("If I get another roommate paper . . ."), and swap ideas about teaching.

I want to stress the importance of this water cooler. When I directed the program, visitors would occasionally ask about the curriculum. We had "official" material for them, but I was tempted to suggest they stand by the water cooler, for it was there that the curriculum for the program was made and remade each day. While the directors could sometimes change the guidelines, these changes were given substance (or they were successfully — sometimes wisely — defied) in the casual talk around the water cooler. I came to see this oral culture as the primary form of instruction for new teachers.

But, unfortunately, new teachers cannot stand, indefinitely, by the cooler waiting for the right advice. Teaching is a strange profession because even as a beginner you are often expected to do everything — plan the syllabus, develop daily plans, confer with students, and grade their work. While we use the term "teaching assistant," new teachers in our program assist no one but themselves. So we decided to put together some of the program's folklore for the benefit of new teachers. As director, I knew which of the program's teachers were constantly being "stolen from," and I asked them to write chapters on their areas of expertise. As we read the results, we felt that even experienced teachers could use the book. Previously the folklore had been passed on in bits and pieces; that, after all, is how an oral culture works. In these chapters we saw how each teacher fit practices into a coherent approach. We could now steal more coherently.

The book is not an official curriculum that everyone in the program follows. It is a series of snapshots taken in the early 1990s. It is a dipping into a largely oral culture to describe the range of practices and to bring them into a kind of order. And it too will be added to, modified, and selectively rejected around our water cooler and, we hope, around water coolers in schools across the country.

We have tried to put together a book that is unabashedly practical. We see ourselves and our readers as fellow teachers who roll up our sleeves and teach writing. For me, this interest in the practical comes naturally. My father regularly told the story of how he picked the quotation for his high school yearbook picture. His classmates combed *Bartlett's Quotations* (and the speeches of then-popular Elbert Hubbert) for suitably uplifting statements like "Nothing great was ever done without enthusiasm." My dad chose "Cleanliness pays." This became a family fable, a moral teaching about the value of the seemingly mundane.

The Purification of Freshman English

In this introduction I want to trace the institutional and intellectual developments that led to the snapshots in this book. This look at the central issues in one program can, I think, serve as a case study that illustrates the evolutionary development in composition teaching over the past twenty years. This evolutionary change followed the revolutionary changes of the late 1960s and early 1970s.

The central question in this history is: what is the function of a writing course in the institution that requires it? The United States is, after all, unique among English-speaking countries in requiring college-level writing courses that are separate from academic disciplines. Even the physical location of the third floor at Hamilton Smith Hall, its isolation, its relative inaccessibility, points to this central question—how does a writing course fit in?

To some this is not a serious question. The writing course is designed to help students write in their other courses, enabling teachers in the academic disciplines to teach their subjects without the distracting obligation of teaching writing too (as if discourse and subject content were separable). We are to clear student writing of errors; we are to teach the conventions of academic citation. I kept a file of letters from faculty who complained that we had sent students out unprepared for their courses—consequently the faculty had to "waste" time teaching writing.

I'm sure that administrators and most faculty view the writing course as a service to the academic disciplines. But what happens if those chosen to teach the course come to reject many of the features of academic discourse, particularly the impersonality and exclusivity that seems to characterize much of it? What happens if a writing course pits itself against the institution that surrounds and supports it? Can a writing course in the academy be antiacademic (which is not the same thing as anti-intellectual)? It is this tension—call it the "third-floor problem"—that I will explore here.

The late 1960s and the early 1970s must be seen as a time of fundamental change in the teaching of writing. It was during this period that Donald Murray purified Freshman English at the University of New Hampshire. The change was radical and total. What had been a two-semester course in which students wrote about other texts became a course that focused single-mindedly on the act of writing. The term given to this shift—"teaching the writing process"—did not suggest the full scope of the

3

changes Murray initiated. The concept of "process" was, of course, part of the transformation. Reading finished texts does not reveal the processes that produced the texts. In fact, the finished text is something of an illusion; its very orderliness hides the disorderliness of the creation. Murray argued that we need to let students in on this disorderliness—and he began to formulate (and reformulate, and re-reformulate) the elements or stages of the process.

Yet if this were the major change, it could have been easily assimilated into the course as it stood. Students could have been given more guidance in the process of writing about literary texts (in fact, some of the introductory literature courses have become more process-centered). He was proposing a bigger change than this: he was calling into question the very model of the writer that informed the traditional composition course.

The writer in the traditional course was an initiate into the world of academic discourse, writing about established texts chosen by the instructor. The student was on foreign turf, the teacher's turf. The student was not writing as an expert but as a neophyte, mimicking a language and authority he or she did not possess. In Murray's view this was an inversion of the position of writers outside the academy—where the writer, not the reader, is the expert on the topic.

Murray's truly radical move was not to stress the writing process but to claim that the professional writer should be the ideal around which the course should be constructed. The title of his first and best-known book, *A Writer Teaches Writing* (1968), announced this new ideal. Freshman English, from this time forward, might be technically *in* the English department, but it was no longer *of* it. It looked elsewhere—to established writers—for insights about teaching and learning.

One practical consequence of this transformation was the invitation to students to choose their own topics. Murray assumed that students come to composition classes as experts in some areas of their lives (or willing to become experts about questions that interest them). If they are to write, as writers do, from a wealth of information and from emotional and intellectual commitments to their topics, they need this freedom to pick their own subjects. The writing course was no longer about any specific subject (i.e., literature); it was about a process of making and shaping meaning. In one of many quotations from writers' testimonies, Murray cites James Baldwin on this point:

> One writes out of one thing only—one's own experience. Everything depends on how relentlessly one forces from this experience the last drop, sweet or bitter, it can possibly give. This is the only real concern of the

artist, to recreate out of the disorder of life that order which is art. (Quoted in Murray 1982, 134)

If this was true for the artist, Murray argued, it was true for the student. And because this experience was to be the center of the writing course, Murray, during his short term as director of Freshman English, virtually banished the use of published writing from the course. The texts that mattered now were those that the students were writing—and the texts of their lives from which they drew.

Murray also introduced the conference system to Freshman English and argued that one-to-one meetings between teacher and student should be the central instructional event in a composition course. While the class might be a useful forum for discussing literature, it was not a particularly good place for writers to get the feedback they needed. This feedback would come in weekly or biweekly fifteen- to twenty-minute conferences, which have been a regular feature of our writing courses for the past twenty years.

In his many descriptions of the writing conference Murray is careful to stress the active role of the student. The conference is not a time for mini-lectures or specific direction from the teacher; the student is to be responsible for diagnosing writing problems and offering solutions. The teacher does not absolutely hold back, but his or her role is to comment on the student's comments, to push the student's own analysis. "The instructor and the student earned each other's respect as they worked together, and this relationship did not diminish the authority of the instructor for he re-earned his authority each time he read a student's paper and reacted to it honestly" (Fisher and Murray, 1974, 170).

The writing course that emerged was stripped of much that, in Murray's view, interfered with the act of writing—assignments, a common syllabus, the common reading of published writing, even classes themselves. The first move in the course was to teach students to look within. Using rhetoric that came to be almost automatic in the program, Fisher and Murray wrote:

> We drove students back into themselves, urged them to write what they knew. . . . The range of subject matter was as varied as their backgrounds, experiences, and ambitions. They were minor authorities on their subjects; they were individuals who deserved individual response. And as our students began to discover they had something to say, they began to hear a distinctive voice, their own, saying it. (170)

It was this vision—of students suddenly put in contact with their own lives, their own voices—that energized the Freshman English program (and to a considerable degree still does). Yet within a few years, Murray's reconceptualization began to be challenged in the professional literature and slowly modified within the Freshman English program.

Critiques of "The Writing Process"

As I noted earlier, the writing-process approach at UNH was defined as *in opposition to* writing practices of the university. The term "academic" became a term of disapproval — meaning overly abstract, elitist, dull, pedantic, obscure. The model became the writer who operates outside the university. But in the 1980s, some composition specialists began to reconceptualize the place of composition within the university. This did not mean a return to the writing course as a mere "service" course that took care of mechanical problems, nor a return to the writing course that was really a watered-down literature course. It did mean that "academic" was no longer a term of disapproval; the slowly gained skills of analysis and interpretation came to be viewed as empowering for the student. The awkward early attempts at academic writing were honored as important first steps in this empowerment — and not condemned as pompous, dishonest posturing. Take the following sentence from a student paper:

> As one will notice, the definition of rape has not only become more complicated since its' first upheaval, but the pressures on the victim have also become enhanced.

In *Errors and Expectations* (1977) Mina Shaughnessy taught a generation of composition teachers how to read a sentence like this one. The student is trying a complicated not-only-but-also construction (and seems in control of it). She is also trying on language that doesn't quite fit. "Upheaval" is not quite right, though it does convey the idea of suddenly made visible. "Enhanced" is also close but carries a more positive connotation than the writer probably intended. The solution is not always to urge writers to make it simpler or to avoid words they are not sure of but to encourage the risk taking, the trying on of this new language, even if it leads to some errors.

The most influential articulation of the academic role of a Freshman English course came in David Bartholomae and Anthony Petrosky's *Facts, Artifacts, and Counterfacts* (1986). The image of the writer in their book is vastly different from the one in the early writing-process literature. Murray urged writing teachers to ally themselves with the student — against the academy. Once the student was out from under the shadow of the academy, and in touch with personally meaningful subjects, the struggle with language would have been essentially won. The writer, organically in touch with his or her subject, would discover a voice (and corresponding ease of expression) that would keep writing from becoming a struggle. The struggles and awkwardness of student writers were often the consequence of trying to mimic an inappropriate model.

The teachers in Bartholomae and Petrosky's University of Pittsburgh program did not ally themselves against the academy; the course was designed to "give students access to the language and methods of the academy" (9). Struggle, and the awkwardness and failure that accompany struggle, were inevitable as students tried to appropriate this language because it did not exist neutrally, in some dictionary, available to all. "The acquisition of discourse is like the colonization of another's property, for words are never unclaimed lands awaiting our discovery. They are owned by someone" (McCarthy and Fishman, 1991, 420, summarizing Bakhtin). For Bartholomae and Petrosky, the writing classroom is not a place where the writer is pushed back into a self, but where the self is transformed in the drama of appropriation:

> ...we are presenting reading and writing as a struggle within and against the languages of academic life. A classroom performance represents a moment in which, by speaking and writing, a student must enter a closed community, with its secrets, codes and rituals. The student has to appropriate or be appropriated by a specialized discourse, and he has to do it as though he were easily and comfortably one with his audience, as though he were a member of the academy. And, of course, he is not. (8)

This struggle for a new language is justified by the conceptual control that the academic skills of analysis and interpretation offer the student. They allow students to challenge the "givenness" and literalism they bring with them to the academy and perhaps ultimately to challenge the academy itself.

In addition to its marvelous specificity, *Facts, Artifacts, and Counterfacts* has reopened the question: what is the relationship of a beginning writing course to the discourse of the institution? It presents a considered justification for the writing expectations of the the academy. But one problem with Bartholomae and Petrosky's position is their tendency to treat "the academy" as a unified phenomenon with a relatively uniform language and set of intellectual tools. But if we view the academy as a confederation of discourse communities with a wide variety of language practices, it becomes more difficult to imagine how one course can find the center, the common-ground, in this confederation. The business course wants brevity (time is money) while the literature course wants discursiveness while the psychology course wants the accurate use of terminology—and the list goes on. The academy of *Facts, Artifacts, and Counterfacts* seems, not coincidentally, most like that part of the academy we know best, the liberal arts (or the English department)—or perhaps an idealized version of that part of the institution.

Peter Elbow (1991) has recently raised other questions about the renewed focus on academic discourse. If academic discourse is as exclusive as Bartholomae and Petrosky claim it is—a community with its "secrets, codes and rituals"—shouldn't a writing course focus on more broadly useful abilities, ones not limited to this closed community? If by academic writing we mean the ability to present information, to read critically, and to both render and analyze experience, these can hardly be viewed as confined to a closed community.

Like Murray, Elbow argues that writing programs should not be confined by a concept of academic writing. "Life is long and college is short." Few students will write academic discourse after college; and, even within college, few will enter the kind of academy Bartholomae and Petrosky describe. The course should be open to "nonacademic writing" (like the personal narrative—writing that renders experience); being encouraged to make this kind of personal investment, students may develop the lifelong habit of *wanting* to write.

Yet despite real differences between the Pittsburgh course and the one described in this book, both attempt to reconcile the pedagogical revolt of the late 1960s with institutional expectations for a writing course. Both might be viewed as reactions to or revisions of the purified writing course.

To my mind, the most compelling critique of early writing-process descriptions centers on the seeming lack of instructional focus. In *Research on Written Composition* (1986), George Hillocks challenges the effectiveness of the strategies he calls "natural process," a term that Murray, Elbow, and others in this classification would oppose. According to Hillocks the natural process approach is characterized by striving for very general objectives (increasing fluency), writing for peers, and revising written work. Hillocks argues that the natural process pedagogy is inferior to what he calls the "environmental approach," which has clear and specifiable objectives and in which "materials and problems [are] selected to engage students with each other in specifiable processes important to some particular aspect of writing" (122). Elsewhere I have questioned whether experimental research provides the sound support for the environmental approach that Hillocks claims it does (Newkirk, 1987). Nevertheless, Hillocks does point to a problematic assumption that underlies much of the rhetoric of the writing process—the assumption of latent fluency.

In the archetypal writing-process story a student comes into our class with a history of past failure. To add to the drama, the student's early attempts are described as dismal. With the encouragement of the teacher, the student begins to write on a topic of deep personal interest and importance and suddenly there is an eloquence and power that the writer's early work did not even suggest. This fluency was latent, suppressed. The teacher did not teach this fluency but created conditions, particularly a relationship of trust, that enabled the writer to dip into this rich territory.

Some cognitive researchers (like Hillocks) would find this assumption entirely too mystical. Proponents of academic literacy may dismiss it as irrelevant to the task of mastering the discourse of the academy. But I have seen it happen too often to dismiss it. And I feel that it is pedagogically healthy to assume that all students can produce writing that is genuinely effective and not simply a fair approximation of someone else's language.

Still, the latency assumption cannot explain how students can move into new territory. When students do write with newfound authority and power, they are often using discourse forms they have heard or read. They have schemas, internalized patterns—usually forms of narration—for rendering their accounts. Even the student who is "freewriting" will often draw on these patterns. But what if the student is asked to produce a type of writing that is less familiar, one for which the writer does not have a strong intuitive sense of form? What happens, for example, when a student is asked to write an extended analysis or argument? At points like these, the writer often needs the structured assistance of Hillocks's environmental model.

The writing-process approach that we describe in this book has certainly not abandoned a belief in latency or in that fluency that comes when writers are emotionally and intellectually connected with their topics. But at the same time, it is not as passive as the "natural process" pedagogy that Hillocks criticizes. The dozens of writing exercises described in this book are precisely focused; the conferences and evaluation systems are carefully structured to teach students to comment on their work; the chapters on the research paper and on writing about literature provide careful and thoughtful guidance for the student, who is often working in new territory. This is not "hands-off teaching" that merely frees the student to discover an inner self. It is hard and careful work.

Thomas Newkirk

Questions About Purification — A Personal Story

I began teaching in the Freshman English program in 1977. Previously I had taught at the University of Texas, where the course had been laid out for me. As I recall, it was a combination of modes and aims arranged in a sequence that began with a classification paper and worked toward an evaluation paper. There was little time for revision. All papers were graded. During class time we discussed essays (the reader was chosen for us), or I explained points from the rhetoric textbook we were all expected to use. This approach came to be stigmatized as the "current traditional paradigm" — but whatever its faults, it did provide a measure of security for new teachers (and perhaps students).

From this highly structured program I moved to one of almost intimidating freedom. No common syllabus. No types of required writing. No common texts for the program. No grades on individual papers. The only firm guidelines were that students write five pages per week and that we meet with them each week for a one-to-one conference. This was Murray's purified Freshman English course.

As a beginning teacher in this program, I found the freedom both exhilarating and frustrating. The students clearly wrote better because they were given choices of topics; at Texas they were always trying to figure out how to fit the requirements of the mode for that week. But it was difficult to discover, in all this freedom, the conceptual guidance for constructing a *course.* Most skill courses (swimming, skiing, photography) move from less complex to more complex tasks; there is a developmental principle, a theory of difficulty, that underlies the progression. But if assignments themselves are an unwarranted and counterproductive assertion of teacher power, any sense of *sequence* seems to go out the window.

The insistence on student choice also came to seem limiting. How can students choose the unfamiliar? I found that, given a free choice of topics, students regularly chose to work in narrative structures with which they felt comfortable. Within these structures I could work with them on detail, focus, use of dialogue, incorporating reflection into the narrative. But without some push from me (i.e., some assignment) they would not spontaneously attempt a movie review or a profile or an argument or a research paper. So students were choosing, but too often they were choosing within the narrow perimeter of the known and the comfortable.

Finally, the exclusion of reading seemed to empty the course of intellectually engaging material. While I agreed that the primary texts should be the students' own writing, there were strong reasons to bring in other read-

10

ing as well. For one, students need to develop their ability to read texts that are more difficult than their classmates are likely to write. Outside reading is also necessary to bring into the classroom diverse, even discordant voices. There are extremes of experience that students may not confront if they only read the work of their peers (though they will find some extremes there). Particularly at a school like ours, which does not have a diverse student body, and in which most freshman sections are made up primarily of eighteen-year-olds, there is a need to move outside the range of experience that students can, to use their own term, "identify with." Reading becomes a vicarious encounter with "the other," new territory that students can write about.

Over the past fifteen years, directors of the program have worked to reintroduce many of the elements that had been eliminated from it—but to do so in a way that allowed students to retain the authority so critical to the major shift of the early 1970s. I know that we all felt the delicacy of this position. There were two significant changes to the guidelines that directors introduced to clarify (and extend) the expectations for the course. One was the requirement for a research paper, the other a requirement for reading-response papers. The current guidelines, though still terse, suggest a general progression:

> Typically, writing in the first part of the course focuses on the student's experience, recollections, and observations. There is a shift in the second part of the course to types of writing that are not *directly* about the self (research, analysis of reading). But ultimately we want the student to see that all good writing is personal—it begins and is sustained by the writer's personal connection with the material.

This explanation attempts to accommodate the individualistic core of writing-process pedagogy with a developmental principal that qualifies the radical freedom of earlier course descriptions. Patricia Sullivan's chapter describes a sequence comprising three composing cycles—the first on writing a personal essay, the second on writing about reading, and the third on writing the research paper. Not all teachers in the program follow this model (for example, Donna Qualley describes how she uses reading *throughout* her course), but it does provide an instructive example for thinking about sequence.

This general progression, like that in the course developed at the University of Pittsburgh, suggests a "turn" toward what is generally called expository writing—and negotiating that turn is a key challenge. The mere mention of the "research paper" (or worse, "term paper") evokes memories of obligatory note cards, arcane bibliographies, and estimating space for footnotes at the bottom of the page. Worse still, there is the danger of a reversion to the evacuated style that teachers in our program work so hard to counteract.

There is also a conceptual problem about integrating a research requirement into a composition course. Typically we do research from a base of knowledge about the general field in which our question is located. In fact it is difficult to imagine how we *could* research a question without some sense of the lay of the land. In a traditional academic subject the required readings and lectures provide (at least in theory) the context for a research project. But how can a writing instructor expect students to master the context, and pose and research a question, all within a three- or four-week period?

Over a number of years, with Bruce Ballenger leading the way, the program began to view this paper not as the kind of heavily documented paper we find in the writing handbooks, but as an investigatory paper. Library resources play their part, but students are encouraged (and in some cases required) to include their own experiences and interview information. This semester, one of my students wrote on tattooing; he described his own experience of getting a tattoo, provided background on the extent and techniques of tattooing in this country (e.g., more women are getting tattoos these days), and interviewed the owner of a shop—who had his name (Hobo) tattooed on the inside of his lower lip. This personal connection with the material was the link with the earlier writing in the semester.

Similarly, the requirement for a response-to-reading paper (or papers) pushed the staff to develop ways of integrating this assignment into the course. Again the danger was a regression to the boilerplate five-paragraph theme writing many of our students learn in high school. The requirement itself is purposely vague:

> [Students] should have the experience of writing about reading (fiction, essays, or nonfiction). They should have the experience of making observations or raising questions about a text—and then exploring these observations or questions. Instructors may choose to have students write one of their five-page papers about a text, or they may choose to have students write a number of shorter responses.

Teachers in the program are encouraged to find their own strategies for meeting this objective. Sue Wheeler sets up groups in her class and has each group focus on a particular author; in addition to writing about the work of that author, the group members make a presentation to the class. Other teachers may have students highlight passages that puzzle them and then write journal entries exploring this puzzlement. In general, the teaching staff has not viewed this writing as an introduction to a particularized academic discourse. We do not, for example, teach literary terms. We typically try to show students that they possess a language that they can use to talk about texts. Donna Qualley's chapter in this book will show a variety of other ways in which this colloquial language can be a resource for engaging with texts.

Other chapters in this book reflect what I call "bottom up" changes, ones initiated by staff members that are becoming part of the lore of practice. One change is the increasing emphasis on the discourse of self-assessment. While teachers have traditionally urged students to comment on their own writing in writing conferences, current approaches formalize this expectation. Students often evade the opening question asking them to evaluate their own paper. They say something like "It could use more detail" (safe ground here—freshmen think we have an insatiable desire for detail). Becky Rule presents an approach that requires students seriously to consider the strengths and weaknesses of their own work.

In many sections, students use the discourse of self-assessment when they turn in their portfolios. Traditionally, the portfolio in our program was a folder of the student's best work that would be turned in for a grade. More recently, instructors have asked students to include more in that folder (e.g., pieces of informal in-class writing; writing they have done for themselves; significant writing in other courses; perhaps writing they did in previous courses). This wider set of writing then becomes the text for student commentary. Elizabeth Chiseri-Strater describes ways in which the portfolio can engage students in a reflective look at their own literate development.

Finally, there is the question of errors. Traditionally, composition teaching was pathologically focused on errors, so those advocating a more comprehensive view of the writing process typically argued that teachers should deal with errors in the context of a student's paper—and then only in the editing stage. A premature concern for error inhibited the composing process, directing attention away from more global concerns. Such was the new orthodoxy.

But in practice this new approach created such a small window of attention that it was difficult to deal with student errors (or even sentences) in a systematic or sustained way. It was very easy "not to get around to" mechanical problems. And, as Jane Harrigan argues, students are interested in learning the conventions of written language. Those who are unsure of sentence boundaries, who place commas when they take a breath, feel an underlying insecurity when they write. Students appreciate Mina

13

Shaughnessy's (1977) assertion that errors are "unintentional and unprofitable intrusions upon the consciousness of the reader" (12) (and, one might add, they intrude upon the writer as well). Harrigan suggests numerous engaging possibilities for helping students get inside their sentences.

Many of these recent changes in the course have moved it toward some of the long-standing institutional goals. Yet I like to think of Freshman English as not fully integrated into the academy—set off, as it is, on the third floor. At its best it is a burr under the saddle, a point of critique. Linda Brodkey (1987) has written that the academy (to the extent we can speak of it as a unity) has a limited tolerance for human stories. I have even heard of English departments—which owe their existence to the power of stories—that have tried to outlaw narratives in Freshman English. The academy that freshmen see is often large, impersonal, and alienating. Students are taught and tested "objectively." They make few decisions in their learning. A good writing course can stand in opposition to this prevailing pattern, emphasizing the integrity and significance of students' lived experience.

I like to see writing teachers in league with other faculty who manage to overcome the passivity, the pseudo-objectivity, of many introductory courses. I keep coming back to a paper written by a Freshman English student several years ago. It's titled "Philosophy Is Messing Up My Life" and begins with the anxiety the writer felt about taking an introductory philosophy course. The professor at first appeared intimidating, with "a strong philosophical nose, and eyes that could eat a question mark right through you." When the roll was called, the writer could barely manage an audible "here." Once the class began the student opened his notebook and expected the professor to begin by providing a definition of philosophy. He didn't. Instead, he asked questions that showed, in the student's words, that philosophy is "a process of questioning and answering things you don't understand in an attempt to arrive at the 'right answer' which usually doesn't exist anyway." This process of questioning has taken hold and started to "mess up [his] life." He writes:

> I started out by asking questions about life. I've come up with some disturbing answers. . . . The reason I called this paper "Philosophy Is Messing Up My Life" is because most of my answers make me look bad. Realizing that I have a philosophy has opened up a new world that I never knew existed. I'm not sure I'm ready for truth yet. But I've made truth my responsibility. . . .

It's this kind of engaged "here" that we're after.

References

Bartholomae, David, and Anthony Petrosky, eds. 1986. *Facts, Artifacts, and Counterfacts: Theory and Method for a Reading and Writing Course.* Portsmouth, NH: Boynton/Cook.

Brodkey, Linda. 1987. "Writing Ethnographic Narratives." *Written Communication* 4:25–50.

Elbow, Peter. 1991. "Reflections on Academic Discourse: How It Relates to Freshmen and Colleagues." *College English* 53:135–55.

Fisher, Lester, and Donald Murray. 1973. "Perhaps the Teacher Should Cut Class." *College English* 35:169–73.

Hillocks, George. 1986. *Research on Written Composition: New Directions for Teaching.* Urbana, IL: National Council of Teachers of English/ERIC Clearing House on Reading and Communication Skills.

McCarthy, Lucille P., and Stephen Fishman. 1991. "Boundary Conversations: Conflicting Ways of Knowing in Philosophy and Interdisciplinary Research." *Research in the Teaching of English* 25:419–68.

Murray, Donald M. 1982. *Learning by Teaching: Selected Articles on Writing and Teaching.* Portsmouth, NH: Boynton/Cook.

———. 1968. *A Writer Teaches Writing: A Practical Method of Teaching Composition.* Boston: Houghton Mifflin.

Newkirk, Thomas. 1987. Review of *Research on Written Composition: New Directions for Teaching* by George Hillocks. *Teachers College Record* 89:155–57.

Shaughnessy, Mina. 1977. *Errors and Expectations: A Guide for the Teacher of Basic Writing.* New York: Oxford University Press.

1

Charting a Course in First-Year English

Patricia A. Sullivan

WHEN I first meet with new teaching assistants before the start of fall semester, I tell them that the philosophy driving the University of New Hampshire's Freshman English program brings good news and bad news. The good news is that the TA's get to design the course themselves—creating their own writing exercises and assignments, selecting their own reading materials, constructing their own syllabi, deciding on evaluation criteria, etc. The bad news is that they get to design the course themselves—creating their own writing exercises and assignments, selecting their own reading materials, constructing their own syllabi. . . .

Many composition programs in this country require new teachers to adopt the same textbook and to work from a syllabus that has been planned in advance. In such programs, teachers bring their own personality and experience to a curriculum that is otherwise uniform across individual sections. At UNH, on the other hand, even textbooks and course design are left to the discretion of the individual teacher. It's probably only a coincidence that "Live Free or Die" is emblazoned on New Hampshire license plates, but our composition program does grant extraordinary freedom and autonomy to its new teachers. The directors of our writing program over the last twenty years have all subscribed to the belief that student writers gain most from an instructor who has been personally involved in planning his or her course from the very beginning. Such freedom is quickly experienced by many new TA's as a mixed blessing, however. The prospect of planning a fifteen-week course that one has never taught before is both liberating and daunting.

New teachers in our program are not expected to "invent" a composition course *ex nihilo*. A packet of materials, including guidelines, sample syllabi, and suggested textbooks and anthologies, is sent to all new teachers well in advance of fall semester to help them prepare and plan their courses. From the guidelines, TA's know they are expected to teach three components of the program: the writing process, the reading process, and the research paper. They will ask for five pages of writing a week, meet regularly with their students in conferences, and schedule time for students to read and respond to one another's drafts. They know their students will practice planning, drafting, revising, and editing; will learn various ways to read and respond to other texts and to other writers; will learn how to search for information, locate library resources, and weave their own developing ideas with those of other authors. Their students will be encouraged to find their own voices but to gauge the effect of their words on an audience; to experiment with style but to respect convention; to discover meaning in their personal experiences but to use these insights to engage the discourses of others in the university and in the culture at large. The teachers know, finally, that they must transcribe these general guidelines — this amalgam of departmental philosophy, composition theory, and practical advice — into a syllabus, a plan of action. But here lies the rub. Even with the help of sample syllabi, the new teachers must generate a plan of action before they have participated in the action itself. They must navigate a voyage that they have not yet embarked upon, equipped only with the charts of more experienced travelers.

My purpose in this chapter is to "think through" a first-year writing course with new teachers, to translate the surface features of a syllabus into their underlying purposes and principles. I will focus on the first five weeks of the course, when I take my students through the elements and stages of the writing process that will set other elements in motion for the rest of the term. What follows is a way of thinking about teaching writing rather than a prescription for what teachers ought to do day by day. My hope, in fact, is that new teachers reading over my shoulder will be able to adapt and revise the specific features of my course as they go along, inserting their own ideas and strategies wherever their own practices will better help them meet their own or their department's curricular objectives.

Plotting a Course

One of the keys to planning a course in composition, I'm convinced, is to think of the course as a whole at the outset, that is, to think of the processes of reading and writing that we teach as a complex but coherent pattern composed of an interlocking chain of events. What lends a pattern to these myriad activities and events are our objectives—our aims and purposes in teaching. Some teachers frame their objectives in terms of critical thinking: they assign increasingly challenging pieces of reading and writing to expand their students' cognitive and rhetorical capacities for invention, analysis, and argument across a range of academic fields and genres. Other teachers take as their principal objective students' active understanding and appreciation of good writing: literary and nonliterary works as well as students' own writing are used to help students explore, practice, and refine the creative and communicative possibilities of the written word. Still other teachers build their courses around a specific set of social issues or theme: students read and write to explore firsthand the various perspectives that can be brought to bear on a social problem or cultural phenomenon and to locate their own positions among those they and their classmates have constructed as a community of writers and thinkers.

Over the years, I've revised my own objectives many times, taking into account developments in composition theory and research, the particular institutional setting in which I was teaching at the time, and my own evolving beliefs as a teacher. In the current course I teach, my implicit goal is to expand my students' ways of seeing as readers and writers—to make visible, to unsettle, and to augment their customary habits of thinking and expression so that they may become more active and reflective participants in the various cultures that comprise their world. My course is thus informed, to some extent, by all three of the objectives I have sketched above. The main point I wish to emphasize here, however, is that by formulating our purposes and aims in advance of whatever other planning we do, we can help transform what might otherwise be construed as a series of unconnected acts of reading and writing into a unified sequence, into segments and links of a larger pattern. And the better we are able to articulate our objectives to ourselves, the better we are able to convey a strong sense of purpose and commitment to our students—many of whom are taking our courses, as they will almost too readily admit, merely because composition is a university requirement. Our objectives can help us to erase the "merely" from our students' minds, to put our students in charge of their own literacies and learning.

While I'm convinced that it is important to think of the course as a whole at the outset, this whole can only be "seen," I am also convinced, in terms of its parts. In this sense, the course we are teaching mimics the very subject we are teaching—composition. We have to imagine a product (or outcome) in terms of its constituent processes and stages, allowing new insights to emerge as we proceed. In preparing a fifteen-week course, I find it helpful to divide the semester into three five-week segments and to see each segment as a minicourse that focuses on one of the three major processes I am teaching: writing, reading, and research. The structural image I have in mind for the course is not three distinct lines but a single spiral with three loops. The focus of the first five-week loop is writing, the focus of the second is reading, and the focus of the third is research. The second and third loops each retrace, but at a higher level, the writing (and reading) experiences that students have practiced in the previous five weeks.

In the first five weeks, students explore and practice what we have come to regard as the basic elements or stages of the writing process: prewriting, drafting, and revision. They freewrite; brainstorm; compose drafts of a personal-experience essay in response to a topic that I give them; share their drafts with others in the class; compose short reflective pieces in which they analyze their own writing; revise their drafts; workshop them again; and hand them in. They then repeat the entire process; only this time they choose the topics and modes for their essays, and the "pace" of the process is quickened; the turnaround time for the second essay is somewhat shorter.

The next five-week segment of the course focuses on reading. Students practice the same writing processes (planning, shaping, workshopping, revising, and reflecting) they worked on in the first five weeks; only now, the texts they are writing are transactions with the texts they are reading, and their reflective essays take into account both the comments of other students in the class and the voices and ideas of the authors with whom they are engaged, dialogically, in their essays.

When students enter the third and last loop of the spiral, the research process, they have already been practicing writing, revision, and reflection for ten weeks, and writer-reader transactions — processes of interpretation, imitation, appropriation, response, and criticism — for five weeks. They are now poised to do research, to view themselves as agents or makers of knowledge. They choose both the topics and the sites of their inquiry. They formulate an issue or problem in which they are personally invested as a result of previous work in my class or another class they are taking, and they explore and/or attempt to solve the problem through methods they have selected from a range of research strategies. I ask them to locate at least three sources in the library as supports or foils to their hypotheses, but they are otherwise free to conduct surveys, interviews, case studies—whatever methods they need to accomplish their research. The three-part structure of my course is both sequential and recursive. Each exercise and assignment imparts new skills by building on what has come before it, but each also anticipates what is still to come. One of the freewritings my students do in the first week of class, for example, will become the point of comparison for a freewriting in the fifth week. And the collecting exercise they do in the third week will help many to generate topics for their research essays. Throughout the semester, I frequently remind students of where we have been, both theoretically and practically, as we move on — to new readings, new assignments, new lessons. I try to make the emerging structure of the course visible to the students themselves.

The following outline lists the topics and assignments for the first five weeks of my course as they appear on my syllabus. The schedule is based on two class meetings a week, each lasting an hour and a half. I should point out that I do not require a composition textbook in my course, preferring to assemble course materials from a variety of sources, including the work of former students who have given me permission to photocopy drafts, finished essays, and journal entries.

Schedule

Week One: Beginnings

Sept. 5 Tu	Introduction
	Assignment: Read Macrorie's "The Poisoned Fish" and "The Language in You"
7 Th	Discussion of Macrorie; freewriting; overview of writing process
	Assignment: Write personal-experience essay (4–5 pages)

Week Two: A Sense of Audience

Sept. 12 Tu	Freewriting; workshop: sharing writing; reflective writing
	Assignment: Reflect on writing process (2 pages) Read Murray's "Internal Revision"
14 Th	Seminar on revision; in-class exercise on revision [Conferences]
	Assignment: Revise personal-experience essay (make 3 copies)

Write reflections on revision seminar in notebook

Week Three: Revising and Collecting

Sept. 19 Tu   Freewriting; revision workshop (descriptive responding)

Assignment: Write final draft of essay

21 Th   Final draft of essay due; class workshop on effective writing [Conferences]

Assignment: Write reflections on workshop in notebook
Collect ideas to write about

Week Four: Beginning Again

Sept. 26 Tu   Workshop on possible paper topics

Assignment: Begin writing new essay (aim for 5 pages)

28 Th   Sharing workshop: essays in progress; finding a lead and focusing your writing

Assignment: Complete essay (make 1 copy)

Week Five: Back to the Future, or, Revising and Reenvisioning

Oct. 3 Tu   Revision workshop (descriptive responding)

Assignment: Revise essays to hand in
Reflect on writing process (2 pages)

5 Th   Final draft of essay due; discussion: tying the course together [Conferences]

Freewriting; comparing freewritings of Sept. 7 and Oct. 5

Reading and discussion: Olds's "Photograph of a Girl"

Assignment: Write reflective essay (2–3 pages) on changing perceptions

Write (1 page) in notebooks about what you "see" in photograph to be distributed

Week One: Beginnings

Let me confess right away that I used to approach the first day of class full of eager anticipation mixed with a heavy dose of stage fright. In retrospect, I think the set of rituals I planned so carefully ahead of time were as much for my benefit as for my students'. I would introduce myself, call the roll, ask students about their backgrounds and academic interests as I read their names, distribute and read aloud my syllabus, and then say, with all the hope and cheer and promise I could muster in my voice, "See you tomorrow." As I walked out of the classroom, I felt relieved, to be sure. I had taken care of business, down to the last detail. But I also felt that something, some connection, was missing.

In *The Making of Meaning* (1981), Ann Berthoff offers a maxim that has come to have, for all its apparent simplicity, a profound effect on my own teaching: "Begin with where they are" (9). When I used to simply get down to business on the first day of class, calling the roll and eliciting from my students what amounted to their name, rank, and social security number, I missed the opportunity to learn more about where my students *were* as writers. I didn't give my students a chance to talk about their previous experiences with reading and writing, their attitudes toward writing, their self-perceptions as writers, their goals.

To begin with where our students are means, I think, that we give our students the chance to teach us about their personal literacies — the extent to which reading and writing are a part of their lives and the importance they attach to each. I now adopt Berthoff's maxim, beginning with the first day of class, to find out as much as I can about my students' reading and writing experiences both in and out of school. I learn the names of texts they've recently read, the kinds of texts they most often read, the kinds of texts they find the most and least accessible, their favorite and least favorite reading materials. I learn similar things about their writing: what they like to write, how often they write, what kinds of writing they did in high school classes or on the job, how good or bad they think their writing is, and why they think so. To begin with where our students are is to enlist our students' help in building the foundation for the course we are about to teach. Their literacies rather than our agendas become the point of departure for the journey we are about to embark on together.

There are numerous ways to find out about students' personal literacies. Some teachers I know have students pair off and interview each other, thereafter reporting to the class what they've learned. My own strategy is less imaginative perhaps, but it fulfills its purpose: I pass out note cards and ask students to write down their responses to a series of prompts I give them; then they use their notes to introduce themselves. (I collect these cards at the end of class because they help me to acquaint myself with individual students before our first conference.) A dialogue between and among students inevitably replaces the first few "monologues" as students identify with one another's high school experiences, discover mutual likes and dislikes, and ask each other questions to explore other common interests and points of intersection. When the last student introduces herself or himself, I reintroduce myself and share some of my own personal literacies (my addiction to the morning newspaper, for example, and my fondness for writing letters to friends that explore the limits of nonsense). I then continue the conversation by distributing the syllabus and weaving students' own experiences and expectations into my discussion of our course objectives and philosophy. As we cover practical matters like writing assignments and deadlines, classroom and conferencing procedures, formatting requirements for papers, and evaluation criteria, I point out how each of these turns on the students' active involvement and participation in the class; I emphasize that they have the major role, and the major responsibility, for shaping the course and making it work to their ends.

The syllabus lists an initial assignment that throws the ball squarely into the students' court. They will read Ken Macrorie's "The Poisoned Fish" (1970) and "The Language in You" (1968).

I like beginning our second class meeting with Macrorie, with the chapters he has written for both his high school and college textbooks, because he speaks in students' own terms. *He* begins where they are. And *they*, I have discovered, are more than eager to talk about the personal wells of experience and frustration that he taps. When students read Macrorie, they discover a writing teacher who is on their side. He tells them it is possible to recover and cherish their own voices against the "phony and pretentious" language of the schools. He dubs fancy but ultimately empty academic language "Engfish," a coinage he attributes, significantly, to one of his students. My students, in turn, share stories about good and bad teachers, about being corrected rather than heard, about Engfish they have encountered or have been compelled to write, about writing blocks and internal censors and seemingly impenetrable rules. Because Macrorie understands and begins where students are, he is able to stir them, like no other writing teacher I know of in print, to reclaim writing for their own. When my students read Macrorie, they want to write; they are eager to try their hand at composing again. And they want to write well. Macrorie not only gets students talking about the individual processes and institutional contexts that engender or inhibit writing; he elicits students' own perceptions of what makes writing "good" and "bad." He addresses students as writers, but engages their sensibilities as readers as well. Macrorie thus helps me to set the stage in my own course, a stage where students will be both the principal actors and audience. Our discussion of Macrorie forms a bridge between the first day of class, when we discussed personal literacies, and the remainder of the course, when we will build on those literacies.

Since students are eager to write, to try their hand again, that's exactly what they do. I briefly introduce the concept of freewriting to those in the class who are unfamiliar with the term (increasingly, I find, students are doing freewritings in high school), and set them freewriting in their notebooks for five minutes ("whatever comes to mind," "write as much as you can," "don't bother to correct or revise — just write"). I tell them afterward that we will devote five to ten minutes each day to freewriting, sometimes in response to prompts I give them, other times about whatever is on their minds at the moment.

I follow the first freewriting with a second, focused freewriting, asking them to record their first impressions of UNH — as many thoughts and observations as they can — in ten minutes. (This early piece of writing in their notebooks will resurface, and become important again, weeks later; it is one of the links in my course, connecting their earlier and later perceptions of the university, their different "ways of seeing.") When ten minutes are over, I call on some students to share what they've written, and I invite others to compare their own impressions and observations. Students usually write about the visual appearance or size of the campus, their initial reactions to roommates, classes, and teachers, and their opinions of dorms, dining-hall food, bookstores, and registration lines. We also talk about the amount of text each was able to compose in ten minutes and what their freewritings look like: some students will end up with a paragraph, others with several pages. Some writings are arranged in paragraphs, each with its own topic sentence; others are written in a single chunk and are full of arrows, erasures, crossed-out phrases, sentence fragments, and free associations. We merge the two discussions, of content and form, to talk about their writing processes — about differences and similarities in their perceptions of the university (what they chose to write about) and the extent to which each was actually able to generate prose when given the opportunity to write without having to pay heed to inner critics or censors or internalized rules. I help them connect this piece of writing to the issues we discussed in our reading of Macrorie, and I use it to present an overview of elements of the writing process we will practice in the next few weeks — generating and developing material, drafting, workshopping, revising, and so on.

At the end of class, I distribute the following assignment:

Patricia A. Sullivan

Personal-Experience Essay

For this writing assignment, I'd like you to recall an experience you've had in the last two years or so that strikes you as particularly significant, one that has changed the way you are or the way you think about things. I want you to describe this experience as completely as you can, providing your readers with all the details they'll need to understand what happened. When you've finished telling us what happened, reread your essay to be sure you've explained how and why this experience was a "significant" one, that is, how and why it affected you as it did. Your essay should be about four or five pages long.

This is a rough draft, not a finished paper, which means that you can go back and change things later. In fact, you will be given several opportunities to revise this essay. For now, work toward a complete essay but not necessarily a polished one.

The topic of this first essay is open in the sense that students choose the event they want to write about, but the event must have personal significance or a lasting meaning, which the act of writing will help them explore. I tell students that in our next class meeting, they will break into groups of three and will read their drafts aloud to the other two members of their group.

Week Two: A Sense of Audience

We begin the second week of class with a "warm-up" freewriting on anything the students want to write about. I do a freewriting along with the students and then read mine to the class, its flaws, missteps, and restarts intact. I invite others, when I've finished, to read theirs. In my ten years of teaching, this invitation has yet to go unanswered: there are always students who can outfreewrite me and who are eager to give their teacher her writerly comeuppance. And many times a student will freewrite about an experience or issue she wants to take up with others in the class. But the main purpose in reading my own freewriting aloud is to help break the ice for the sharing workshop that's about to take place.

After our warm-up freewriting, I break the class of twenty-four into groups of three (alphabetically, using the class roster) and ask each member of the group to take a turn reading his or her personal-experience essay to the other two members of the group, whose only job is to listen. The classroom quickly fills with noise as eight writers simultaneously read their work to two listeners. Rather than join one of the groups, I stay at my seat and write as I listen to their voices, occasionally glancing around the room to observe the various readers and their audience.

I can't overemphasize the importance and value of this initial exercise in sharing, which, like many of the workshops I now use in my course, I've borrowed from Peter Elbow and Pat Belanoff's *Sharing and Responding* (1989). First of all, this workshop serves as a much-needed icebreaker for students, transforming a class of twenty-four students just getting their bearings in the university into a community of writers practicing their craft. Most students are afraid or at least hesitant to share their writing with their peers. This exercise helps them get beyond this fear by confronting it directly—within a context that is utterly safe. As a writer reads her draft aloud, her voice melds with those of seven other classmates reading their essays, and she knows she will receive no criticism whatsoever from her listeners (unless of course she specifically asks for their comments and suggestions). This early workshop not only helps to familiarize students with workshopping itself—one of the staples of my course—but forges an atmosphere of support and respect among the students as it prepares them for the more interactive workshops that will occur later on. Secondly, students are reading their writing to actual, utterly attentive listeners– to a real audience. Their readings are met with occasional sighs, nods, laughter, groans, expletives, and in some cases, blank stares and fidgeting as their listeners register their honest reactions to the story they're hearing and to the meaning it has for the writer. As I've watched students reading their drafts aloud, I've noticed that a writer will often pause to correct an error or rewrite a phrase so that it "sounds" better, will interject that "this part still needs some work," or will announce, several pages into the story, "maybe I should have just started here." In short, this workshop helps to instill in students an early consciousness of audience, an awareness of the social nature of writing even when the topic of their writing is a personal experience. It situates students not only as writers reading their work but as writers listening to two other writers at work. Each is attuned to the piece of writing *as* a piece of writing, tacitly noting elements and features that strike a particular chord. Through this sharing workshop, they are learning the importance of making meaning of their experience for another, and in the process they are discovering relationships between audience and craft.

The workshop takes thirty to forty minutes in all, allowing for the spontaneous comments and conversation that inevitably occur in most groups. When all readers have finished and voices have begun to die down, I ask students to write for ten minutes in their notebooks on their workshop experience—on reading their own drafts aloud and listening to the other two writers in their group. The purpose of this "reflective" writing is to get students to put into words or to make visible their own learning as it is happening.

To convey a sense of the kinds of things students are learning at this point, I offer these extracts from freewritings that students have shared with me in our conferences:

> I didn't know how to end my paper so I just kind of slapped on this ending, this saying from a TV commercial about how friends don't let other friends drink and drive. But then, when I heard the way Shelly ended her paper, it was more personal or something. It just sounded better. I think maybe I should try something like that.

> I noticed Kevin used alot more descriptive words than I did. To be honest I think the experience I was writing about was more interesting than his. Maybe I'm just not into hockey or other sports . . . but in terms of writing his was definitely more interesting to listen to. I need to spruce mine up a bit.

> I read my essay a bunch of times to myself before class. But when I read it out loud, I realized I had left things out, things I needed to say or explain or my story wouldn't make sense to someone else.

> Matt wrote about his brother's suicide and it was awesome. I mean not just the story, which was really powerful, but the way he wrote it. He told it from his brother's perspective, like his brother was talking to him and trying to explain why he did it. Kelly (the other person in our group) and I both asked him when he was through how he did it, what made him think of writing the essay like that? He said he started over four times and wrote tons of pages and then his brother's voice just sort of "took over."

> Ugh! My essay sounded like Engfish. It really did! I heard it as I read it out loud. It was horrible! I even asked the people in my group when I finished reading and they both sort of nodded. I'm thinking about starting completely over. A whole new topic and everything. I got some great ideas from listening to the other two papers.

While students may lack our vocabulary to talk about their writing at this point, they are already attuned, as these comments suggest, to sophisticated matters of voice, structure, clarity, diction . . . and to writing's power—its potential as a tool of discovery and its ability to affect others' perceptions and emotions.

When students have finished their in-class reflections on their workshop experience, I hand out their writing assignment for the next class: a short (two-page) reflective essay in which they extend the insights of their in-class writing. The assignment asks them to bring their writing process and in-class sharing experience to bear on this very essay: that is, to comment on their essay so far, its hits and its misses.

Reflective Essay

In "The Poisoned Fish," Ken Macrorie defines "Engfish" as fancy and pretentious academic language that is not really a kind of communication because the writer does not write about what truly counts for himself or herself. But Macrorie also says there is another kind of Engfish—simple, everyday words that say nothing because the writer keeps his or her experience private. For your first writing assignment, you were asked to recall an experience that has changed the way you are or the way you think about things. You then shared your writing with other writers by reading your work aloud, and you listened as other writers shared their work with you. I would like you to write a short essay (two pages) in which you reflect on what you have learned about your writing, about yourself as a writer, as a result of reading your work to others and listening to the way others wrote about their experiences.

For this piece of writing, you might ask yourself questions like these: How did the experience of reading my work aloud change the way I feel about my essay? What might I want to do differently? What changes might I make so that I can be sure I am including my readers in my experience? What did I learn from listening to other writers' essays that might be useful to my own writing? What did each of the other writers do especially well? What did I do well? What can I improve?

I also distribute an essay they will read for the following class, Donald Murray's "Internal Revision: A Process of Discovery" (1979). I ask them to highlight or underline three points in the essay that stand out for them and to note, either in the essay's margins or in their notebooks, their reasons for choosing those points.

Our next class is devoted to a "seminar" in revision, a session in which students work as a class (rather than break into groups) to formulate and test their own theories of revision. Murray's essay forms the centerpiece of our theoretical discussion. I like "Internal Revision" as a seminar piece because Murray announces early on that "rewriting is one of the writing skills least researched, least examined, least understood, and– usually— least taught" (30). Research on revision actually abounds in composition journals and textbooks, but as a rhetorical gesture, Murray's statement helps me invite students to formulate their own theories of revision—to fill the "gap" in our knowledge by drawing from their own experiences and knowledge as writers. Also, Murray proposes that "prevision," "vision," and "revision" be used in place of prewriting, writing, and rewriting to emphasize the idea that "writers use language as a tool of exploration to see beyond what they know" (32). Thus his essay helps me relate the purposes of this "seminar" to our larger purpose in the course — to discover what our customary habits of thinking and expression are so that we can begin to stretch the limits of our thinking, to see beyond the customary.

After stating that rewriting "almost always is the most exciting, satisfying, and significant part of the writing process" (31), Murray analyzes revision in terms of its "two principal forms": "internal revision," in which the audience is "one person — the writer," and "external revision," in which the writer imagines the perspective of his audience and reads his draft as an "outsider" (36). Murray concludes by describing "four important aspects of discovery in the process of internal revision": content, form, language, and voice. Many students will disagree with Murray's claim that rewriting is the most "exciting" or "satisfying" part of the writing process as they initially reflect on their own writing processes. But most will agree with Murray that rewriting is important to the process of discovery and will cite specific examples from their own drafts or from their reflective essays. One of the key points of contention in students' discussion of Murray's essay is his idea that during the process of internal revision, "beginning with the reading of a completed first draft" (36), the writer's imagined audience is still the writer himself, even if this self reads the draft as an "outsider." Some students vigorously defend this idea (and claim that they always write only for themselves), while others argue that if a writer didn't have another audience in mind, he wouldn't bother to revise at all. ("*I* know what I mean," one of my students offered; "I'll only change my wording or add something to a draft if I think someone else won't, someone who isn't me.") Students seldom reach a consensus as they explore their theories of revision and their conceptions of audience, but the very purpose of this seminar is this kind of dialectical interchange. Through their agreements and disagreements, they help each other to articulate what revision is, what it's for, and whom it's for.

Immediately following our theoretical discussion of revision, I distribute a draft of a personal-experience essay written by a former student and ask students what suggestions they'd make to the writer for revision and why. My purpose is to get students thinking about what revision can do, that is, how and why it changes the textual features, focus, and meaning of a draft. I deliberately choose an essay that is (or was), by the writer's own admission, loaded with problems. Students' theories about revision's role in the writing process quickly turn into particular suggestions for rewriting, and their suggestions come fast and furious. Even students who have been relatively silent in class up to now will jump into the discussion to help whip the essay into shape. Oftentimes, students' suggestions for revision will conflict with one another, stirring discussion (and debate) about the writer's intentions and returning us once again to Murray's essay. One student, using Murray's terminology, will defend the writer's draft, accusing another student of concentrating only on "editorial details" of "external revision" and not getting into what the writer was trying to say. Another student will counter by saying a refusal to criticize the draft won't help the writer to revise or change anything; what the writer needs is specific feedback about content, grammar, organization, and so on. Like the theoretical part of this seminar, the practical part is meant to get students to reflect on their own writing processes but also, looking beyond them, to acknowledge their personal investments in the essays they have written and, in addition, to invest themselves as writers in the literacies of others.

The students' assignment over the weekend is to write a page in their notebooks about the revision seminar—whatever thoughts they have about revision at this point—and to revise their personal-experience essays. I ask them to bring three copies of their revised drafts to class: two for the members of their writing group, who will workshop their papers, and one for me.

Week Three: Revising and Collecting

The revision seminar of the previous week turns into a responding workshop this week, with students offering one another feedback on their revised drafts. After a warm-up freewriting, I distribute a handout entitled "Descriptive Responding" and take some time to explain its language and purpose to the class. (Again I've borrowed this workshop from *Sharing and Responding* by Peter Elbow and Pat Belanoff[1], making some minor changes of my own.)

Descriptive Responding:
Pointing
Summarizing
Listening for What's Almost Said or Implied
Finding the Generative Center

When you're working on a piece of writing, you may want to hold off receiving any criticism for a while, but you'd still like some feedback to find out how your work is coming across to a reader. Oftentimes, your

---

[1] Copyright © 1989; published by McGraw-Hill, Inc.; reprinted by permission of the publisher.

readers can give you ideas about how to rethink and reshape your work. It helps if your readers/listeners think of themselves as your allies or co-writers. Here is a group of ways that you as a *reader* can give descriptive, noncritical feedback to a writer:

Pointing: Which words, phrases, or features of the writing do you find most striking or memorable (or which do you like best)?

Summarizing: What do you hear the piece saying? What's the main meaning or message?

Listening for What's Almost Said or Implied: What do you think the writer is going to say but doesn't? What ideas seem to hover around the edges? What do you end up wanting to hear more about?

Finding the Generative Center: What do you sense as the generative center or the source of energy of the piece? (This center might *not* be the main point or the "thesis." Sometimes an image, phrase, detail, or digression seems to give special life or weight to the piece. The center might be something minor that is "trying" to be major.)

As its name implies, this workshop offers the writer descriptive, non-critical feedback. Readers write responses that echo the writer's own attempts at meaning and expression. They underscore an essay's strong points, summarize its implied or explicit message, note its allusions or out-right gaps, and locate the source of its "energy" or potential power. This workshop, I should note, also serves to introduce students to the concept and activity of close reading: they must get inside the piece of writing to articulate its moves, locate its strengths, and interpret its message. When my class reads professional writers' and students' essays in the second segment of the course, I remind them of the analytic and interpretive skills they already have as readers.

I ask students to break into the same groups they were in for the initial sharing workshop and to exchange their essays, offering any information they think might be useful to their two readers before they, and their readers, begin writing their descriptive responses. Readers write their responses directly on the copy the two writers have provided—in the text and margins as they read along and in the space at the end of the last page. I try to provide ample time for students' readings, rereadings, and responses, and I read as many of my copies of their essays as I can as they read one another's. When all members of the group have finished responding to the other two essays, they give back their drafts and comments to the writer. I provide additional time for the students to read their reviewers' comments and to jot down any notes to themselves they think might be useful toward revising their final drafts. We then "open the field" to any questions or problems individual students want to raise for the entire class to work on. One writer, for example, might have received conflicting messages from his two responders and would like to hear a third opinion. Another may simply wish to know whether an error she spotted in another student's essay is really an error. I conclude class with some "descriptive responding" of my own, summarizing what I heard some of the essays saying as I read my copies of their drafts and pointing out features of writing that were especially effective or memorable.

The students' assignment for the next class is to write a final draft of their essay to hand in to me. (While I don't grade this initial essay, I do write comments on the students' papers. Some students will decide to include this essay in their final portfolios and may wish to revise it again on their own later in the semester.) I ask them to attach their reflective essays from the previous week, as well as a brief note to me about how they would like me to read their essay: What would they like me to focus on or to pay the most attention to? What misgivings or questions, if any, do they still have about their writing? What kinds of comments would be most helpful to them at this point? (I use these notes and their reflective essays to confer with students individually about their writing in our conferences.)

Students come to the following class with their finished essays, and I come with a handout I've prepared from their drafts. The handout is made up entirely of "successes" from the students' drafts—instances of effective prose from every student in the class. The twenty-four entries on the handout range in length from a single sentence to several paragraphs and include beginnings, endings, titles, well-wrought metaphors and analogies, finely tuned anecdotes and descriptions, passages that create suspense, a sequence of ideas that creates surprise, or simply a well-placed word or phrase. My purpose is to make visible to my students my own perceptions of what makes writing good, to let them in, so to speak, on the mind of the reader/teacher who will be commenting on their essays. But also, and more importantly, I want to demonstrate to each student and to the class as a whole what they are capable of as writers– what they can do and how well they can do it. My handout deliberately accentuates the positive; it records their talents and strengths, even their lucky accidents. It is deliberately meant to displace their assumption that whatever else I might say, I'm mainly concerned with error and its correction. Later on we will analyze a handout composed of errors and missteps from the students' essays as part of an editing workshop. But concentrated attention to error at this point would only derail the more important lessons about process and audience that students are learning. Error, at this stage, is often a sign of risk taking and growth, and thus a necessary part of learning. My handout of "successes" is timed and geared to take advantage of students' eagerness to write rather than their eagerness to please. But even as it reinforces their individual attempts to write well, it asks them to consider what it is that makes writing effective.

Students already know, as we discuss each entry, that I think it's an example of good writing. Their job is to explain why it is effective by analyzing how it works. (I provide, when necessary, the context for a passage or sentence on the handout either by glossing the essay or by reading from the surrounding text.) Each entry poses a different task of analysis, and the qualities that make it good are seldom, if ever, self-evident. I tell students at the outset that they will not always see the same things I saw, indeed that there are no "right" answers. Their job is to explore and formulate their own criteria for what makes writing good and to test their criteria intersubjectively with others in the class. This exercise consumes a full class period, but I think it rewards both the teacher preparation that goes into it and the class time invested. Students come away with both theoretical and practical knowledge of language's inner workings, what we usually refer to as style. They have generated and articulated their own understandings of the relations between meaning and form.

I ask students to write a page in their notebooks over the weekend about three things that stood out for them from the in-class workshop, focusing on those ideas they found most useful or relevant to their own writing. I also distribute an exercise to help them gather potential paper topics for their next essay, which they will begin writing the following week. The handout asks them to collect ideas in their notebooks by responding to a series of "prompts."

Collecting

One of the purposes of your notebook is to collect ideas and topics that you might like to explore later in a more sustained piece of writing. This exercise is meant to stimulate your thinking about people, events, and issues in your life. It can help you discover — in your own experience, knowledge, and attitudes — potential paper topics that are personally meaningful to you. Over the weekend, I'd like you to list ideas in your notebook in response to the following "prompts":

ten things you like

ten things you dislike

five things a friend would say you're an authority on

ten things you'd like to know more about

five people you admire

five influential events in your life

five . . . (create a category of your own)

Have fun! But please put thought and care into this exercise. We will use your lists in a brainstorming workshop that will help you choose and develop the topic for your next essay.

This exercise will produce seven lists — and fifty potential paper topics for each student. When their lists are completed, I tell them, they should go back and circle one item from each that they think would make a fruitful paper topic — and jot down their reasons.

Week Four: Beginning Again

Composition textbooks and handbooks contain an array of invention strategies and heuristics to help students generate and explore paper topics on their own. Over the years that I've taught writing, my students and I have tried our hands at "topic trees," "word maps," "idea clusters," "Aristotelian topoi," and "tagmemic grids" — on the blackboard, on paper, on-line. But only a few students have ever actually reported success at finding and developing a topic through such means, and I confess I've yet to put my own mind or pen through any such paces to help me generate ideas for an essay, even in the most desperate of times.

While the weekend collecting assignment would seem, at first glance, to be one more example of the same, it is actually based on an assumption that runs counter to those underlying the invention exercises found in most composition textbooks: ideas for papers don't arise in a social vacuum — or in an individual psyche. My students come to class with lists of potential topics, but what transforms those ideas into topics for writing is the social interaction that occurs in the workshop that follows. Working in groups, students help one another articulate and elaborate their ideas, probe their ideas for significance and meaning, select and discard relevant and irrelevant information, and decide on avenues of inquiry that might be fruitful.

In new groups of three, the students in turn share what they came up with for each of the prompts on the handout and for the created category. (Even allowing for overlapping ideas among the students' lists, this exercise generates over a hundred potential paper topics for each group.) The listeners are allowed to "thieve" from a reader's lists if an item stirs their own memories or imagination. Each student then talks about why she thinks the circled item on each list might make a good paper topic — and, if she likes, why she might consider writing instead about a topic she has just thieved from another student's list. The students then work together as a group brainstorming "brainstorming strategies"; that is, they help one another decide what they should write about and why and suggest ways each writer might go about developing her ideas. This moment of the workshop marks the essential point of difference between theories of invention that impose a preconceived set of strategies across groups of writers and the situated theory of invention operating here: students, as writers situated in the same rhetorical context (writing a paper for this class), are coming up with strategies to help one another select, discard, and develop ideas according to their specific backgrounds and interests.

When thirty or forty minutes have passed, I ask students to freewrite for ten minutes about one of their potential paper topics, or, if still undecided, about any item from one of their lists. The students' assignment for the next class is to begin drafting their essays, aiming for five pages by the next class period.

We begin the next class with another sharing workshop; only this time, students talk through their work in progress with their two listeners rather than read their drafts aloud, and they invite feedback from their listeners. A writer has ten minutes to talk about his topic, his purpose, and his plans for the piece of writing as well as problems or questions he has that his fellow writers might help him with. The students are in the same groups as in the previous class; by the time they hand their essays in (the following week), they will have worked as a "team" to plan, shape, and revise their individual essays.

For the second part of class, our attention turns from the writing process to the writing itself—that is, to the text the writer is crafting. Since students are beginning a new essay, our focus is on an essay's "beginning"— or what journalists call the "lead." And since they have chosen both the topic and the mode for their writing (some are writing narratives, others expository essays or issue papers), I encourage them to think about their leads as determined by their purpose. One writer might begin with a thesis or controlling idea, introducing his subject as well as his stance or attitude toward the subject. Another writer might begin with an anecdote or a setting that imparts a particular mood. I try to tease from my students' own reading experiences the importance of a good lead: how it engages their attention and makes them want to continue reading. And I draw from writing experiences they've shared with me in conferences or in their reflective essays to underscore how finding a lead can also help them find their focus as writers. Often, I tell them, they will discover a lead several pages into their essays: they will find their true topic and focus only after writing several pages or even when they go back and read a completed draft. Following this discussion, we workshop leads using a handout I've prepared from the essays students handed in the previous week. The handout contains the introductions or beginnings from nine or ten of the students' essays, and they are decidedly mixed: some are a single sentence, others a full paragraph long; some are full of Engfish, others are full of crisp detail; some avoid getting to their subject as if the writer is just warming up, others charge out of the starting gate and leave the reader clamoring to hear what comes next. I ask students to choose their three favorite leads and to discuss the reasons for their choices. As disagreements arise, I call on students to make a further case for their own choices and then invite others in the class to decide whose case is most persuasive. Once again, this exercise actively involves students in their own learning: they are forming and testing their own hypotheses about what makes a particular lead effective rather than looking to a single, authoritative source—their English teacher—for the right answer. We eventually move from this specific exercise to a more general discussion about style and audience. I help them connect the specific features that make a lead effective to the principles of craft that enhance a piece of writing's overall effect on a reader, reminding them of the criteria they formulated to analyze the examples of good writing on the handout of "successes" the previous week.

The assignment over the weekend is to complete their essays and to make one extra copy for the student who will respond to their essay in a revision workshop the following week.

Week Five: Back to the Future, or, Revising and Reenvisioning

The responding workshop that begins our class this week continues the work of the previous class: it trains students' attention on principles of craft and their relation to audience by situating the students (once again) as writers responding to other writers' work. In this case, however, the students are working with a full text or piece of discourse rather than a partial text that is an instance of style. This workshop is another exercise in "descriptive responding" and is again adapted from Elbow and Belanoff's book. It asks students to describe what is going on in the piece of writing they are reading rather than to evaluate its strengths or weaknesses.

Patricia A. Sullivan

Descriptive Responding:
Structure
Voice, Point of View, Attitude Toward the Reader
Level of Abstraction or Concreteness
Language, Diction, Syntax

In literature classes, we tend to describe what is going on in a story, poem, or novel rather than judge it or find mistakes. Inherent in such an approach is respect for the text. The result is learning—allowing the text to speak on its own. You can benefit from asking for that kind of respect for your writing and from showing that kind of respect to the writing of others. But it isn't easy to describe what is going on in a piece of writing or to discuss how the piece works. It helps to use categories to describe important dimensions of a piece of writing.

Structure: How is this piece of writing organized? Note that there's no such thing as "no organization." You can always describe what serves as the beginning, middle parts, and the end.

Voice, Point of View, Attitude Toward the Reader: How would you describe the voice you hear (e.g., tentative, concerned, self-centered)? What is the writer's point of view or stance on the subject? Does she speak from an objective position or as an involved participant? (And does she speak in first, second, or third person?) How does she seem to treat the reader?

Level of Abstraction or Concreteness: Are the writer's generalizations appropriate to his subject? Are there places at which you feel you need details or an example?

Language, Diction, Syntax: What kinds of words are used (technical, down-to-earth, rich in metaphors and images)? What kind of sentences and phrases? Are there sentences that confuse you because of their word order or the way they are punctuated?

Because this kind of feedback requires acts of analysis, readers cannot give it after just hearing a piece of writing; they need the text in their hands so they can go back over it. Be sure, as a reader, to describe the text in as "descriptive" or nonevaluative terms as possible—not praising or criticizing. For example, instead of saying "Some of the sentences in this paper are too short and choppy," tell the writer *where* the short sentences are and what effect they have on your reading.

I take a lot of time to explain the four categories on the handout as well as the responder's role in the workshop. The "English-teacher" terminology of the categories is initially off-putting for some students. I help them connect each concept to what they already know and can do as writers, citing examples from their own essays, and I remind them of ways they have used the same ideas, if not the same words, to discuss their own and others' writing in their reflective essays.

The workshop itself takes considerable time, usually the entire class period. Though students are in their same groups of three, each will have time to read and respond to only one essay if they're also to have some time to talk, as a group, when the workshop is finished. I also give them the option of composing their responses in a letter to the writer. (Many feel more comfortable writing letters to each other; it helps them get beyond the formality of the exercise.) When students are finished, they keep the writer's essay but give back their pages of feedback, which the writer can then use for her final revision.

The students' assignment for the next class is to revise and polish their essays to hand in, and to write another informal piece (two pages or so) in which they reflect on their writing processes. I ask them to think about what they've learned so far about their writing—and about themselves as writers—from their own processes, from their readings of other writers' work, and from the feedback they've received. I ask them to include this reflective essay with their final revision, which we'll discuss in our conference the following week.

Our next class concludes the first five-week segment of the course, and I treat it as a day of connections: we retrace some steps and take a few others. I begin by asking students to share some of their discoveries and insights about writing from their reflective essays or from other moments in the course that they recall. I try as much as possible to let the students talk at this point, to shape and to carry the conversation. But I also listen for opportunities to help weave various strands of the course together—recalling points that were made about Macrorie and Murray, insights individual students shared in conferences or in class, and questions about writing that were raised in workshops but were never quite resolved.

At the end of this conversation, I ask students to freewrite for ten minutes on their impressions of UNH now that they've been students at the university for five weeks. Once again, I encourage them to write as much as they can, whatever comes to mind, without stopping to revise. When ten minutes have passed, I ask them to read their freewritings to themselves and then to flip to the page(s) in their notebooks where they recorded their first impressions of UNH. I ask them to compare their freewritings: what has changed? Some students start laughing: the "huge" campus and "far-away" buildings they wrote about before now seem small, a short walk away, familiar. Others shake their heads: they definitely misjudged their roommates, for better or for worse. Some now see UNH as a giant social club and they are only too happy to be members. Others have discovered that the university's lush greenery and constant hum of activity mask a cold heart; they feel alienated by large, impersonal classes, distant teachers, oppressive workloads, impossible exams. Many students comment on the importance of this class in their lives: Freshman English has become an important touchstone or grounding point for their other course work in the university.

What most students notice in comparing their freewritings– their earlier and later observations of UNH — is that what has changed is them. The self who wrote five weeks ago is a different self now. This self sees and encodes and judges things differently. As we explore these differences in their ways of seeing and try to articulate what accounts for the differences, I gradually substitute the word "reading" for the word "seeing." I suggest that we might think of the university as a text. If they are all reading the same text, I ask them, how is it that their readings are different — from one another's and from their own reading five weeks earlier? Most will acknowledge that their experiences of the university are different now because they themselves are different and thus their readings and writings — their "takes" on UNH — have changed. Their different experiences of the university have led to different observations and impressions; they see things in the "text" they didn't see or pay attention to before, and they have revised previous interpretations. One of my purposes in having students compare their freewritings is to help students "see" that writing and reading *are* ways of seeing, that they entail acts of perception and interpretation. My other purpose is to help them understand that reading, like writing, is essentially a meaning-making activity, one in which the perceiver — or reader — plays an active role.

To demonstrate these concepts and to introduce students to the processes of reading we'll be exploring in detail during the next five weeks, I distribute a poem: Sharon Olds's "Photograph of the Girl" (1988). In this poem, Olds describes a photograph of a young Russian girl who is starving to death in the drought of 1921. Olds tells us that the caption beneath the photo says the girl will die "that winter/with millions of others." In the last lines of the poem, Olds writes: "Deep in her body/the ovaries let out her first eggs,/golden as drops of grain." I've chosen this particular poem for many reasons: its subject matter is emotionally powerful; it is accessible even to those students who think they "can't read" poetry; and the poem is short, enabling us to discuss it deeply and fully in the amount of class time we have. Most importantly, the situation of the poem is such that it "models" the very processes I am trying to introduce. Olds is "reading" the photograph she is looking at in order to write about it. Through a series of questions, I elicit from students a description of what Olds is doing, what the poem is about, and where its affective power lies.

As Olds describes what she sees, she enables us, as her readers, to form an image of what she's looking at. But as students notice, her descriptions are selective: she has included some details and left out others, so that while we can form our own images of the girl in the photograph, we can't visualize exactly what Olds sees. Students also notice that Olds describes what she sees in her "own" language; another writer might have chosen different words. Many students will point out that Olds moves from a literal description of what she sees to an interpretation, especially in the last lines of the poem. She makes meaning of her own perceptions, embellishing her literal description with what she sees in the mind's eye. And some students will suggest that it is the meaning Olds imparts to the unseen—the significance she "reads into" the photograph—that gives the poem its power.

Olds's poem helps me to initiate students into a conversation about reading much as Macrorie helped me to initiate a conversation about writing. As we read and discuss the poem, we simultaneously explore what it means to read, how reading is a form of writing. Our discussion thus helps to lay the conceptual groundwork for the weeks ahead, when students will read and transact with various kinds of "texts," from photographs to essays, in order to respond to those texts as writers and to explore and reflect on the processes involved in reading itself. While the course takes a different turn at this point (we are rounding into the next loop of the spiral), the "new" territory in which students find themselves will still seem at least somewhat familiar because they will be employing the processes of writing, reflecting, and responding that they have been practicing all along. As we invite other authors into the classroom and attend to their ways of seeing, their ways of reading and writing the world, we will continue to build on the students' own literacies–reaffirming them at times, calling them into question at others. But always our eyes will be fixed on that space where learning emerges.

References

Berthoff, Ann E. 1981. *The Making of Meaning: Metaphors, Models and Maxims for Writing Teachers*. Portsmouth, NH: Boynton/Cook.

Elbow, Peter, and Pat Belanoff. 1989. *Sharing and Responding*. New York: Random House.

Macrorie, Ken. 1970. "The Poisoned Fish." In *Telling Writing*. Rochelle Park, NJ: Hayden.

———. 1968. "The Language in You." In *Writing to Be Read*. Rochelle Park, NJ: Hayden.

Murray, Donald M. 1979. "Internal Revision: A Process of Discovery." In *Research on Composing: Points of Departure*, edited by Charles Cooper and Lee Odell. Urbana, IL: National Council of Teachers of English.

Olds, Sharon. 1988. "Photograph of the Girl." In *The Dead and the Living*. New York: Alfred Knopf.

2

Conferences and Workshops

Conversations on Writing in Process

Rebecca Rule

I read one of my short stories to a receptive crowd. People laugh at the stuff that's supposed to be funny. They applaud at the end. They compliment me. But deep down, I think they're just being polite: nobody throws tomatoes at these affairs after all.

Writers are an insecure bunch. (It's not just me, is it?) And student writers are particularly vulnerable, often coming to us with little or no history of writing success; believing, in fact, that they can't write well—never could, never will.

As a teacher and a writer, I accept that discussions about writing in process can be awkward and uncomfortable. But by talking with their teachers and peers about what's effective and what's not, students learn how to elicit criticism, how to use it, and, eventually, how to be their own best critics. In conferences (one on one) and workshops (large- or small-group discussions of student writing), students learn the hard lesson of seeing their writing as it really is on the page, not as they wish it would be.

Some teachers shy away from full-class workshops, from small-group workshops, and even from direct criticism of student work in conference. Some of us have had our writing "torn apart" by readers. We know what a painful experience that can be and wish to protect our students. Certainly, in every workshop, small group, and conference both the student and his work are exposed. My experience tells me, though, that the benefits of such exposure far outweigh the risks. Conferences and workshops can build confidence while providing feedback that allows the student to improve the work and to grow as a writer.

I asked my colleagues what they thought a good conference or workshop accomplished. They told me that the writer leaves the session with increased and justifiable confidence, enthusiastic about the work, and, as Donna Qualley put it, "itching to write."

Conferences

Scheduling of conferences varies among teachers. Some meet each student each week; some meet students every other week; some will schedule several conference several weeks in a row, then a break, then several more. I give students a written schedule along with the syllabus, indicating when papers are due, when grades will be given, when conferences and small groups are scheduled. Right away, then, they see the overall structure of the course, the working model — a cycle of writing, feedback, more writing.

On nonconference weeks feedback may be provided through peer conferences (pairs of students critiquing each other's work), workshops, self-evaluation (guided by formal questions), written responses from the teacher, or — one of my favorite in-class activities — a paper exchange. In this activity, each student brings two copies of her or his paper and attaches cover sheets with two or three questions. All the papers are laid out on a table. Readers select a paper to read, then write a response to one of the questions. As soon as the reader finishes with one paper, he returns it to the table to exchange it for a second, a third, and so on. In this way, students get to see what others are working on, get to choose a paper to read according to interest, and writers get several responses.

The Issue of Ownership

Most conferences run fifteen to twenty minutes. Some teachers read papers in advance; others read while the student sits in the office. Some teachers make lots of marks on manuscripts; others return them clean, encouraging students to make their own notes. Lots of marks may mean a teacher is paying attention, reading carefully; or they may mean the teacher is appropriating the work, rewriting for the student. The density of marginal comments, questions, corrections is not the issue. What's at stake is ownership—and that depends on the spirit in which the advice is given, and the spirit in which it is received. I want my students to feel, ultimately, that they direct their own revisions; they make key choices to shape the final product. They are responsible for that product. I'm the coach—experienced, full of ideas and encouragement, but on the sidelines; they are the players, on the field, putting theory into practice.

Except for editing conferences (when a student and I fine-tune a page of writing, word by word, comma by comma), my marks tend to be minimal, reminders to myself of sections I'd like to revisit, spots where I have questions, examples of recurring problems. I mark phrases, lines, paragraphs, that strike me as particularly strong and will often read these aloud to the student, explaining what appealed to me. Tom Newkirk asks students to draw lines in the margins—a double line for strong sections, a single line for weak ones.

These and other cues from students are important. Before I open my mouth about a paper, I want to hear from the writer. If she will tell me—for example—what progress she's already made and what she plans to do, then I am able to read more efficiently, with a better idea of what she is ready to learn. If a student can articulate where and how a paper could be improved, then a potentially negative experience ("my teacher ripped this essay apart") turns into a positive one ("I know what this paper needs; I figured out what to do"). Instead of receiving teacher criticism, the student demonstrates her own knowledge and practices self-evaluation.

Which is *not* to say that teachers should simply sit and wait for student revelations—sometimes revelations never come. But we can make room for them and, in some cases, elicit them.

Give and Take: Some Examples

Listening—simple active listening, making encouraging noises, asking a question now and again—is sometimes all the room revelation needs. The student says: "I think my lead's too long—what do you think?" "It was easier to write about this subject because _____." "I got onto a different track right here—and I think I like this idea better—but _____."

Which is not to say that student revelations constitute the whole of any conference. Teachers make suggestions and observations, too. Specifically, we disclose our reading: "When I read this section, I was thinking _____." "I was confused by this phrase—what did you mean?" "So your main point then is _____."

By disclosing our reading, we let students know how we understand their messages. Revision can begin with the discrepancy between what a writer is trying to say and what is actually coming through to a reader. Seeing what they've actually written can be, for some writers, all they need to move forward.

My colleague Amber Ahlstrom offers this model conference:

Student: Hey, Amber, I really worked hard on this paper. I think it's almost where I want it to be. (*Silence while teacher reads the paper*)

Teacher: Umm. You chose a difficult topic.

Student: I think it's more complicated than I thought. Anyway my point is clear, but I'm not sure about the order of the paragraphs.

Teacher: Yeah. Your point is that _____ .

Student: Right.

Teacher: Okay, try this exercise to check for organization.

In this conference, the student takes charge, coming up with an idea for revision (order of paragraphs). The teacher lets the student know how she understands the paper ("Your point is") and gives a specific process suggestion ("Try this exercise").

Of course, writers don't always know what they're trying to say, especially in early drafts. Through the writing—and sometimes through talk in conference—they discover what they think, what they mean. Bruce Ballenger emphasizes this discovery principle in his teaching. He says:

> A "great" conference begins when I find some line or passage in the student's draft that dips below its surface, suggests some unexpected meaning. Then I find the questions to ask that challenge the student to think more about the idea. I often hope they'll reach a point of confusion about what they think—that's the starting place for revision.

Among the questions Ballenger asks to get his students talking in conference:

> What do you understand about this now that you didn't understand then? Have your feelings changed?
>
> What else has happened or have you observed that is related to this?
>
> What's the most important line, passage, or paragraph; the one the draft couldn't be without?
>
> What surprised you most when you wrote this?

Overlapping Agendas

Once a discrepancy is revealed or the "dip below the surface" experienced, then the door is open for specific practical advice about how to proceed. Again, if the student can advise herself, so much the better, but I feel perfectly comfortable giving advice, especially once a need or direction is established by the student. I want my students to learn about focus, about supporting generalizations with specifics, about anticipating reader questions, about creating a tone appropriate to audience and purpose, about leads that intrigue the reader, about endings that do more than simply restate, about conventions of grammar and punctuation. The agenda for conferences over the semester reflects my agenda for the course — the writing skills I expect my students to master. Amber Ahlstrom warns: "Don't be coy. It's hard to find a balance between telling them what to do and leaving them confused. They need to know what you think and how you respond as a reader and as a teacher."

I look at the student's weekly writing and listen to the student's comments about that writing as a guide to what one aspect of my agenda (occasionally, more than one) might be addressed in conference.

It's very easy, too easy, for conferences to fall into the traditional pattern of the all-knowing teacher telling the all-too-amenable student just what to do. We have to work hard to avoid that pattern if we want students to believe in themselves as writers and critics. Dianne McAnaney, another colleague, gives this advice for teachers working to empower students:

> Try not to impose your ideas/solutions when a student feels confused or discouraged about his/her writing. (Ask questions; listen — actively, attentively.) Do not use positive support as a substitute for listening to where the student wants to go with the paper. It's one thing to say, "This is a good start," and quite another to say, "This is a wonderful paper," especially if your words become a substitute for allowing some moments of silence while the student explores his/her ideas and begins to make connections and discoveries.

When All Goes Well

I assume the writer knows her work better than I do. She placed the words on the page. She knows what's there. She knows, or is in the process of figuring out, her own intentions. What she may not have is distance. Our conversation may allow her to *see* what's happening on the page and what's not. That is my primary purpose in any conference: to help the student step back and really see.

Rebecca Rule

Barbara Tindall, another UNH instructor, says: "In a great conference, a student shows he/she can read a draft in process. I'm there to throw in a question or different point of view if needed." That's a good approach. I throw in questions like: Where are you in the process of writing this? What are you pleased with? How does this compare with your other work? What did you learn from writing this? What are your plans for revision? And, especially: How can I help you? What are your questions for me? Through questions I hope to make room in the conference for the student to speak. Through questions I give him permission to speak and (when all goes well) engage him in the process of responding to and evaluating his own work.

Preparation

This business of conferencing can be intimidating for students: sitting alone in a room with a teacher's full attention—like a high-intensity lamp—focused on the student's work. The student is on the spot and may perceive a puzzling reversal of roles: What do *I* think? Didn't I come here to find out what she thinks? The student may not—initially—believe in her own knowledge, her ability to evaluate her work, her ability to make choices in revision. She may, in fact, resist.

So, I ask students to prepare for a conference by writing questions and comments ahead of time. In these "progress reports" (about a page double-spaced), students write generally about their progress in the course and specifically about the work they're handing in. I ask them to let me know what they're working on, what's easy, what's hard; to reflect on assigned readings, class discussions, small groups; to comment on the work they're handing in, listing questions they'd like discussed.

Early on, my students tend to ask global questions: Did you like it? What do you think of it? How can I improve my writing? (Translation: How can I get an A?) These questions, they soon learn, do not draw particularly coherent responses from me. I don't think of student writing in terms of "like" or "dislike." I don't understand the question, What do you think of it? It is too open-ended. And as for, How can I improve my writing? I say: Any piece of writing can be improved in any number of ways.

I turn questions back on students: Do *you* like this paper? What do *you* think? You say you're planning to revise: what specifically are you planning to change? why? This kind of reversal can make room for what Bruce Ballenger calls "the opportunity to confess that the paper was 'easy' to write," followed by a "challenge to take risks."

Later in the semester, their questions become more specific: Are you confused in the part where _____ ? Do you think the ending is too quick? Is this two papers in one? Do I have enough specifics about _____ ? How do I know when I've rewritten too much?

They learn to ask these questions from hearing my questions, from listening to other students, and from realizing what kind of feedback they need and what questions will elicit that feedback.

A student recently handed me two pages of an unfinished paper. He said, "Read these and tell me what you expect on page three." I was pleased. This student was using me as a reader (not looking for the right answer); his question made me think, made me work, led to real conversation between us.

Kim wrote in one of her progress reports:

> I have tried to recreate the day on which the tragedy occurred. At some points it is difficult because I feel I have tried to block some of it out.... I am sure as I continue to write and revise the memory of the day will return.... This draft is clearer to the reader on what happened to Tommy than was the first. However, it still is sketchy in some places. I am unsure whether I am going to include more of my pain, or just keep the paper focused on Tom.

This report suggests several places for the conference to begin. We could talk about the ways in which this draft is clearer than previous ones. We could look at where it's sketchy—determine some particular passages for her to expand. She is obviously struggling with focus—who's the paper about, Kim or Tom? Can it be about both? What sections seem to be about Kim? What sections are about Tom? Which sections does she think are stronger? Why?

Based on Kim's progress report, I would expect the conference to deal with issues of meaning, translation of personal experience through selected detail, focus. Kim's fundamental question seems to be: What do I want to say about the death of my friend? At this conference, I would probably not bring up issues like writing a more intriguing lead or a fuller ending. I would probably not bring up Kim's problems with sentence variety or comma use. These issues can be addressed later when Kim is more satisfied with the overall content of her essay and is ready to think about refining her presentation.

UNH instructor Dot Kasik writes that in successful conferences students are willing to take responsibility for their own writing and research. This, she says, is most apt to happen if they've prepared for the session beforehand by evaluating their papers before I see them. The amazing thing is that they can almost always point out their own problems with a draft, and when they do, they're more willing to rewrite.

The issue of responsibility that Kasik raises is an important one. Students might like to hand responsibility over to teachers: Read this, tell me what to do, and I'll do it. But for a student to know how to write, the student must know he knows. That is, ownership must remain intact through all the drafts. These are his ideas, his revisions—the ultimate success or failure belongs to him. As his teacher, I must be careful not to take over—because the minute I do, the success (if there is one) becomes mine, not his—and the learning is diminished. I can contribute; I can guide; I can brainstorm with him; I can suggest exercises; I can offer models; I can tell him where the comma goes; I can support him wholeheartedly. But I must not take over.

Having students write about their drafts beforehand provides a foundation for the conference. The student "speaks" first through her progress report or commentary sheet. Amber Ahlstrom asks her students to write down answers to the following questions before each conference:

1. How would you describe your process in working on this paper (where did you get your idea, how did you develop it, did it come easily or with difficulty, how long did it take you)?
2. What do you see as some strengths of this paper?
3. Is there anything in the paper that seems weak to you?
4. What did you learn (about yourself, the subject, writing, or the world) from doing this paper?
5. If you were to do another paper like this, what would you do differently?

Responding to the Student's Response

Access to this kind of information puts the teacher in the position of responding to the student's response—rather than to the paper itself. Tamara Niedzolkowski, another colleague, structures her conferences this way: "The student talks about what he or she is trying to do in a paper and I start responding to *that*. It's like we both brainstorm on the paper. Coming up with suggestions of things to try, different strategies for getting certain effects."

In his progress report about a first draft, my student Todd wrote, in part:

I feel sometimes that when I write that I sort things out in my brain. When I wrote about my father in this paper, I have had some confusing thoughts about him. My self-confidence had been lacking lately and it was mainly due to the fact that my father has put a lot of pressure on me to be like he was through college. . . . Lately I have just not felt accepted by him and it was really paining me every day. This paper was almost like therapy. . . . I read through it and it actually helped. I feel more confident about my relationship with my father. As far as writing it went, the only way to make something like this interesting would be to include personal stories with a little dialogue. Humor also came through as I was writing the piece.

Todd's comments are an invitation. Clearly the essay is important to him. He even has some ideas about how to make it more interesting—personal stories, dialogue, humor. We can discuss where those stories might fit, where his humor is evident already, the technicalities of writing dialogue. Before his fifteen minutes are up, though, I must ask: What are you trying to say about your relationship with your father? Unlike Kim, Todd is not struggling with focus—he doesn't recognize the need yet. Unless his focus narrows, though, how can he decide which anecdotes to include?

I use the discussion of anecdotes that he initiates to move into a discussion of focus, something I believe is essential to his success with this paper, and his progress in the course. He seems to have many different, sometimes conflicting ideas about the relationship. We talk about those ideas, what's coming through to me, what he'd like to express more forcefully. We begin with Todd's agenda, and his agenda leads to mine. *I do not withhold important observations about drafts*; but, ideally, the student leads the way.

As a follow-up to conferences, Amber Ahlstrom asks her students to write postconference remarks on the commentary sheets. She also keeps her own record of student conferences: "topics, issues we talked about, things I want to watch for in the student's writing, etc."

I ask my students to keep a "conference record," which includes a summary of each conference along with brief what-happens-next remarks. What happens next may be revision, delay, abandonment; or it may be a workshop—small-group or full-class. The hows and whys of these are discussed in the following section.

Workshops

Conferences serve as models for workshops. In workshops, small-group or full-class, students become teachers offering oral and written feedback to other students on writing in process. The way the teacher responds in conference — positively, specifically, with questions and comments that show respect for the writer's intent and the writer's knowledge of her own work — will eventually influence the way students respond in workshop.

Conferences develop over the semester as students learn what's expected, internalize reader questions, gain confidence, accept responsibility. In the end, the student not only sets the agenda for his conferences, but may decide when he needs one. I make conferences optional for the last three or four weeks of the semester, telling students: sign up when you feel you need to. This tactic doesn't necessarily cut down on the number of conferences I do in a week, but it normally ensures that my time and the student's are well spent; the student knows what kind of feedback she wants, and asks for it when she needs it.

Workshops develop over the semester, too, as reading and critique skills practiced in conference begin to carry over, as students learn to trust one another, as the writing community coalesces, and as the anxiety level drops.

Early full-class workshops, where one student's essay is copied for everyone to read, tend to be stiff — with just a few students making careful remarks, following the ground rules with sidelong glances at me to be sure they're interpreting the rules correctly. Later, more students will speak more openly. Not everybody speaks at every workshop, but by the end of the semester, I hope all but the shyest will feel comfortable contributing what they can. In early workshops, tension runs high. When nothing too dreadful happens workshop after workshop, everybody relaxes, and workshops become useful, even fun.

Presenting Strong Work

Carl read his work aloud in a full-class workshop. The class laughed appreciatively in all the right places. Someone said, "I loved this — I think it's the best thing I've read all semester — don't change a word." Carl — a nontraditional student doubtful about his academic ability — glowed. The workshop continued with give and take about structure, confusing language, places where readers wanted more detail, details readers found particularly strong.

Carl told me the following week that the workshop had been the highlight of his semester. His confidence increased, his motivation increased: he had witnessed the effect of his good writing on an audience and he wanted to do more.

I choose strong work for full-class workshop. Ideally, this work is finished enough for its strengths to be obvious, but unfinished enough that the writer still has questions, is genuinely curious about audience response, and plans another draft so information gained can be put to good use. Not every workshop will be as positive as Carl's was; still, one measure of the success of a workshop is, for me, the extent to which it builds a writer's belief in the value of his work, the extent to which it motivates him to write.

Workshop is sometimes a scary prospect for writers — in some circles it is seen as a forum for discussing what's wrong with a manuscript. I challenge my classes to see what's right — what's working and why. It's easy to discourage, difficult to encourage, when our natural tendency is to discount compliments and take negative criticism to the grave. Certainly writers need to know where a draft goes astray — and workshop is one place to find out. But that information must always be in the context of where the story is on track, where it is strong — *always* in that context.

The first speaker in another workshop, Prescott, tells the writer, Carole: "Two things I thought worked really well in this—the structure, moving from the general stuff to the really specific stuff and back; also your details were great." He lists some of the outstanding details. Carole confirms his perception of structure and explains why she set the piece up that way. Prescott's enthusiastic recognition of Carole's effective organization ties directly to his struggles with organization in his own work. He sees a pattern. He hears Carole's rationale, gains insight into her writing process. The next step for him is application.

The Teacher's Role

Full-class workshops are like conferences with lots of readers, so the writer has the benefit of many points of view. Not all the readers will be as skilled as the teacher at articulating their thoughts and expressing them tactfully, but they learn these skills with practice. In workshop, as in conference, the writer sets the direction by laying out one or more agenda items for the group to discuss.

I, as teacher, am one among many readers. I try not to speak first. I try not to speak more than others in the group. Sometimes — when the workshop is going especially well — I don't speak at all. Usually, though, I participate in at least three ways:

1. I ask the writer, What are your questions for us? and then remind the class of those questions at key points in the discussion.

2. I remind the students to point out what's working generally and specifically in the draft; I explain why I think this is a strong draft, emphasizing some techniques or approaches that other students might try.

3. I summarize or synthesize: This is what I'm hearing. . . .

I am, therefore, usually an active but not a dominant participant in the full-class workshop, one among many readers.

Sue Wheeler, in an unpublished text written with Mary Peterson and Elizabeth Chiseri-Strater, says:

> The worst insult to any writer who has worked hard on a paper is silence. Second worst is a breezy, "I like it," or "I hate it," with no explanation. Be generous with your criticism and you'll receive in kind. The generous critic thinks of the writer: the generous critic is not afraid to risk opinion to help someone else. (147)

In full-class workshops, I can ensure that explanations are given: What do you like specifically? Show us where are you confused. Can you give another example? Did anyone else stumble here?

I talk with my classes about this notion of generosity, offering examples of when readers have helped me with good advice. I urge them to give the kind of feedback they would like to receive, tempered by the cues they get from the writer. If a writer says, "Be brutal—I know this is a strong essay and right now I really need to know where my argument has holes, even little ones," then, by all means, tell her your feelings, point out any holes you notice. If a writer says, "I've been working on this for five weeks. I think it's almost done, but I'm not sure my point comes across in the end," then talk about what is coming across in the end and what is not. But don't suggest a total reorganization or shift in thesis—clearly the writer is not open to these suggestions and they will not be helpful. The point is not to create perfect papers through unrelenting criticism; the point is to allow writers and readers to hone their skills through discussion. The short view is: let's make this a stronger paper. The long view is: let's all learn about writing and reading from one another.

Preparation

Not every reader speaks in workshop. Short of calling on students one by one (which seems a bit regimented to me), I see no way to make every student speak—and really no point in it—especially if they have already responded to the work in writing. This system works for me:

54

Conferences and Workshops

1. A paper is handed out during the class before the workshop is scheduled.

2. The writer may present questions at that time or wait until the workshop. In the absence of specific questions from the writer, the students are instructed: Mark the paper as you read. Use clear editing marks to indicate favorite lines and details, points of confusion, problem areas. Write notes in the margin to help the writer know how you read (I love this! This seems true. Did I miss a reference to this person earlier?). Write a letter to the author about what's working generally, what's not working, and what's working specifically. Sign the letter.

3. During the workshop, the writer reads part of the paper aloud. If there's time and the paper is short, he'll read the whole thing. Occasionally, the writer asks that someone else read the paper or that the class read silently.

4. The writer asks his questions; the class responds.

5. The class hands the writer their marked drafts and letters.

6. Afterward, I go over the written responses with the writer (or sometimes just on my own), noting readers who helped and those who need further instruction in helping.

Constructive Criticism

The class has read in advance three drafts of Todd's essay about his relationship with his father. They've written letters to him. Todd opens the workshop by asking whether readers think the third draft is really better than the first. He thinks he may have lost some of the passion of the first draft through his revisions. The class acknowledges that the first draft is more "emotional" than the third. Readers go on to say that the third draft is, however, stronger — because it is more focused, more detailed, clearer. They suggest incorporating some of the examples from draft one, specific lines that might recreate some of that initial passion. Many readers talk about the guts it takes to write so honestly about family problems; they praise Todd for his willingness to write honestly about a risky personal topic. I see three significant results here:

1. Todd's intuitions were confirmed and his confidence level raised. Yes, the third draft was less "emotional"; he was right about that. Both his first and third drafts had strengths; he knew that, too.

2. Those strengths could be merged — and his readers had some specific suggestions about how that merging could take place. So Todd got specific, practical help with revision — which he was able to use.

3. The students saw the payoff for taking a risk, writing honestly and specifically on a tough, personal topic. This was a turning point for many writers in the class: in the weeks that followed, other students would take similar risks.

Students are interested in what their peers write. This interest tends to make them read the work carefully, perhaps better than they read the work of professional writers (from whom the student reader — any reader, I suppose — feels a certain respectful, inhibiting distance). There is, of course, the hurdle of "feelings." Some students are reluctant to say much at all about a peer's work for fear of hurt feelings.

Yes, I've had students angry or in tears after workshop (during conferences, for that matter). Usually these reactions have more to do with the frustration of perceived failure than anything specific a reader has said. One student told me (weeks later) that she cried after our first conference because I hadn't specifically said I liked her essay — I hadn't used those exact words, which she'd waited the whole, interminable fifteen minutes to hear. Another student became very angry over the idea of revision. Later he wrote a letter about all English teachers, our general intolerance, but especially the intolerance of this one English teacher in high school. . . . His anger was, I think, unavoidable. Too many bad associations.

Michelle approached me after class recently to say her group (two other women — good writers) had "destroyed" her essay. We talked at length about the alleged destruction. As it turned out, Michelle had presented an essay that had been giving her a lot of trouble. She'd been working on it for several weeks and couldn't seem to find a focus. At last she found one, revised the essay one more time, then presented it to her group. She was, in fact, finished with that essay; she couldn't work on it anymore. And to hear from her group that there was room for improvement — any room at all — simply overwhelmed her.

Sometimes students will hear ten encouraging comments in a workshop, but recall only the one blunt, negative remark.

Sometimes students are upset by the responses they get from me or their peers. More commonly, though, students say their readers just don't give them enough feedback. Tell me more, they say. Answer my question fully. Explain yourself. Take my writing as seriously as I take it, as seriously as you take your own.

Small Groups: Sequencing and Setup

Some teachers use a few full-class workshops early in the semester as models for small groups. The students learn how to critique in the big group, then apply their knowledge in the small ones. This way more papers can be discussed during class time. Some teachers begin small groups right away, saving full-class workshops (if they use them at all) for later in the semester when the papers are stronger.

Many of us see small groups as an alternative to conferences—a variation on them—and schedule groups on nonconference weeks. From Donna Qualley and Barbara Tindall I learned the technique of combining conferences and small-group workshops by meeting in my office with two students at a time for a shared conference. I find this allows me to be freer in my comments because they are balanced by the comments of the other reader. I can respond to the paper, to the reader, to the writer, to the reader's response to the paper or the writer, to the writer's response to the reader's response. There's a lot to talk about.

Usually I schedule thirty to forty minutes for a shared conference—and we'll talk about a paper from each student during that time. This creates a more leisurely pace than scheduling two fifteen-minute conferences in the same time slot. These meetings combine the intensity and teacher guidance of the conference with the energy and variety of the small group. Qualley prefers shared conferences or in-class small groups to full-class workshops:

> Small groups ensure that everyone talks. For me, talk is essential for learning, for working out what you think. So I guess I try to set up opportunities for this to happen in my class. In whole groups, I find it is too easy for me to dominate, for them to let me dominate and direct. . . . In small groups, everyone is a reader and a writer at the same time.

There are many points of view about the "best" setup for small groups, many questions to be considered:

Should there be two, three, four, or five students per group?

Should the groups rotate or remain intact for several weeks or the whole semester?

Should groups deal with one paper in great detail during a half-hour or hour session or should they spend less time on more papers so everyone gets a turn?

Should teachers assign membership—and, if so, should each group contain at least one strong writer or should the groups be more homogeneous, students of equal ability working together?

Should teachers drop in on groups or keep out of the process?

And the answers are: I don't know. And, all of the above. Just about anything can be successful if the students are willing to work and if they know what they are expected to do. If students are *not* willing to work — for whatever reason (lack of responsibility, maturity, engagement, commitment), then small groups are doomed — and all the structure and clear expectations in the world won't save them. But I've found that small groups usually do work. And when they work, the class takes off. Students help students, everybody participates, the writing process is illuminated, products improve dramatically, and the community thrives.

Amber Ahlstrom offers:

> I have tried so many combinations: three to six people, groups they select, groups I select, groups that change membership. I start with four people per group, their choice, and ask at some point if they want to switch. Since I figured out how to train better, the logistics don't matter so much.

Dot Kasik assigns students to stable groups, formed about the third week of classes. Members bring copies of their work. They comment orally and in writing. She says:

> I used to hand out a critique checksheet to follow for these sessions, but more recently, we talk as a class long enough at the onset of each session to formulate a checklist for the day. That seems to work better because it focuses on whatever we've currently discussed and affords a more pointed evaluation.

Donna Qualley's groups meet during nonconference weeks, three or four times over the semester. She, too, has experimented with stable groups but says: "Lately, I . . .switch them around just so they can have the experience of working with a number of different people." In class each student shares a draft of a paper that needs more work. Then:

> After reading and talking about the papers, readers take their copies home, reread them (another reading skill), mark them up with questions and comments, and write an overall response to the writer. They return these to the writer next class. When the writer receives all of her written feedback, she writes a writer's response (for me) on the help she received.

Keeping Small Groups on Track

Training and *accountability* are critical to the success of small groups. Students need to know what they're supposed to do and how to go about doing it. Reporting back to the teacher (by checklist, in a progress report, or, as

Qualley suggests, through a writer's response) keeps the teacher in touch and allows him to intervene on an individual or group level. For the student who says, I'm just not getting enough good feedback, I say, Demand feedback with your questions. If readers say they're confused, follow up with: Where? What words confuse you? What can I do to clear up the confusion? For groups that seem to be wasting time, I can offer a checklist or discussion guide; I can cut down on the time allotted; I can reassign members.

In full-class sessions, the teacher may choose not to dominate, but she may (usually does) control discussion with questions, reminders, comments. She may end discussion when it seems to have run its course.

By giving the class over to small groups, a teacher gives up quite a lot of control. He can't personally monitor every group; he may, in fact, choose to steer clear of them all. My presence in a small group influences discussion. Students wait for me to speak; look to me to decide when to move on to a new paper; tend to take my responses more seriously than the responses of other members. Naturally, I'm curious about what's going on in the groups—but I want them to function independently. My solution is to stay in the room, reading or writing, looking up now and again (so they know I'm listening), joining a group only when invited.

Many of us give fairly rigid instructions for early small-group sessions, easing up as the students become more comfortable, more aware of what can be accomplished. For a first small-group experience, I instruct my students simply to read their papers aloud to one another. That's it. I tell them the purpose is for them to hear their work as others hear it; and to get an idea of what others are working on.

At the next session, writers might again read aloud; then listeners would simply list what struck them about the reading, what they remember—details, ideas, phrases. Pat Sullivan assigns a reflective essay after such sessions. Her instructions:

> You . . .shared your writing with other writers by reading your work aloud, and you listened as other writers shared their work with you. I would like you to write a short essay (two pages) in which you reflect on what you have learned about your writing, about yourself as a writer, as a result of reading your work to others and listening to the way others wrote about their experiences.

She also lists questions students might ask themselves as they compose:

> How did the experience of reading my work aloud change the way I feel about my essay? What might I want to do differently? What changes might I make so that I can be sure I'm including my readers in my expe-

rience? What did I learn from listening to the other writers' essays that might be useful to my own writing? What did each of the other writers do especially well? What did I do well? What can I improve?

In this case, students are made accountable for their work in small groups through a formal writing assignment. Other forms of accountability include an oral report to the full class, written feedback to the writer (to be passed on to the teacher), a written report of highlights (some teachers have a list of questions to be completed), and informal discussion of "what the group said" at the next conference.

Training in small groups is done on the job. By beginning the semester with a lot of structure, with specific instructions on what to do and how the groups will be held accountable, teachers show students how groups can work.

I might ask my students to look first at leads, talk about what the lead makes them expect from the rest of the paper, then read the paper to see if those expectations are met. If we're working on persuasive writing, I might write four tasks on the board:

1. Explain to the writer why you agree, disagree, or can't make up your mind.

2. Brainstorm counterarguments.

3. Answer any questions the writer has.

4. Be prepared to report back to the class at least one example of each of the five principles of persuasion discussed last class.

This on-the-job training reinforces class content while helping students develop a vocabulary for discussing process and product. By the end of the semester, the teacher-imposed structure can be eased because the students will impose their own structure — appropriate to the needs of members.

After a few sessions (or sometimes as a kickoff to the groups), I ask the class about these and other groups they've been involved in — what worked, what didn't? Together we develop guidelines. I want students to be aware that the success or failure of the group rests with them. Listed below are some typical guidelines from a class brainstorming session:

Let the writer establish the rules for discussion of her paper. The writer should speak first.

Keep an open mind. Listening to new ideas doesn't necessarily mean you have to use them. Listen to all suggestions and write them down; sort through them later.

Offer honest, constructive criticism. Before you offer any criticism, think about whether what you're about to say will help the writer with the work in question and over the long haul.

Be specific and clear.

Ask questions of the writer.

Offer suggestions on how you think the paper can be improved, but listen to the writer if he explains why he did something and perhaps offer a new suggestion considering what the writer just said.

I also ask the class what to avoid in small-group workshops. Here are a few of their suggestions:

Don't be "nice."

Don't just be a negative critic.

Don't say the work is "perfect" or "excellent" just to be kind to the writer or because you are afraid the writer will no longer like you.

Don't cut a piece down because you would rather have it "this way."

Don't make comments on the writing until you have thoroughly read the work.

Don't lie.

I periodically survey the class to find out whether they feel time spent in small groups is worthwhile. I will increase or decrease the frequency of sessions depending on student response and my sense of the effect of the groups on the writing.

At the heart of any class I teach is the workshop: full-class and small-group. I like the energy of workshop, which comes in part because we are dealing directly with our most important text, student writing. There's a lot at stake in a workshop. Workshops also, I believe, benefit everybody in the class simultaneously — readers and writers.

Benefits for Readers

1. *Readers get new ideas about topic and technique that serve their own writing efforts.* Student essays inspire student essays. Each paper presented in workshop expands the territory of the class as a variety of forms and topics are reviewed. Todd's Dad essay will generate more Dad or Mom essays. Michelle's argument about disposal of insulin needles and misconceptions about diabetes will generate more arguments, perhaps

on very different topics. After Jim, the jazz musician, attempts to translate the energy of a jam session into words, others will write about music or art or dance or gymnastics using the time-expansion technique that he used so effectively.

2. *An increased awareness of process results from these workshops—it becomes clear that no one stands alone in this struggle to communicate.* As the writer reveals the steps she took to create her draft, as she talks about obstacles and successes, readers identify. They recall their own struggles with last week's assignment and the essays they are working on now. A sense of community develops, a sense that we are all learning new ways, refining old ways of translating what's in our heads onto the page. As the writer describes how he came up with the topic, what research was necessary, how he cut three pages of background, how he tried five different leads—as the writer reveals how the draft came to be, readers will recognize steps, attitudes, maneuvers that might be useful in streamlining or enriching their own processes. In responding to the work, readers become part of the writer's process; they invest in the work, developing a sense of the class as a writing community.

3. *Readers practice recognizing strengths and weaknesses, solving writing problems, using a writer's vocabulary.* Readers have automatic objectivity when critiquing someone else's work. They can see what's on somebody else's page better than what's on their own. Without distance, we see what we want to see on our own pages, rather than what's there. Workshops allow readers to practice seeing, to practice the articulation of what they see. It is often the student struggling to include more detail in his own work who recognizes the need for more detail in someone else's. The student who claims he never knows how to end a piece pays particular attention to other people's endings. When the talk turns to rhythm in a well-turned sentence of Sarah's, Norman perks up: "What's this rhythm stuff? What do you mean by rhythm?" Suddenly, he can see why Sarah made certain word choices for the way the words sound together—something Norman's almost ready to tackle on his own.

4. *Workshops establish standards.* Students in any course know they must figure out what's expected, what the standards are. Grading is one kind of practical information on expectations and standards. So is the full-class workshop. Since I present strong papers in workshop and explain why I consider these papers strong, standards become explicit. Anthologized essays by professionals may provide interesting models for stu-

dent writing and may stimulate their thinking, but strong essays by other students provide a practical basis for comparison. Readers ask themselves: Is my work this detailed, moving, thought-provoking, honest, risky, logical, persuasive, graceful, carefully edited?

Benefits for Writers

1. *Workshops bring an audience to life.* Through the workshop a writer sees the effect of his words on an audience. He sees that a whole roomful of people cared enough to read his work, cared enough to write comments and discuss it. It is one thing to say we write to communicate, another to face our audience. Ideally, readers will have read the material before the workshop, will have marked the pages with their thoughts as they read along, will have written a letter to the writer or filled out a comment sheet. I ask writers to read part (or all, if it's short) of the essay aloud in class to help us remember what we might have read a day or two ahead of time, to help us focus on the essay.

   Reading aloud also puts the writer in direct contact with her readers. She can hear them sigh, laugh, shuffle their feet. She can hear the silence when they're engaged, the rustle when they're not.

2. *The writer gets advice about what's working, what's not, how to improve.* She asks her readers the same kinds of questions she might ask the teacher in conference — questions she knows will help her move forward with the draft. I encourage writers to ask about strengths; I encourage readers to talk about strengths; I will step in and direct the discussion toward strengths if need be. The writer will also want to know where the draft needs work. Her questions will guide readers to the problems she is ready to tackle. What about the ending? the writer asks. Is it too abrupt? Do you need more information on this particular law? Do you want more examples? I think I have a problem with long sentences. Which sentences trip you up?

   As in conference, the writer sets the agenda for the workshop — which is not to say that an item on the writer's agenda can't lead to a different item on the reader's agenda. Students who model my conference methods (and for freshmen this may be the only model they know) will use the writer's questions as jumping-off points. A question about the ending may lead to comments about theme: How is the theme, for example, represented in this ending? What if you cut the last paragraph? How would that change the meaning of the essay?

A writer learns what questions evoke useful answers. He learns that readers disagree about problems and solutions. He gets lots of feedback (I was confused here, I laughed here, I could relate to this idea because . . .) and lots of advice (how about introducing the neighbor sooner, this paragraph would make a good lead, I'd cut that whole dialogue). My primary role — a role the writers eventually take on themselves — is to ask for examples and clarification; I want to be sure the writer understands what the readers are saying. (I want to be sure readers understand what they're saying, for that matter. I want everybody to think about what's being said.)

To begin a workshop I say, Dave, what are your questions for us? How can we help? Dave, then, directs his workshop. I moderate, usually with questions: So, is this what I hear you saying . . .? Can you give an example of where he makes an effective transition? What page are you on? What do you mean by flow? Sometimes I summarize or interpret: Jenn and Michelle seem to be saying the same thing in different ways. Mark thinks that line is effective because . . ., but Cathy sees it as a repetition of the point you made in paragraph three. To end a workshop, I encourage readers to list what they thought worked best, particulars, to leave the taste of success in the writer's mouth.

3. *A distance is gained between writer and page.* In a conference, my primary purpose is to help students gain objectivity; same thing in a workshop. I do not expect the class or small group to rewrite papers. I do not expect a writer to take all (or any) of the advice she is given. I instruct writers to listen, maybe to take notes, to pay attention to any advice that makes sense, to disregard any that doesn't.

What I expect is that the workshop will help the student see her paper in a fresh way. I hope she will see a host of possibilities for revision. I hope she will see the paper as others have seen it — while at the same time retaining her sense of ownership and intention.

To this end I make sure that during every full-class workshop, readers at some point address the question: What do you think this writer is trying to say? This is also the question I recommend most often for small groups.

One way or another — through a full-class or small-group workshop or a conference — I want a writer to see how his work is being interpreted. I want him to understand what's coming through. Ultimately, I want him to see for himself what he's written, to see the possibilities open to him, and to develop a repertoire of techniques and skills that will allow him to communicate with confidence.

Reference

Wheeler, Susan, Mary Peterson, and Elizabeth Chiseri-Strater. *Writing Matters.* Unpublished manuscript.

Exercises for Discovery, Experiment, Skills, and Play

Susan Wheeler

Some people believe exercises are tedious, repetitive, and remedial tasks, or something an unimaginative teacher relies on to fill time. And yet painters sketch and musicians practice scales. Why shouldn't writers practice, too? A good exercise lets writers write without hearing their internal critics say their prose is boring, full of mistakes, or dumb. Fear of failure and a need to perfect first drafts constrict many writers; exercises can change their attitudes. We can tell our students that we expect, we *want* their writing to be rough, exploratory, that this is "only an exercise," an invitation to take risks and fool around. A good exercise provides a direction, a specific challenge, and a safety net for writers so that they dare to experiment. Often exercises result in ideas for longer papers.

Exercises can stir or jar imaginations, provide chances to play with ideas and words, lift students out of the midsemester doldrums, and teach specific writing skills and forms. They can encourage good writing habits and build a writing community.

I rely on exercises partly because I feel uncomfortable when I talk too long about writing; I'd rather let writers write and learn by doing. When students have specific work of their own in their hands, talk about writing becomes more dynamic and effective.

There is a sequential pattern to the exercises I present. There are wide variations from class to class, of course, but each term a pattern emerges based on what I see as the writing needs of the majority of students; and their needs tend to follow somewhat similar patterns.

In the first week or so, I use exercises to help students gain confidence and find subjects that fascinate and challenge them. Then come exercises that give writers experience with specific skills — writing tools — designed to help them gain insights into their subjects and write clearly. There are several exercises that encourage students to make major conceptual revisions and others that help with fine-tuning. I present revision and fine-tuning at very different times in different semesters: sometimes with major revisions, about week three if most students have found strong subjects and need to revise, more often about week six of our fifteen-week course. I discuss fine-tuning on an individual basis in conferences when the timing feels right, as well as in classes and in small groups. Usually I present fine-tuning exercises in the middle to last third of a term. Also, about one half to two thirds of the way through a semester, come exercises that introduce different forms. And throughout a course, again depending on the needs of the majority, I use exercises to loosen students up, to get their imaginations going, to give them fun and experience with freewriting, with words.

Like many teachers, I occasionally refer to my own writing process and products as we discuss exercises. I might read a short excerpt from my work to illustrate a skill: an awful first draft, a middle draft or two, the final one that works. Some teachers give students a paper or poem or story they're working on and ask the class for help. This is a wonderful way to show students that everyone in class is a writer, learning and sharing experiences.

The most successful exercises are often the ones we invent. We're enthusiastic about our own inventions, and this counts. So does confidence. Confidence is as important to teaching as it is to writing. Each of us comes to teaching with specific strengths. We should capitalize on these. If you have an exercise you want to try, try it right away. Or, if exercises feel strange and wrong somehow, do something else at first. As the semester goes on you can add new ideas and strategies.

Points to Consider Before Presenting Exercises

Does the exercise address the most pressing needs of the majority of students this week?

Take notes from time to time as you read students' papers each week so that you know which writing problems are most important to address when.

Exercises for Discovery, Experiment, Skills, and Play

Once you know what the majority of a class needs, you can invent a way to address it or use an exercise someone else has devised. The exercises that have flopped for many of us are those that sounded great but weren't relevant for our classes on the weeks we presented them.

What is the main purpose of the exercise?

Before I introduce an exercise, I try to say in a sentence or two what it will accomplish. The best ones often accomplish several things, and many of the results surprise me, but I like to fulfill at least one goal.

Do students understand why you're doing each exercise?

Not only teachers but students need to understand the purposes. Students should know why they're asked to do what, and where exercises fit into their writing and reading experiences in this class, in other courses, and in their lives after college. It's easy to neglect the *why* from time to time.

Is the exercise time-efficient?

As a semester gathers momentum and complexity, we sometimes in our rush make projects unnecessarily convoluted. We need to value our students and our own time. There are two good questions you can ask. First, do you need an exercise to demonstrate this point? If the skill is easy to assimilate, a straightforward skill such as going back and forth in time in personal essays, why waste time with an exercise? Just explain the skill, read aloud from some writers who handle it well, and let students experiment and make discoveries on more important material. Don't be afraid to throw out an exercise in favor of a short explanation of the principle. Second, is there a way to shorten the time spent on an exercise and still accomplish its goals? The best exercises are often simple and straightforward. Bruce Ballenger says he's wary of exercises that take "elaborate twists and turns."

Is it valuable to read from published and student prose to demonstrate a specific skill or idea that you're presenting and that students will practice in an exercise? If so, when? Before or after students write the exercise?

Try different methods. Find what works best for you when. Sometimes I read aloud to students before they write, sometimes after, sometimes not at all. The decision rests on my sense of what will work best for a given class with the given exercise. At the beginning of a semester, if most students in a class are writing safe, corseted prose, I'll likely read before the students write.

When I read aloud, I choose several examples that illustrate different ways of thinking, seeing, and writing. In this way, I don't send a message that one way is right. Always, I use examples I love just because I can't imagine reading aloud from material I disliked or didn't believe in. Students are inspired by literary prose just as people can be inspired by beautiful paintings and music. It's important to balance numbers of women and men writers and use some writing that comes from minority groups, from different countries. I read from different forms, showing how often several forms are contained within one piece of prose. I also use good student prose–and treat it seriously. I might read from four pieces to illustrate a form or skill: two student pieces, two published works. With student writing, I always say that these pieces have been revised many times so that my current students won't be intimidated. (Save good student writing; it will help you the following semester.)

Sometimes I read aloud and give short handouts so that students can see *and* hear. Sometimes I read without distributing the text. It's important to use both methods. Sometimes I ask students to bring in writing they love that illustrates a specific skill, and they read aloud.

Should students revise their exercises? Should you and other students see their exercises?

Often the answer to both questions is no: some exercises should remain private, and sometimes you won't have time to read the exercises. However, there are certain exercises that teach critical writing skills and forms. I don't want to discuss these skills with one student after another, week after week, in conference. I just can't stand it. And why should students waste weeks stumbling about when a specific skill or form can help them write precisely, which in turn can lead them to insights? For these critical skills, I ask students to write in class, and then, as we discuss what has happened, maybe some of them will read from their pages. Then they swap their exercises with another writer, rework the exercise, and type it at home. Finally they show the exercise to me in conference.

I always tell students that they don't have to swap if their material is confidential. When they do swap, I remind them that these exercises are quickly written rough experiments. Polish doesn't count. Each reader is to look for what works best in the exercise and offer one or two suggestions to make it better.

Should you write along with students in an exercise or not?

Some teachers feel strongly that they should do what they ask students to do. That idea is wonderful, but I write at home each day, and I just don't want to write again in class.

Specific Exercises[1]

I. Writing with Confidence/Involvement/Authority

The purpose of the first two exercises is to show students that they have important things to write about and that involvement in a subject can lead to strong prose. Students experience the energy of writing honestly.

A. Write letters to a person you love and to a person you can't stand

At the end of class on the day before you present these exercises, tell students the following: Think of someone who is very important to you right now; for example, someone you love or admire, someone you might want to be like some day. Think also of someone you can't stand, who gets you riled, churned up, infuriates you; even better, someone who infuriates you but whom you love; or a person you're jealous of.

Tell students to bring these two people inside their heads to the next class. Tell them that if their choice of persons isn't clear in their minds before they start, they'll waste ten minutes wondering whom to write about when they could be writing. At the beginning of the day I give the exercise, I remind students that they were to have been thinking about two persons, so that as I discuss the exercise, the students will reestablish those two people before they write.

Ask the students to write a letter to the person they love and to tell that person every single thing they ever wanted to say, including things they never dared say. Assure them ahead of time that this is confidential. No one will ever see this. Not you, not anyone in or out of class. They can tear up the letter later. Probably they should. And they must write fast with no regard for careful sentences. They can leave out words if they like, and punctuation; they can break into lists — whatever. They must use the person's name — Dear Carlos or Bets — write fast, and tell *all*. After they've finished, ask them to write a letter to someone they can't stand. Again, assure absolute confidentiality before they write.

When you stop them from writing, ask how they felt as they wrote. Ask them to compare the strongest letter they wrote to a paper for another course where (1) they didn't care, (2) they didn't have enough information, and (3) they were bulling their way through. They'll see that the writing is much easier, more satisfying, and the product is stronger when they know a lot and care.

---

[1] The exercises are arranged roughly in the order in which I tend to give them.

Next, ask them to imagine that the person they can't stand, or have conflicting feelings about, has died. They must write a letter of sympathy to that person's parents. How hard this would be: they couldn't be honest; they couldn't use lots of specific information; they would lack conviction. Don't have them write this letter. They've written enough bull, and this is a class where that stops.

Discuss the differences between writing about people they feel positively about and writing about those who cause tension, conflict. Probably they feel more strongly about the latter. That's because we often talk about positive things. Many people don't talk much about ideas and people that bother them, so there's intensity when these subjects burst out on the page. More importantly, we understand why we admire someone, and so the prose is a rehash. When we're in conflict about someone, we likely need to understand more, to examine and rethink, to revise. Conflict, lack of knowing, and a need to see more clearly are wonderful occasions for writing.

B. Write about an issue or idea you feel strongly about
In the class preceding this exercise, ask students to think of an idea or issue they feel strongly about. They must know a lot about the subject, too: for example, drinking at school, sexism in high school sports, homeless people, snobs, noise in the dorm, lack of financial aid, football scholarships, a prejudice they feel about any person or group.

Tell students that they may but don't have to address a person or group—such as the editor of the student paper or their three roommates. In this exercise, the purpose is to get down what they know fast. Interestingly, many students do address a specific audience in this exercise; because they feel strongly and know their audience, they usually address it appropriately.

Before they write, I tell them to title the piece in a way that asserts, for example, the need for more courses in the music department or the need to lower the noise level in the dorm. After they've written, you can suggest they might want to expand on this, read up on it, interview people, write more. Students often think their ideas are worth little. This exercise shows them they have things to say and that they can ask questions, find new information, and make more discoveries.

C. Respect different writing voices
This exercise encourages students to have confidence in their subjects and in their writing voices. Gather about ten pieces of prose from your all-time favorite writers who have distinctive voices. Include types of subjects to show a wide range of writing topics, styles, voices, approaches. Use essays, feature articles, narratives, persuasive pieces, etc. In class, read aloud first

paragraphs or short sections from each writer. I read from a taut, bare-bones writer like Joan Didion, then follow with a writer whose prose is lush with details, like Gabriel Garcia Marquez or Katherine Anne Porter. I'll read a passage by traditional, rather formal writers like Elizabeth Drew, Stephen Gould, and Mark Helprin and follow these with the gutsy voices of Gloria Anzaldua, Toni Cade Bambara, Tim O'Brien, and Grace Paley. Students need to see that a writer's experiences, subject matter, and ways of seeing the world result in a distinctive writing voice. Some students have an awful tendency to write in a would-be academic voice that's deadly to read and surely must make their eyes cross as they write; these people are relieved when they know their experiences, backgrounds, and ideas count and should be put on the page.

Often I'll ask students to bring in strong-voiced pieces to read aloud for the following class.

II. Finding a Subject

I want to help students find subjects that are worth their time to write, subjects that are of central importance to them. I want them to see the difference between an ambitious subject that will challenge them because they need to learn and make connections, and a subject that's not a challenge because it's a review of what they already know.

A. List your major concerns

I talk about what makes a good subject, about how appealing it is to read something where the writer obviously is fully engaged with a subject that's critically important to her. I sometimes mention a couple of issues going on in my life that would be good for me to write about. I mention one or two things that were very important to me in college and would have been ideal subjects for a paper then.

I tell students that most people are most interested in their own lives. I think almost all of them know those subjects that most fascinate them. The question is, and I say this out loud: Will they write of these things? I discuss the courage it takes to tackle tough subjects, to write honestly, and the courage and discipline to search through complexity to find truth. I say that it's hard to write; why not grapple with a subject that counts in their lives rather than slide over surface concerns?

Students list the one, two, or three concerns that have been in their minds in the last few weeks, concerns that feel critically important to them. They don't have to show me their lists unless they want to; they aren't committed to write about these subjects. I always hope they will tackle one or two of them.

I think it's important for new writers to write about their strongest subjects that first week, and I tell them why: they'll learn writing skills, make connections and discoveries when they're highly motivated. They can spend two or three weeks developing that strong subject, go on to others, and return to the first one for polishing at the end of the semester after they have more skills. Often, they want to hoard their strongest subject for later, after they know more about writing. They need to know why that's a mistake: their "best" subjects will often lead to even better ones.

I tell students why, for now, we'll use only this first method of finding a subject. I want them to develop a habit important to writers: acting on the knowledge that if you look within yourself or look at the outside world with your own eyes, you can discover what's important to you; and that your ideas, interests, and experiences count. I tell them that other ideas for finding subjects, such as making up lists, diagrams, and flowcharts, can work; but I ask them, Why not use the direct route for finding a subject: the process of thinking *first* about what interests them, and in that way tapping into their strongest material? I assure them we'll try other ways of finding subjects later if they haven't found challenging ones the first week.

Sometimes I extend this exercise. I have them take one of the subjects, think for a couple of minutes about *the* part that most interests them *now as they sit here,* and then write for a few minutes about that just as fast as they can, without regard to order, logic, and other conventions.

B. List nine key words

Students' strongest papers result from their writing about themselves: family, friends, jobs, schools, hobbies, activities, ideas, dreams, goals. I write this list on the board. Students write down the words on their pages and jot down sentences, phrases, or lists that come to mind for each word. Afterward, I sometimes have them get in groups of four or five and discuss possible subjects. They ask each other questions, explore possibilities.

C. List many words or phrases

On the board, write these and other words or phrases you think of. Leave spaces between them. (Note: I don't always use all of these.)

conflict   tension   love   hate   joy   sorrow   anger   grief
jealousy   courage   greed   competition   triumph   pride
defeat   humiliation   strength   weaknesses   determination
discipline   laziness   forgiveness   pain   kindness   meanness
ambition   the end of something   the beginning of something
separation   loss   fighting   reconciliation   compassion

moments of insight   confusion   despair   hope   excellence
prejudice   beliefs   illusions   being duped   equality
inequality   fairness   unfairness   fear   cowardice   courage
respect   admiration   disgust   challenge   ideas   dreams
goals   generosity   seeing something or someone in new ways
competence   incompetence   misunderstandings   missed
opportunities   stupidity   intelligence   clarity   connections
curiosity   passion

Ask students to write these words or phrases on several pieces of paper, leaving large spaces between them. Have them look at each word or phrase on their pages and write down any names of people, any ideas or events that have meaning for them and are associated with each word or phrase. I usually spend about three minutes jotting down words on my list on the board. A name like *sister* may appear under a number of headings, such as love, fighting, jealousy, competition, courage. *Soccer* may appear often; or *trip to Colorado* may appear under both the fear and courage categories. Some headings won't reverberate for a writer; in that case, the writer goes on to the next. I explain that if an event, person, or idea appears under a number of headings on the list, quite likely there's an idea for a paper here.

Students work on these lists for about fifteen minutes. Then I ask them to circle the names or events that appear most often. Sometimes, after this, people talk in small groups about a subject that seems promising.

D. List everything you do

Mary Peterson, an instructor in our department, thought of this exercise. Ask students to brainstorm, listing the activities that make up their lives on a piece of paper. It's important to write down anything that comes to mind, even idiotic things like "brush teeth." Often, after several trivial activities will come good ones.

For instance, after "brush teeth," a writer might think of conversations in the bathroom, people who appear with terrible hangovers. This might even lead to a paper on drinking or alcoholics. Some people list items down the page; others would rather use sentences. Lists are usually best. I give students examples: soccer practice, set the alarm clock, argue with roommate, walk around town with a gang or alone, eat at a dining hall, study, cram for tests, do laundry, worry about money or a friend, listen to music, waste time, go to library, and so forth.

This takes about ten to fifteen minutes. Then students circle the items that interest them most. They start a new list with the most interesting item, and under this heading—such as playing the clarinet, fighting with roommate—they list everything they can think of to do with this new heading. Finally, they take what seems to be the main point of this new list—such as, How much benefit am I getting out of all the time I spend practicing the clarinet? Is it worth the time? or, Should I try to change roommates?—and write these key concepts on top of a blank page of paper. Then they start listing ideas that go with this subject.

E. List subjects and ideas you want to know more about

These lists can include anything from how to prepare mentally for a gymnastics competition to questions about the effect of alcoholic parents on teenagers to divorce in a family to finding out about the health care system in your home state to shelters for the homeless to opportunities for handicapped people in school to care centers for the elderly. Some students may want to learn about the life of a favorite painter or writer or musician, or find out how a coach regards her job or how players on a team regard their coach, or measure the extent of sexism or prejudice of some kind in school.

As in the list above, students write fast and include even seemingly foolish ideas. Then they circle the ideas that interest them most and discuss one or two of the best ideas with a group. The group asks questions, which often give a writer more ideas.

III. Finding an Angle on a Subject

Some new writers need to know what "an angle" means. Often I'll give students a very quick example from my own life to illustrate this and to show how I find an angle. For instance, say I want to write about my twelve years of living in Montreal. My family moved from the States to Montreal when I was six years old, and I had all my precollege schooling there. I could talk about how the city is built on a volcanic island in the middle of the Saint Lawrence River. It's a wonderful city, primarily French-speaking, with one of the best newspapers in the world—Le Devoir. I could talk about the French and English plays, the concerts, the old city with its marketplaces, the cathedrals, the museums, and the narrow cobble streets. It's one of the largest fishing ports in the world. And/or I could talk about the schools I went to, how we wore uniforms even though this was a public not a parochial school: short black dresses high above the knee, black stockings, black bloomer pants, and white oxford shirts. The boys and girls had separate classrooms, even had separate entrances to school. We started homework in the third grade. By high school, we had at least two and a half, often three hours of homework. And studied seven subjects in different classes each day, having at most one free period a day, usually only one or two free periods each week. We studied French starting in grade school because the majority of people in the Province of Quebec are French-speaking. I could talk about how I was very shy until I joined the field hockey team and worked on the school newspaper. I could write about my friends. If I write about so many aspects of Montreal and my schooling there, I'll write a summary; the writing will lack point and meaning. I need a focus here, a way into the material, a hook, an angle, to give me a reason for writing. When I have a worthwhile purpose—that is, an ambitious one that challenges me to solve a problem, to make meaning of those years in Montreal—then my writing will be more directed and purposeful. Readers will want to keep turning the pages when they know a paper has a reason for being, a purpose.

I give students two or three possible angles for the Montreal subject and I say that the one I choose will be the one that seems most interesting and that presents the greatest challenge to me *now as I sit down to write*. I actually go through this process (quickly) with the class, discussing two or three possible angles until I settle on one. I make sure the class sees why it's the most challenging to me *now*.

I'm careful to say that two years ago or many years from now another angle would have been or will be more appropriate.

A. *Make up new angles for a published essay*
Students who need to find new approaches to subjects will see from this exercise that there are many possible angles. Sometimes I refer to a very short reading we've all looked at; for instance, Joan Didion's essay "On Going Home." We pretend that we're Didion, who in the essay has just brought her baby home to her mother's place, and who, over the course of the visit, resees and revises her old ideas about the meaning of home, family, and the traditions she can pass on to her daughter. We brainstorm other angles we might have chosen: a comparison between going home in college as a single person and going home now, with a family of our own; a comparison of our relationship with our mother when we were in high school, in college, and now, when we have a child; an examination of the similarities and differences between ourselves and one parent; an exploration of what good traits we picked up from our parents and what we want to pass on to our child, as well as the traits we want to discard.

Sometimes I mention a paper that a student in class has written and that everyone has seen in workshop. The writer discusses why he chose the angle he did and we all discuss other angles he might have chosen.

B. *Brainstorm new angles on an old paper*

I ask students to think of one of their papers where they liked the subject. In one sentence they write down the angle from which they handled the subject. Then they write five other possible ways to approach it. Next the students get into groups of three. One writer tells the other two the subject of her paper. The others then list five possible angles that they think would be interesting. Everyone compares lists.

IV. Specific Information, Facts, Details

A. *Compare vague and specific sentences*

This activity illustrates for students what we mean when we talk about specific information, facts, and details. It makes clear the value of being specific. Find specific sentences in an essay, short story, novel, and newspaper feature article that you love. Rewrite the sentences, making them vague and occasionally throwing in ordinary details that readers will forget. Read aloud your vague version; then read aloud the writer's specific sentence. Students will hear the differences fast. Then hand out a sheet with a number of vague-specific sentence pairs so they can see and hear the differences as you read. Here is an example:

> *Vague sentence:* It was pleasant outdoors.
>
> *Specific sentence:* It was about seventy degrees in Hyde Park with just enough wind to fly a small kite.

After we've reviewed the list, I ask them to take out one of their papers where they've been vague, where they may have used too few details, or where the details were ordinary or not essential. They rewrite one of their pages. Then they swap pages with someone in class and offer advice.

B. *Make horoscopes specific*

Dan Halliday's hilariously specific horoscopes appeared in *The North American Review*. I converted this to an exercise.

Clip a fistful of horoscope predictions from newspapers. Pass them out to students. Then read a couple of the vague newspaper predictions, and right after, read your specific versions. Here are some real horoscope entries, along with my students' revisions:

Scorpio

Newspaper horoscope: "Situations that have hemmed you in will be somewhat alleviated today. On a modest basis you'll be able to lessen pressures and call your own shots."

Class response: "When your VW doesn't respond to your prayers this morning and you miss the 7:45, your boss will call to inform you that Harvey, his son-in-law, has been promoted to your position as Assistant Vice President in Charge of Interplanetary Diplomacy. Despair not! Aunt Bertha Mae has fallen into the gin vat and the distillery in Critter Creek, Kentucky is all yours."

Pisces

Newspaper horoscope: "Show a willingness to make sacrifices to benefit others today. If you do, they may be more apt to act in your behalf in problem areas."

Class response: "Kiss ass."

For this exercise, students work in pairs; it's more fun that way. After they've rewritten their passages, we go around the room, and one partner reads the vague newspaper sentences and the other reads the revised version aloud. I give them about ten or fifteen minutes to rewrite the passages. It takes another ten minutes or so to go around the class reading aloud.

I've often used this exercise right after Thanksgiving or spring break if students seem to need a review of basics. It pulls a class together quickly. It's a wonderful way to pull a class out of a midsemester swamp.

V. Writing Leads

I explain the importance of a strong lead. It's the first notes in a symphony, a door opening into a house you've never been before, a strong accurate first impression of your new roommate. A lead should be honest and point to the heart of your paper.

"Start with the good stuff," Andy Merton, a writer and a professor at the University of New Hampshire, often tells his students. Start with the piece of information, the idea or the moment that excited you about the subject, made you decide to write it. This energizes you; you'll want to keep writing. Readers will want to read on, too. If you start with boring background information and write up to the point of real engagement, by the time you get to the good stuff you're tired. You'll lack the energy to write well. Remember, you can always go back in a later draft and fill in the gaps, rearrange things.

A. Read aloud from ten favorite leads

Choose your all-time favorite leads. These can be from essays, newspapers, magazine articles, fiction. A mix is probably best. After you've explained strong versus weak leads, and I think this can be done in about three minutes, read your good leads, one after another. How to write good leads is, after all, a fairly simple, accessible skill. So I tend to be directive with them and use longer methods if the students don't catch on right away. Usually they catch on quickly.

B. Copy leads of students' papers
This is a wonderful exercise if your students have trouble writing strong leads. Tom Newkirk introduced this method. Photocopy leads anonymously from each student's paper during one week. Pass them out in class. Ask people: What are the best two or three leads? Why do they work? What's wrong with the ones that don't work?

C. Ask students to revise their own leads
Ask students to bring to the next class a paper of theirs that starts slowly. They should like the subject and want to revise it. After discussing leads, or copying student leads to distribute in class, each writer revises her or his own. Then students swap with another person to check out the improvements. Several students may want to read their first and revised leads out loud.

VI. Using the Skills of Essayists, Journalists, and Fiction Writers
The five skills that I think are most helpful to writers working on personal essays are writing description; writing scenes; using flashbacks; commenting, evaluating, making meaningful statements; and finally, playing with time in compositions: stretching a short period of time to a page or more of writing, summarizing a long period into a paragraph.

Some new writers think that writing dramatic scenes or wonderfully visual descriptions is for cosmetic purposes, to help the reader enjoy the paper. But skillful use of craft helps writers resee more clearly, relive more fully and accurately, think more precisely and deeply about what happened; therefore they are much more apt to reevaluate and come to greater meaning than if they handled their material in a clumsy way. Using the writing craft skillfully can lead writers to meaning.

Students may have heard that writing scenes, using flashbacks, and so forth, are for published fiction writers only, but that's not true.

Before students write, we talk about what an essay is. I refer to an essay we've read in class and compare it with a short story and feature article so that students see how many similar skills and techniques are used in all forms, see that forms blur.

I talk about writing personal essays that have shape, point, and meaning, that challenge the writer to think hard and come to new insights. Essays must avoid a superficial rehash of an experience. They must answer that rude question, So what?

Exercises for Discovery, Experiment, Skills, and Play

I tell my students that certain writing techniques that once were almost entirely the domain of fiction writers are now used by essayists and journalists. These skills empower writers, helping them to grapple with complex ideas and come to insights. As the students practice these skills, many of them will get ideas for longer papers. In addition, the skills will give them practice in forms they'll use for other papers: for instance, they will compare and contrast how they now regard an experience with how they regarded it earlier; they will persuade readers of the truth, importance, and believability of the worlds they create; and they'll analyze the evidence they record to see what actually did occur and to understand the meaning of an event.

The exercises are arranged sequentially, an idea I hit upon my first semester of teaching. I once belonged to a repertory theatre acting group that followed the method acting exercises Stanislavsky had arranged in a sequential way for his students. Later, in my first year of teaching composition, it seemed the idea of sequential exercises could be applied to writing. The sequence I present here (I tell this to students, too) springs from my assessment of most new writers' needs: they need first of all to use specific information well, to use facts and details in order to describe people or places. Writers make use of the five senses, especially the sense of sight. Writing scenes comes next because students want to render their most dramatic moments vividly. The motivation to write scenes effectively is high. When students write scenes, their prose suddenly takes on life, has impact. Then comes using flashbacks, then playing with time. In each exercise, I also discuss how writers can comment on and evaluate their material.

I mention in class that many new student writers tend to give almost every moment and episode in their papers approximately the same weight or emphasis. The students usually know some moments need to be stressed; they just don't know how to do it. Some writers feel trapped in the same chronology in which their experiences took place: according to clocks and calendars, the and-then, and-then syndrome. To escape this, they need to be able to write a scene, to slow a moment of time, to skip over or summarize long periods of time, and to use flashbacks.

A. Describe a person or a place
Students think of a person (or sometimes a place) they feel strongly about: for instance, someone they love or can't stand or are jealous of or all the above. They should have the person and place fixed in their minds when they come to class. I give them an example of a person who's on my mind, a place that fascinates me. In mentioning a place, I tell them to limit themselves to a house or a rock or a room, not all of California or Europe.

I concentrate on the descriptions of people because they're harder for most students to write than the descriptions of places. We discuss creating a strong first impression. I read from descriptions by my favorite essayists and fiction writers. We talk about the differences between a surface description and one that captures essence, that has purpose and meaning, that reverberates deeply for the writer and reader. I mention how many writers, like John McPhee, use lists. I read several of his lists aloud. We also talk about how writers can step into a description with commentary—interpretations, questions, speculations, or impressions about a person or place—as does Isak Dinesen in *Out of Africa.* Toni Morrison and William Faulkner will comment sometimes for pages in their novels. Students need to be encouraged to do this, too. They tend to fear they'll say something obvious or silly or sentimental. That's all right; no one in this class will laugh at them. Most writers say foolish, embarrassing, or obvious things from time to time. They go back and make changes.

I read from different writers and point out the details I especially love, ones that seem essential, outstanding. I emphasize those places where a writer comments either in a short phrase or passage or at length about a character.

Here's an example of a description of a person by student Dawn Boyer in "The Wine, the Soap, and the Words:"

> He'd swagger down the street, rolling up a magazine, tapping it against his hand. He wore a brown leather jacket and a hoop in his left ear ("I think it makes me look kinda swanky," he'd lilt while I'd tuck my arm through his and think, "That's how he looks all right"). I was intrigued he taught at Boston University. We'd go out for Mexican food and he'd tell me how he'd been involved in everything from dealing drugs to publishing stories. All of it was wonderful: the midnight phone calls, staying up until five in the morning, having flowers delivered to each other with cards that read, "It's nice knowing you." The whirlwind, the giddiness of being together.

How much better this is than, "He was tall and thin and rather daring, eccentric." We know not only things about his character; we know how the writer regarded him, and therefore her character is revealed, too.

B. Write dramatic scenes

Ask students to think of one argument or important discussion they had with one person in one place. They must feel strongly about the person as well as the argument or discussion.

These are the elements of dramatic scenes that I present in one class period: setting the stage, dialogue, action/reaction, the thoughts and feelings of the writer at the time the scene took place, and if indicated, the writer's thoughts and feelings now, as he looks back. However, this isn't a formula. There are scenes, for instance, with only dialogue or with almost no dialogue, with long reflective passages or with none. I tell students that if writers learn to use each of these elements, they'll have a wide range of skills from which to choose.

It takes about fifteen minutes to go over the elements of scenes, about twenty minutes or more for students to get a good start into writing them. They finish their scenes at home and bring them to the next class or conference for feedback.

1. Setting the stage   Writers use essential "props" so that readers can see the key people and the place in which a dramatic event occurs and so that the writers themselves can examine the effect of that place. I tell students that place is part of context: it affects how people think, feel, and behave; and it affects outcome. I read from scenes I've admired, stopping occasionally to discuss how some writers use much detail, some hardly any at all.

In the following excerpt, student Judith Noyes writes of returning as an adult to St. Paul's school where she had been on scholarship in the summer program. In this paper she compares her experiences in school with her experience at the reunion. She still has much less money than her old schoolmates, but for the first time feels that the subject of money has become important. Before the dialogue begins, she makes sure readers can see the setting:

> We returned to Bill's apartment where a delicious display of bread and fine cheese awaited us. We gathered around an old lobster trap table as two bottles of Bordeaux began to circulate. It was the same scene we had played before, five years ago, only the props were changed. The apple crates we had sat on were replaced by a plush couch and large cushions, the no-name potato chips had transformed into Brie and Camembert, and the French wines replaced the warm Riuniti we used to buy for a few dollars.
>
> I was the only one who still wore faded jeans. Theresa's cotton dress came from Milano. Roberta bought almost exclusively Gloria Vanderbilt and even Bob, who prided himself on being practical and simple, bought his pullover at L.L. Beans for a price that would have fed my cat and me for three weeks. I leaned back into the shadows and lifted my glass to my lips.

2. Dialogue   Dialogue is not used to feed information; it's used to show what people do to each other's feelings, ways of seeing, guts. A grotesque exaggeration of dialogue used to feed information is, "Look, Andre, over your left shoulder is a window and, with the temperature in the 90s, perhaps you should open it." Readers know that's fake and lose faith in the writer's ability to tell the truth. Writers should just tell readers that it's 90 degrees outside and Andre opened the window.

Another thing to watch for in dialogue: don't let people talk too long. New writers often rely too heavily on dialogue; it's easy for many of them, and they get carried away. Writers can feed much information indirectly as does Robert Lindemann in the essay included below in exercise 4 ("Thoughts, comments, interpretations, feelings"). I tell students to get to essential dialogue fast and skip the hi-how-are-yous.

3. Action and reaction What people do, how they lean forward or pull back and stare at their hands on their laps, how they gesture or don't move as they speak and listen, reveals them. What we writers do and do not observe or choose to record reveals us. We should include actions and reactions in most scenes and be aware of their significance. Again, I refer to some of my favorite scenes or to scenes the class has read in essays in order to show different approaches and effects.

4. Thoughts, comments, interpretations, feelings I remind students to record only their own thoughts and feelings; if they go into other people's minds, suddenly the essay is fiction, or has slipped into the literary journalism genre of fiction/nonfiction. Some teachers, however, encourage writers to use other points of view to gain distance and understanding. The writers then return with new insights to final drafts and include only their own perspectives. A scene can rely on mostly external observations, as many Didion and Hemingway scenes do, or writers can interrupt at any point to reflect, as Maxine Hong Kingston does in *The Woman Warrior* or *China Men*. It's easy to stop a scene cold at any point and remark — at length or in short phrases — about what is going on. Students need to be told this. Often they get so swept up in the drama of what happened that they forget to comment. A note here, though: perhaps it's best for some writers to write that scene fast at first, no comments. Later they can go back, slow down, and examine more deeply what occurred. They can also include what they thought at the time the event took place, and compare what they thought and felt *then* to how they think and feel *now as they write.*

Below, student Bob Lindemann writes about giving his father a bath. The father has emphysema and has recently recovered from a cancer operation. In this scene, Bob interrupts the dialogue to record how he regarded their relationship at the time of the bath, and he occasionally reevaluates how he perceives the relationship now as he writes.

"I'm giving you a bath," I said. "Come, let's go."

I help [my father] struggle from the bedroom, across the worn rug-covered hallway and into the small bathroom. We move slowly together. My steps are short and slow, mimicking his painful shuffle. He takes off his pajama tops and unsnaps the bottoms. The elastic waist band separates under his navel. The pajamas cascade down and drape around his thickly veined feet.

"Can you stand there okay?"

He nods. I get towels and soap, making sure the transparent green floral shower curtain is tucked inside the tub, hoping stray water doesn't seep into the duplicate second floor apartment directly underneath.

"Here, let me help you." I grasp his arm firmly, support him, as he gingerly lifts one leg, then the other, over the yellow porcelain tub edge.

"You gonna sit down?"

"No! I want a shower."

Pop Pop is a men-don't-eat-quiche and a heads-of-the-household-don't-do-dishes kind of guy. "Men take showers," he once proclaimed after mother had commented on the lack of a tub in my small one-room apartment.

I see and feel his frailty. I realize that I can handle him physically, that he will fall if I don't hold him. He has always been the strong one in the family, the boss, the one to give orders. I am no longer afraid of him, only afraid of becoming like him. Now I am the strong one, but am I strong enough to tell him of my hurt?

I want to say, "You didn't love me, Dad. You never praised me, encouraged me. I didn't get a chance to fight for your affection. You had no affection to give. I want so much to love you, to be friends, to be able to look you in the eye and tell you I love you, but I can't."

The sound of running water brings me out of my trance.

"Not so hot!" he says.

5. Insert essential background information. I tell students that knowing how to insert background information — that is, using flashbacks — in a dynamic way saves writers from slogging through dull information in the first pages. They can start with strong material, then go back and fill in the gaps.

Flashbacks should contain only information that's critical to clarity and meaning and/or that adds to the tension in the essay. New writers often include unnecessary information.

The use of the word *had* tells readers that this is background information. For short flashbacks, writers often use the word *had* only once. In some cases, not at all. For long flashbacks, they may use *had* three or four times.

Some writers make the mistake of delivering just one sentence to begin a story ("I sat down on the brown bench by the railroad tracks and looked at Bill") and then move on to a two-page flashback (on the relationship with Bill). This won't work. Readers must be pulled substantially — they should be given at least a paragraph — into a situation and want to read on before being jolted into the past.

Before introducing a flashback, a writer often gives her readers an unforgettable moment or detail. Then, when returning to the main story action after a flashback of a paragraph or several pages, she can mention that strong detail or moment.

D. Control time in compositions

l. Time stretch   Students take a one- to five-minute experience they feel strongly about and write a page or more about it. This exercise helps them learn to recognize important points or moments in their work and emphasize them. It helps writers include their readers in an experience by using specific facts and details, by relying on the five senses, especially sight. It teaches writers that when they observe and record accurately, they will remember even more and they will often discover insights.

At the end of the class before the one in which I will present the exercise, I ask students to think of a one- to five-minute experience they feel strongly about. I give examples: seeing someone they love wheeled into an operating room; seeing someone hit by a car; waiting for the curtain to rise on a play in which they had the leading role; two minutes of specific skating routines that were particularly difficult to execute in the state championships; being told by someone they love to go to hell; reeling in a fish. This time period must be engraved in their skulls.

When I present this exercise I stress taking control of time, manipulating it in writing. In life we're caught in chronology. Writers are freed from this. We can slow two or three minutes of a critically important experience and write several pages about it and, if we want, dismiss years of unimportant events or material in a phrase. New writers need to be aware of this power.

Sometimes, to illustrate the point, I make up a two- or three-minute story that starts, "The alarm went off and I awoke to the sound of my beagle barking outside my room." In this made-up story, each section gets equal weight: brushing my teeth, driving to the mountain, climbing out of the car, climbing up the mountain, and (the climax) saving my brother from falling over a cliff, seeing him for the first time as vulnerable, seeing my relationship to him in a new way. Then I discuss the obvious need for control, for cutting out the alarm clock and the beagle, perhaps cutting the drive to the mountain, too (unless we fought, or behaved in such a way that our relationship was strongly revealed); I discuss writing a long section on those two minutes when my brother teetered on the edge of the cliff.

I hand out a paper by a former student, Judy O'Donoghue, called "The Nursing Home." This was her response to the time stretch exercise. Judy took the exercise home, lengthened it, and revised it many times. It took her several drafts to trust and use specifics and to discover their meaning.

> My father pulled open the heavy glass door of the Nursing Home. Each Saturday he came to visit my grandmother. The time had come for me to see her. The air was stale and warm. He guided me with his hand on the back of my neck into the black-tiled hall. I was ten, and ever since I could remember, I hated how he led me around by my neck.
>
> The hall was wide and long. Light came through the windows but didn't reflect off the dirty floor. A flickering overhead light stretched down the center of the ceiling. It reminded me of a school corridor with rows of windows on either side. Some windows were open, some were shut. The shades were pulled halfway and were stained with large brown rings.
>
> Old women lined both sides of the walls. They slumped in their wheelchairs or sat in chestnut rocking chairs. A silent television rolled its picture in a corner. One old woman stretched from her wheelchair and stroked the screen with bent fingers.
>
> They smelled of urine and soiled clothing. Their clothes were wrinkled and fit loosely about their figures. Gingham dresses were faded, and old sweaters stained and crusty. They wore black leather slippers and orthopedic shoes. In one corner, an old woman clawed through a hamper stamped in red, "Dihnan Memorial for the Elderly."
>
> My father's hand fell from my neck and I followed him almost stepping on the backs of his shoes. I kept my eyes on the floor and counted the number of tiles that my father stepped in. His pace grew faster and each stride covered more tiles. I moved beside him and glanced up to his face. His eyes were fixed on the far wall. The halls were so wide and the old women seemed so small. One woman sat in a large armchair with gray stuffing hanging from the torn seams. . . . She startled me with a tug on my skirt. I tried to pull away. Her hand quivered under the hem of my skirt and her fingers gently touched the fabric. Her hand was thin and had brown spots connected by ribbons of blue veins. . . .

Judy continues this description, then discusses the meeting with Grandmother. She begins to see how much her father resembles the old woman. Finally she comes to this insight, which she could not possibly have come to had she not written precisely:

> The longer I looked, the more and more they looked alike. Grandma's face had fallen and Father's was beginning to pull from his cheekbones. His chin hung down like a hammock attached to his neck.
>
> I shifted my chair and looked up to the clock above the exit light. I wanted to leave. I wanted my father to go away so he wouldn't catch it.
>
> I moved my hand to his and he squeezed hard. It was still tight with muscle. I smiled at his strength and I let his large fingers spread mine apart. I wanted to tell him that I loved him and wished he'd never get old.

In slowing time, it helps to think in "slow motion," as sportscasters say when they replay a high dive by a competitive swimmer. It is this effect of time being slowed that writers should achieve in this exercise.

How? By showing — not telling about — the precise things that occurred during those critical few minutes. That means relying on facts, specific information, details. The external world must be rendered exactly. I warn students that it's tempting to tell about what happened: "I was simply revolted, and also frightened by those old people in the nursing home," Judy O'Donoghue could have written in the extended time stretch. That would have left us out of the experience, and more importantly, Judy could not have examined that short period of time carefully, thus robbing her — and us — of her final insight. Students need to understand that sloppy writing leads to sloppy insights.

Before students write, they title the exercise; for example, "The three minutes it took me to walk down the nursing home hall." This helps them to focus at once on the skill, not waste time leading into the exercise.

After students write, they swap with one person. Before they read each other's work, I reread a paragraph of Judy's paper, then read a paragraph or more from a published writer's work: for example, from Agee's *A Death in the Family* when young Rufus sees Grammaw Lynch for the first time.

This is one exercise students always revise at home and show to me in conference because many of the skills are critical to clear thinking and strong prose.

2. Time summary   Students choose one angle of a long period of time and write only a paragraph or two about it. Often this exercise leads students to include more reflective passages in their essays and to depend less, or hardly at all, on chronology.

Students think of a long period of time they feel strongly about: three years of being afraid of a gang; a year of playing the flute or soccer; the year grandmother lived with them; a month in a terrible summer camp or boot-camp; years of competing with or fighting with a brother or sister; years with a difficult parent or neighbor, with a wonderful coach. They must tap into one dominant attitude they have towards this time period; for example, camp was exciting or hell.

In class, I mention that writers can compress weeks or years of time into a paragraph. To capture the essence of a period of time and render it specifically and dramatically so as to include readers, writers must first establish the time frame. They need to communicate their dominant attitude towards this period of time. Then they write, using outstanding evidence to reveal the nature of that time period. Writers make tough choices with this exercise; for instance, in the paper I quote from below, student writer Denver Moorehead had many examples he could have used to illustrate the tough, demanding summer he had spent working construction with his father; he decided that the following examples best illustrated his strong negative impressions of that period of time:

> [For one summer] I was a gopher on a heavy construction crew. We laid 60″ Reinforced Concrete Pipe through the swamps of Southeast Georgia. Sixteen inch Polyvinyl Chloride Water Main next to I–20, twenty-five feet down in red Georgia Clay. My Dad would wake me up around 4:45 a.m. every morning so we could be at the office by 5:30. Trying to stay awake during the long drive through the unlit backroads of North Augusta and Richmond County was a whole new kind of hell. Every time I drifted to sleep, a punch would dig hard into my biceps. . . . Dad would offer a chew of Levi-Garett. I didn't hate chewing because of the taste — I got used to the gasoline flavored juice — it was mostly the stale piercing smell of tobacco that permeated the truck that made me sick. By the time the sun rose, we'd be slinging pipe. Sunrise comforted me because I could then look for water moccasins instead of feeling for them. By lunch time my hair was crunchy from all the dirt trapped under my hard hat and my lips were parched from the sun. Shade was no relief because the swamp mosquitos seemed oblivious to repellant.

We know the incidents above were repeated again and again because of the word *would*. Notice that the writer drops the *would* after a while when he decides we've caught on to the repetitive nature of these experiences. Before students write this exercise, have them label the page: "Time Summary: One summer of working construction with my father" — or whatever fits.

The published time summary I sometimes read from before students swap their exercises in class is from John Cheever's short story "Good-bye, My Brother." Near the end, there's a long paragraph in which the narrator reflects on all the good-byes that his brother has made.

VII. Revising

The following exercise helps students regard revision not as punishment but as a chance to do justice to a subject they care about. It exposes them to common writing problems that can be solved by major revisions. While using in-class time to revise, they can see and talk with others who are making important changes.

I ask students to bring to class a paper with a strong subject they care about but that has major conceptual problems: it needs to be reorganized, needs a new angle or focus, is too narrow and needs a wider context, is too broad and needs to be narrowed, needs more commentary and fewer specific facts or vice versa.

First, I talk about how often I revise my writing. I bring in one of my early, middle, and late drafts of an essay or story and read from certain parts. I discuss the difference between major revision and fine-tuning. Often I quote writers who talk about writing and revision in Don Murray's book of writers' quotes, *Shop Talk* (1990).

I talk about the five common problems listed below and discuss ways to solve them.

A. *Reorganizing*
Here are two ways to reorganize: Use three-by-five cards. Write down the content of each paragraph in a sentence or phrase on index cards. Arrange and rearrange the cards in a logical order across the floor. There will be gaps that can be filled by jotting down ideas on other cards and adding them to the "train." It's enormously helpful to see these cards all at one glance on the floor, and it's fun to play with the order, see right away the effect of your changes. Or tell students to list the contents of their papers, paragraph by paragraph, on long sheets of paper. Then they can see what they actually have written, which often isn't exactly what they thought they wrote. Just seeing this list is often enough to make them think of new ways to organize.

B. *Finding a new angle or focus*
I review the methods of finding an angle discussed earlier in this chapter (Group II, "Finding a Subject"). Usually I have students try the exercise on brainstorming new angles by making lists of possibilities (Exercise III B). After they've come up with, say, two good angles, they discuss these ideas in small groups.

C. *Making the subject broader*
I invent a hasty story of a student who writes of, say, visiting a junkyard for cars. I say that if he only describes what he sees there, the paper will lack meaning because we don't know why the dump visits are important to him. We need a wider context. If he tells us he came from a family where he was lessoned to death (piano, gymnastics, French, navigation, etc., etc.) and that the only time he had unsupervised was the two hours after Boy Scouts on Wednesdays when he and friends raided the junkyard, then we'll understand the context and care more about the subject.

D. *Narrowing the subject*
Again, I use a little anecdote to illustrate why writers narrow their subjects. I might tell about a plan to write of a trip across the country. It took a

month. Recording each day's travels in a short paper would result in a superficial summary and lack focus and interest. Instead, a writer would be wise to concentrate on the weekend the writer overcame fear by learning to scale cliffs on Pike's Peak.

E. Adding and cutting facts, details, information, and interpretive statements

Writers should know whether they tend to clobber readers with too much information and commentary or whether they are stingy and give too little. By the time I give this revision exercise in class, I am confident that most writers know into which camp they fall. If they are in doubt, they can exchange a few pages with another student and get an opinion.

After reviewing these five points, I ask each student to revise a paper in class. They are supposed to consult each other or me for help.

VIII. Avoiding the Midsemester Slump (or Pulling Out of It)

About a third to halfway through a course, students can get bogged down. Often they have written and revised two or more major papers several times. They need to think about future papers, different challenges, new forms.

Depending on the feel of the class, I may switch now to exercises that give students practice with different forms: persuasion, comparison, and contrast. Some students want to try writing for the school newspaper or local papers. Editing or fine-tuning is great to introduce now, I think. Sometimes I skip exercises altogether for a while and we concentrate on reading responses in class. Or I'll pull out some of the "Finding a Subject" exercises I didn't try earlier.

Here are some exercises that will get classes energized again.

A. List the elements found in strong prose and evaluate your writing and reading (a two-part exercise)

Part l: List the elements that make up strong prose

Students discuss what makes writing effective. They see that the same yardstick isn't always applicable to each piece of writing.

The class gets into groups of four or five and brainstorms about what makes a good piece of writing. They refer to their own and to published writing. They draw up lists. Then the whole class gets together and draws up a master list on the board. Invariably, someone mentions that there are forms, language, and traditions in other fields, such as psychology, that are not appropriate to the form of, say, a personal essay. They need to recognize that fact, and this becomes a good time to talk about good writing in different disciplines.

I type up their list, photocopy it, and distribute it in the next class period, when students do Part 2 of the exercise.

Part 2: Evaluate your writing and reading processes and progress and set specific goals for the rest of the semester

This encourages students to take responsibility for their work. By examining how they've progressed, they can see what they need to work on in the final weeks.

Students bring all typed drafts of all papers to class. They bring their reading responses and journals. Referring frequently to the list we drew up in the exercise above, they write a letter to me in which they assess their writing and reading processes and progress. They quote from their own papers, refer to specific points. They consider their writing strengths and weaknesses now, and set goals for the rest of the semester. This letter becomes another occasion for them to ask me for special help and to say if anything in the course bothers or confuses them.

B. Write your impressions of school

This gives students experience in writing in groups. The exercise also works for individual writers. It encourages students to look outside themselves at their community. It gives them practice in manipulating material into different thematic arrangements.

Students think of people, incidents, small or large moments, that have impressed them at school. These impressions can be anything from seeing prejudice acted out between two people, to rushing to class at 8:00 a.m. to observing friends at a party to waiting in line to sign up for courses.

The students' impressions should be brief and vivid, rather like photographs or short takes with a movie camera. No comments, no statements. Some entries may be a page long, others only a sentence. The students work in groups of four or five. First they brainstorm ideas, pool impressions, and come up with a list. Then they divide up the work. Each student writes her share. One impression per page. When they have finished writing, they gather their entries and arrange them to make a thematic statement. Some entries get cut. New ones must be written. One person takes the collection home, types it, and I photocopy each group's "UNH Impressions" to distribute in the next class.

When the response to this exercise is enthusiastic, we return to group work and do major revisions. Some groups decide to change the ground rules and add comments, sometimes even analyses. Then we photocopy and hand out these later drafts to every student.

C. *Write a story in a group*

This is a group exercise my colleague Dot Kasik invented. It's fun, gets imaginations going, and provides students with easy and positive experiences with group writing.

Dot clips a photo and headline from a scandal sheet. She gives copies of it along with this handout to her students:

> Before embarking on this project, you must solemnly promise that you will never tell anyone outside of class, particularly parents or former English teachers, that you participated in this assignment.
>
> You have been given only the headline and accompanying photo from a story taken from one of our nation's finest newspapers. Your job, along with your writing partners, is to write the story as you imagine it. Do it in the following way:
>
> 1. As a whole group, discuss a possible story line. It may be as wild as you wish, but must agree with the words and picture you've been given.
> 2. Still working together, compose a two- or three-sentence lead to introduce the story.
> 3. Now work individually. Write a paragraph furthering the story line. Be original and be specific.
> 4. When each of you has finished your paragraph, try as a group to put everything together in a logical way. You'll find you must eliminate some information because it doesn't fit. You'll also have to fill in the gaps and make transitions.
> 5. Finally, as a group, write a two- or three-sentence conclusion to wrap things up.

Students write. Later, they read their pieces aloud.

D. *Elaborate on newspaper fillers*

This is an idea Judith Fishman Summerfield (1986) describes. The exercise helps writers trust their own reactions, their own ways of seeing, and helps them recognize that there is no one godlike version of any story, but rather many different versions.

Cut a filler from a newspaper—those three- to twenty-line pieces that tell such things as how Renee Dupuis slipped and skidded over thirty yards of wet seaweed at the Lubec Labor Day Parade and miraculously didn't fall down or how Eldredge Johnson, at his hundred second birthday in a Detroit nursing home, had these words of advice to younger people: "For God's sake, take your life while you can and live it!"

Students will write about the filler in any way they like. Some may comment on the events the filler refers to; others may want to adopt the persona of one of the characters mentioned in the filler or a relative of one of the characters, or a news reporter. Some may write a poem, a short essay, a story. Later, students read aloud and the class comments on the pieces.

E. Write about an object
For students who suffer from an overactive nagging critic in their heads, this exercise reminds them that writing is often, in early drafts, an exploration. Students fool around, see if they can make connections, find some meaning.

Students think of an object that's important to them; for example, an old guitar case, a Chinese hatbox, a wart on their chins, a stick-out ear, their roommate's smelly socks.

In class, we talk about starting to write about something small, like an object that intrigues you, and seeing where it leads; we talk about being susceptible to discovery. I ask students to think about their object, and if they want to start their exercise by making connections between the object and an experience or person, fine. They may want to begin with a large statement, such as "I couldn't bear the mole on my face," and go on to discuss its meaning to them. Later, they can describe that lump if it seems appropriate. Often, though, writers aren't sure why an object is important for them. In these cases, it's wise to start with a careful description of the object, which can lead, as one writes, to insight.

F. Enter the bad-writing contest
The purpose of this exercise is to have fun. Becky Rule uses it on the last day of a semester. I've stolen the idea and use it at about the halfway point. Students work by themselves, in pairs or in threes or fours—however they want—and they write the worst possible paragraph or page on any subject they want. The pieces are read aloud. First prize goes to the worst prose.

IX. Fine-tuning

A. Edit a student paper in pairs
Students practice editing. I make sure we have a very interesting and strong piece of prose from one of my students to edit. Before class, I check with the writer to see whether we can write all over her paper as we edit. (Most students know they have trouble editing and welcome this.)

First we read and discuss the student's paper in terms of strengths, weaknesses, and possible solutions to problems. Then we discuss editing. I talk about *radical surgery*, where we slash whole lines and paragraphs, and *fine-tuning*, where we get each word right. The students and I make a list of editing points on the board, such as:

get a wonderful lead

cut unnecessary words — often this requires getting rid of whole sections, paragraphs, sentences

eliminate clichés

use the right word

be conscious of word and sentence placement: the last word in a sentence carries most weight; the first and last sentences in paragraphs carry most weight

surprise readers by using language in an unusual though accurate way

check for word repetitions

vary length of sentences

use strong active verbs

don't overuse adjectives

beware of adverbs

use punctuation to make meaning

strengthen the ending — keep thinking, making connections to the last word

After we have a list on the board, students edit in pairs. Each pair takes a different page (some pairs may be working on the same page, depending on the length of the paper and the number of students in the class). Partners discuss, argue, and negotiate editing ideas. They do this word by word, line by line. I tell them why they're working in pairs: they learn other writers' editing methods.

If there is time, students take one page of their own writing and edit it with a partner.

B. Cut fifteen words per page

The objective is to cut unnecessary words. Students bring one of their papers to class. Tom Newkirk tells his students to pretend that an editor has just told them their paper will be published in a magazine but they must cut fifteen words (or some other number) per page. It becomes a challenge and fun to cut when students know an editor will be checking to be sure they've cut the required number of words. This exercise can be done in pairs, groups, or solo.

C. Edit in a group

Students do this to learn from one another. They bring to class one page of a paper they want to edit. It should be a paper they like. Students get into groups of five. Each writer edits one of his own pages for about three to five minutes. Then everyone in the group passes his or her page to the person on the left and edits another writer's page. Students keep passing and editing pages until their own work returns to them with cuts from four other people.

D. Punctuate for meaning

The importance of punctuation is the theme here. Several teachers at UNH have students work in groups of five or six. Each person studies two points, presents them to the group, and invents an exercise — usually some sentences to punctuate. This can be carried out throughout a semester or accomplished in one class period.

It's news to many students that writers use common sense and pay attention to meaning when they use punctuation. I read aloud from a funny three-page essay by Lewis Thomas, "Notes on Punctuation," in his book *The Medusa and the Snail* (1979). In this essay, Thomas says things like this: "Exclamation points are the most irritating of all. Look! they say, look at what I just said! How amazing is my thought!" The whole essay reads like this and students learn fast.

I mention punctuation in full-class workshops of student prose. I'll point out, for instance, how a sentence might change if a writer were to use a semicolon instead of a period. I do this briefly, but students tend to remember these tips, I think, because they're placed in the context of a paper written by a class member.

X. Persuading

Students write persuasively. This is a good way to introduce the notion of audience or reader. The exercise often leads to longer papers.

I ask students to think of an issue they feel strongly about and know a lot about: for example, noise in the library, sexism they've encountered on campus.

I remind students they've been persuading their parents to let them stay up late, buy a new bike, etc., for years. We discuss how they have persuaded; why they persuaded one parent in one way, the other in another. After a few minutes I'll start listing on the board things like audience, knowing what your audience knows and needs to know, knowing your audience's prejudices (good and bad), deciding how to appeal to your audience. As we talk, I keep adding to the list. It will include such things as anticipating audience reaction, using outstanding relevant facts, deciding what information to include first, second, third, deciding how to begin and the best tone to use to persuade the specific audience — for example, should the writer adopt a tone that's humorous, angry, sarcastic, or straightforward and factual?

Before students write, they note on the page the audience they want to reach; for example, the college community, "the bums on the third floor of Stoke," the citizens living near a nuclear plant.

After students finish writing, I point out that if they are stumped in one of their longer weekly papers, they should consider who their audience is. Sometimes this helps writers see their material in new ways.

XI. Appreciating Different Voices, Including Your Own

Students listen, and again appreciate different writing voices. They begin to discover and trust their own voices. This exercise returns to and extends Exercise I.C., "Respect different writing voices," which I use at the beginning of the semester.

Each writer brings one of her or his best papers to class as well as an essay, research article, story, or news article having a strong, distinctive voice.

Voice springs from your character, from all that you've experienced and done and thought and felt in your life, and from how you now, as you write, regard and concentrate not on yourself but on your subject. I tell students that at their best they have distinctive writing voices.

Students take turns reading out loud a paragraph of a published writer's work where the voice is strong. Sometimes I read from a favorite writer, too. We stop from time to time to compare and comment on the voices.

Then students find passages or even just sentences in their best papers where their voices are strong and distinctive. We talk about why these sentences or passages were particularly vivid. Usually part of the reason is their commitment to their subjects, a strong point of view, and concentration. They talk about the conviction of their best writing, bred partly of an abundance of information. A number of students will want to read aloud from their good passages, and we comment on them.

By the end of this session, students have been exposed to many different voices. I tell them why I wanted them to write down the strongest passages from their own work: they should take the passages and themselves seriously, appreciate how they are at their best.

I use this exercise fairly near the end of a semester because the danger is that if you use it early in the year, students can become self-conscious about how they sound.

XII. Endings

Students learn that writers think, make connections, and discover new insights as they write, right up through the last line of a paper. I try to rid students of old preconceptions that essay endings are vague summaries of what went on in the main part of the paper.

Everyone brings to class favorite last paragraphs of published pieces we've read during or outside class. (I encourage students to find a writer/ mentor whose work they love; they read from their chosen writer's works throughout the semester. Since they okay their author with me early in the semester, I don't worry they'll bring in cheap romances or detective novels.)

Several students summarize the reading they brought to class, then read the last two or three paragraphs aloud. We discuss each one, noting how and why it works.

I read from essays that end with specific details or dramatic scenes. Then I read from a short story that ends with what many people think of as a traditional essaylike general statement.

I've included an ending of a student paper. This is by Dawn Boyer, who finishes her paper about a boyfriend like this:

> He turned and ran his hand across my cheek, cupping it on my neck: for the first time I felt sorry for him because he might never learn. I moved away, turned on the light and reached for his clothes. He asked what I was doing. I think you already know, I said, that it's time for you to leave.
>
> Without looking at him, I walked into the bathroom, turned the shower knobs on to hot and full force, and closed the door. I tried to wash everything about him away.

Another student writer ends an essay with this reflective statement. The paper is called "Loss of Control" and it's about the student's tendency to get violent when drinking. I point out to my class that this author, like Judy and Dawn, is thinking right up to the last word.

> The one fear I carry and will carry long after I break up with B. or leave UNH is that I could again lose control. Though I have begun to expose my tensions and frustrations before they reach a breaking point, I have not stopped drinking. I do not think I will ever completely stop drinking. I am now conscious that I have a drinking problem. The events of that night exposed the severity of my problem. Now, before I begin drinking, I remind myself of the possible consequences if I reach my "catalyst" stage. So far, this has helped me control my actions. If I slip into my "catalyst" stage I am cautious and try to keep myself from getting excited. However, no matter how relaxed or calm I am, every time I open a beer, I run the risk of losing control. Though I am cautious, I am not free from danger. The potential for a drunken, violent explosion will always be present. It is a possibility I live with and pray will never happen again.

To end this chapter, I'd like to point out that good exercises are chances for students to experiment, try new forms and skills, and play with new ideas without fear of being judged either by themselves or by someone else. I can't think of a better way to generate excitement for learning, experimenting, and making discoveries than having a whole group of people fooling around on their pages without inhibitions or pressure and finding out what works, what doesn't, and why.

One of the reasons these exercises are successful is that they've been discussed, tried, altered, and discussed again by many teachers at UNH, all of whom invent, swap, steal, and improve on one another's teaching ideas. When you try some of these exercises and make changes in them as well as invent your own, pass along your ideas to other teachers; later, you'll find your ideas returned to you enriched.

References

Agee, James. 1957. *A Death in the Family*. New York: McDowell, Obolensky.

Cheever, John. 1978. "Good-bye, My Brother." In *The Stories of John Cheever*. New York: Knopf.

Didion, Joan. 1968. "On Going Home." In *Slouching Towards Bethlehem*. New York: Farrar, Straus, and Giroux.

Dinesen, Isak. 1938. *Out of Africa*. New York: Random House.

Halliday, Dan. Horoscopes in *The North American Review*. Various issues.

Kingston, Maxine Hong. 1976. *The Woman Warrior*. New York: Knopf.

———. 1980. *China Men*. New York: Knopf.

Murray, Donald. 1990. *Shoptalk*. Portsmouth, NH: Heinemann.

Summerfield, Judith Fishman. 1986. "Framing Narratives." In *Only Connect: Uniting Reading and Writing*, edited by Thomas Newkirk. Portsmouth, NH: Boynton/Cook.

Thomas, Lewis. 1979. "Notes on Punctuation." In *The Medusa and the Snail*. New York: Viking Penguin.

4

Using Reading in the Writing Classroom

Donna Qualley

When I first began teaching Freshman English, I concentrated on demystifying "the writing process" for my students. Books like Donald Murray's *Write to Learn* (1984) and, more recently, Bruce Ballenger and Barry Lane's *Discovering the Writer Within* (1989) helped students see how a piece of writing evolves and gave them an opportunity to experience and reflect on their own processes of making meaning. While I was teaching myself how to teach writing this way, I really didn't know what to do with the reading component of the course. At first, I used other writers' essays and stories to model form and technique that I liked and that I wanted students to emulate in their own writing. I told students what to look for in a text. I evaluated students on how closely they identified and followed my reading of the text. However, what I was doing to students' readings was the same thing that C. H. Knoblauch and Lil Brannon (1984) criticized writing teachers for doing to student papers. Knoblauch and Brannon accused writing teachers of judging student work according to their own "ideal text," their mental construct of what a paper on a given subject should look like. I realized I was imposing my "ideal text" on students' reading. I was asking students to arrive at a specific understanding without having traveled. I was not showing them the way to "get there" themselves. Instead, I had them bypass a process in their reading that we had stressed all semester in writing: a process that reveals how meaning is gradually constructed. I emphasized one philosophy for writing—one that encouraged writing as a process of discovery, student "ownership" of ideas, and the development of voice and authority—and practiced a contradictory one for reading.

My first response to this discovery was that I couldn't do everything in a semester. After all, this was a writing course and not a reading course—wasn't it? But then it occurred to me that if I taught my students something about the process of reading, their writing would benefit. I began to notice many similarities between the reading and writing processes. I saw how the ideas and language of one could help explain the other. For example:

- Just as we do when writing, we "draft" a first reading and "revise" or elaborate on it in subsequent readings.

- Readers construct the meaning of the texts they read by degrees; in the same way, writers gradually construct the meaning of experiences they write about.

- Just as writing helps people to discover, learn, and clarify their ideas and experience, writing can help people to discover, learn, and clarify the texts they read.

- My better writers always seemed to be the better readers of their own text. Wasn't revision really a reading skill?

Slowly, my class began to evolve and is still developing into a "writingreading" and "readingwriting" course.

What I Want Students to "Unlearn" About Reading and the Reading Process

Thinking assignments have always bothered me.... I prefer the type of assignment that I can do quickly without putting a great deal of thought into it.

Marnie

Marnie's statement might be humorous if it, unfortunately, weren't so typical of the kind of worldview freshmen hold when they arrive at the university. This outlook reflects an emphasis on ends rather than means—on getting things done rather than on the process of doing them. I spend a great deal of my time helping students "unlearn" a narrow conception of what literacy, especially what I might call academic literacy, entails. Students leave high school, if they are lucky, with some notion of the "writing process." Even if they don't feel like competent writers, many of them have worked in groups or experienced peer editing sessions. Most have some idea of revision (or what I would call editing). However, their understanding of the reading process is very literal and limited. Some of our students' assumptions include:

1. *If you can decode the words, you can read.* There are many ways to read, but freshmen are most familiar with two kinds: reading for pleasure — to experience, escape, enjoy — and reading for the main idea (the gist), which entails reading for information, as they would in a newspaper or manual, or memorizing facts for a test. Neither of these ways of reading is particularly useful for the kind of analysis and critical questioning college requires. Nor are these kinds of reading helpful to writers who are trying to read the "potential text" of their own papers. It is not the words that prevent students from reading well, yet many students think they would be better readers and writers if only they had better vocabularies!

2. *Good readers read quickly.* The misconception behind this assumption is that if you read something once and don't get it, it means you are not a good reader. Related to this notion is the idea that once you read it, you've "got" it (like a vaccination) and you never have to read it again, because you've "done that." Our students' attitudes may stem from having been exposed to many timed reading comprehension tests. "Getting it," however, is not the major goal of the kind of reading we want students to experience in Freshman English. Freshman students don't realize that all readers must slow their reading rate and reread certain kinds of texts. As David Bartholomae and Anthony Petrosky (1987) remind us, it's common for people, while reading complex works, to experience a feeling of incompleteness after a first reading. It is true that some readers may not have enough background knowledge to comprehend some texts, but most readers can usually make some sense out of the things they read. Readers can make more sense by talking with others and rereading. Good reading is not quick. It's careful and deliberate. Readers must work the text like tilling the soil over and over in a garden plot. Rereading is essential if we wish to reap a bountiful harvest.

3. *A text is good if you can "relate" to it.* Two misconceptions contribute to this assumption: interest lies in the topic, and fiction is always more interesting than nonfiction. The underlying idea here is that people

read only because they are interested in particular topics. (And this has implications for student writing. It means writers write only about things their readers — that is, teachers — want to hear). Students have a difficult time seeing that "interest" is determined as much by what a writer says about her subject and how she says it as it is by the subject itself. "Interest" is also generated by a reader's active involvement and participation in the reading process.

4. *No one reads essays except teachers.* In Freshman English, we require students to write in a genre they have had little experience reading. Even if they have read an essay, more than likely it wasn't a personal or reflective essay. Furthermore, students' primary experience with nonfiction (textbooks) may directly contradict what we try to teach in Freshman English. We need to spend time debriefing students who think essays have one meaning and can, as one student commented, "only be written with facts and figures" by exposing them to a variety of new models for nonfiction. Variety needs to be stressed here. Students are quick to want to replace one absolute form with another. Through reading different kinds of essays, students will discover that a "great essay" is not simply a five-paragraph theme.

I had the format down . . .as if it was a mathematical equation: I'd insert the data and out came the results. When I plugged my information into the form (introduction concluding in a thesis sentence, body paragraphs — each with a topic sentence, examples and explanation — a clincher, and a conclusion), a great essay was produced.

Ann

5. *Analysis means search for the "hidden meaning" in a text.* What students know about reading and interpreting texts in many cases will be derived solely from their experience of high school literature classes or from *Monarch Notes.* Freshmen often think that "meaning" is what writers purposely hide in the text for readers to find. It does not occur to them that readers construct their own meanings in conjunction with the text, and these meanings can change over time.

I have finally learned I do not have to agree with what the author writes. He is trying to make me think and debate — to have an intellectual conversation with me! My first opinion of an essay does not have to be my final judgment. I am allowed to change my mind . . .this is a huge benefit to learning.

Diane

The First Four Weeks: Learning the Rituals

When I began integrating reading into my writing course, I found that I couldn't just "edit" my syllabus to include a couple of lessons on reading and require that one of the weekly papers be based on a text. I had to revise my conception and format of the course completely. Instead of emphasizing writing as craft or reading as literature, I decided to put learning at the center of my course. Reading and writing became the language vehicles for my students to make sense of things. Both the reading and the writing processes worked to develop a habit of mind that I wished to encourage: the habit of questioning and making connections.

By beginning my composition course with the reading of a difficult text, I convey the idea that this course is challenging and that I expect students to work hard. When students discover that they can still pull meaning from a text although they stumble over individual words, they are more willing to plunge deeper into all texts, even those that appear "easy" or accessible. What is more, because they now have a model from their reading for probing into a text, they seem to be able to move much sooner beyond the What happened? portion of their personal essays into What does it mean? Most freshmen come from a "write what you know" tradition. This tradition suggests that writing is only a matter of communicating information already on hand and already "figured out" by the writer. "Thinking," in this sense, is only a prelude to the actual "writing." The first experiences my students write about are usually the ones they already understand. Many resist examining these events and situations further. After all, why question what is already clear? It had always taken me a number of weeks to help students understand the difference between writing about experience and examining it. I have learned that if I teach them something about the process of reading first, they are more likely to analyze and reflect on (or "read") the experiences they wish to write about. I no longer spend half the semester asking them what point they are trying to make in their papers.

So, reading and writing begin my course together. To generate ideas for writing, I require students to write twenty or thirty "occasions" for homework in the first week. An "occasion for writing," a concept I borrowed from Donald Graves (Personal Communication), is a short, ten-minute, focused freewrite about something that provokes a need or desire to "wonder" into. It can be external (a moment, event, place, person, issue, conversation) or internal (a feeling, idea, gripe, concern, question). Here is part of one of Jessica's occasions—really more of a gripe to herself:

> It sucks to be a female sometimes. Shaving is such a pain especially in the showers at the dorm. There isn't enough room and my butt hits the wall.... I don't like to go to the bathroom so publicly [Jessica lives in a coed dorm]. The guys have it so easy.... Girls also have to watch their weight. I hate the Freshmen 15! All the guys make fun of their beer bellies and stuff and God forbid a girl having a gut! Yeah! And not to mention if a girl hooks up with a guy for one night, she's a slut. [But] a guy is expected to sleep around.... The guys also expect us to do all these motherly things like laundry and stuff....

At first, students are unsure how to turn these jottings into essays because they lack the skill of knowing how to "read them" for potential meaning. Jessica's first paper (which she continued to revise a number of times) examined the double standard for male and female sexual behavior. She interviewed people in her dorm and found that males' and females' attitudes toward sexual behavior actually ranged along a continuum. She then was able to begin to theorize why such standards still exist.

Of course some students dutifully write twenty occasions and never use them — that's okay, too. And sometimes it is not a specific occasion that produces a topic, but a theme running through several occasions, which students only discover when they read through all of them later, as Gina noted:

> I came across the occasions we were assigned the very first class. As I read them, I remember how I felt. They were a chronicling of the things that were foremost on my mind: coming back to UNH ...and trying to decide if it was important to please myself or other people, mainly my parents.... I questioned the validity of the education I was receiving.... I felt as if I was on the verge of being grown-up, but didn't know what it should feel like.... I did not realize that these occasions would be the very basis for my semester in English. What was happening in me shaped how I read, wrote and learned.

At the same time students are thinking about ideas for papers, they are also learning how readers read: I assign them the introduction to David Bartholomae and Anthony Petrosky's *Ways of Reading* (1987). By the time students draft their first paper, three weeks into the course, we will have talked about the process of reading and experienced the process of reading a difficult essay. They are now better prepared to "read" their occasions and ideas for potential meaning that could generate their own need "to essay."

In order to familiarize students with the form in which most of them will write, I provide examples of short personal essays, two- or three-page pieces that I have collected over the years from wherever I find them — anthologies, magazines, newspapers, past student essays. I purposely choose accessible, high-interest pieces because I know that many students believe that essays are "dry, boring, and objective." I want to discount this notion right away. Here, I use reading to show genre, because so many students do not really know what a personal essay looks like. While students are reading their first selection from *Ways of Reading* for homework, we read and talk about four or five of these short pieces in class. I want students to develop their own understanding (or "sense") of the essay. Gradually over the semester I introduce what professional writers say about the essay, such as this comment by Molly Haskell (1989) in her review of a book of essays by Calvin Trillin:

> What seduces us in an essay has less to do with the subject itself than with the writer's way of curling up with a subject and rubbing it like Aladdin's lamp until it takes on shadings and lights of the writer's imprint and sensibility. (10)

We then try to apply what other people have said about the essay to the pieces we have read, and later students will read their own essays through the lenses provided by these writers.

I also try to introduce the skill of reading work "in process" (their own and other people's) as early in the semester as possible. Freshmen seldom have much experience with being the "reader" as well as the writer of their own papers. They are more accustomed to having other people (teachers) "read" their papers to tell them what is right or wrong. Reading work in process has a different aim; it is not to cast judgment as much as it is to see new possibility for revision, clarification, and elaboration. Before students come to a conference, I want to know that they have "read" their own drafts first. I provide them with a way to do this by requiring a commentary (a written discussion of their draft) for each of their weekly papers. (What Becky Rule refers to as a conference skill, I am calling a reading skill. See her chapter for other ways commentaries may be used in conferences.) I ask students three general questions:

1. What are you trying to say? This tells me if students can articulate their main idea.
2. Which parts work? Which parts need work? This allows me to see whether students are reading their texts like writers concerned about meaning or like students concerned with correctness.
3. What kinds of help do you want?

I have learned that students' first insights and breakthroughs about writing will often turn up in their discussions (or in their commentaries) before these insights actually make their way to their papers. As another teacher, Donnalee Rubin (1983), discovered a number of years ago, students know more than their papers reveal. Often they learn how to "read" what they need to do before they can actually do it. Well-articulated questions in their commentaries coupled with a draft that is vague, simplistic, and predictable tell me that the student needs more time and experience writing — they already have the thinking and reading skills. However, general questions (Do I need more detail? Is this a good essay?) or questions concerned *only* with mechanics (Do I have any dangling modifiers?) more often reflect an inability to read "like a writer." I know these students will have a hard time grasping the concept of revision as "reenvisioning."

Here is part of Ned's commentary on a paper he decided to revise from an earlier narrative describing his first experience rock climbing:

> The first page implicitly describes the focus and entire theme of the essay. This focus is the emotional process of my own anger. The description of me rock climbing shows a male meeting a challenge, getting overwhelmed by this challenge, and eventually achieving his goal. The important thing to notice is the climber's emotional alteration from fear to anger and finally to triumph. I would appreciate any pointers on how I could make my rock climbing experience become your emotional experience. . . . The paper becomes very repetitive on the last page . . . Also it seems to take on too many issues. . . . What do you think distracts?

From this commentary I can tell that Ned is clear about his intentions. His questions pinpoint the source of his problems. Although he is not specific about what is repetitive or where he gets away from the focus, he seems to be a student who pretty much knows what his writing needs.

When students begin to tackle big questions and "messy" subjects in their weekly papers, they experience a new kind of writing. This kind of writing involves a great deal of reading, rereading, and thinking. Because these kinds of papers are complex and challenging, students work for longer periods of time on each paper. At least half of their writing time consists of reading — getting a draft to the stage of understanding what their actual topic is and what they are trying to say about it. Only then can they begin to craft their ideas for another audience.

Sometimes students make headway on their thinking but run out of time (or energy) to bring their efforts to fruition in a finished, polished paper. Carrie worked much of the semester on a paper exploring her own ethnicity and how it was affected by her move to New Hampshire. Sometimes Carrie's weekly papers were complete revisions, and sometimes they merely clarified a previous draft. Halfway through the semester, she laments in her commentary: "I want to talk about my experiences as an Asian person from Hawaii who moved to New Hampshire . . .[but] it keeps changing and changing." What was changing was Carrie's "reading" of her experiences. By the end of the semester Carrie was still in flux. She did not complete the paper, even though she worked much of the semester on it. However, she has learned that reading and writing can complicate thinking in interesting ways, and her need for closure becomes less important:

> . . .for all my desire for situations that will stimulate thought, I can usually work myself up to a point where I have saturated my brain so thoroughly that any possibility of reaching a conclusion is absolutely inconceivable . . .but then I have learned that a conclusion is not always necessary or even feasible. . . .

In the first month of my course, then, I will have used reading to teach writing in at least three ways: to develop a way of thinking through ideas, to talk about what an essay is, and to see how to make a draft more effective. It takes me the first quarter to third of the course to familiarize my students with processes: how to respond to texts (their own and others), how to talk about reading, and how to work in groups. Once the ongoing "rituals" of my class are set in motion, I use specific readings, including student work, to model concepts I am teaching in writing. For instance, I might use three drafts of a student essay to model what I mean by revision. I use examples of other writers' leads, including my own, to show them how to "read" a lead from both a reader's and a writer's perspective. I also keep examples of writing on hand to show individual students when the need arises in conference.

What I Want Students to Learn About Reading and the Reading Process

> Reading involves not only being able to understand the words, but also being able to combine your story with the story the words are telling in order to get the full value. . . . I never thought of bringing my previous knowledge to the text.
>
> *Paula*

Bruce Ballenger and Barry Lane (1989) use the metaphor of climbing and diving to explain the process of writing a personal essay. We dive into our sea of experience and climb the mountain of reflection. We select and connect the specific, concrete details from our "sea" to help reveal and illustrate the meaning or idea we have discovered from our vantage point atop the mountain. In a good personal essay, both the writer's mountain (point) and sea (details) are discernible to readers. I can extend this metaphor to help explain what happens during the reading process. In some texts, readers lose themselves in the writer's sea of experience. The story and the details are so absorbing that readers may be loath to struggle out of the sea to climb the mountain to reflect. In other kinds of texts, the writer may not have provided the reader with much of a sea at all. The reader is immediately confronted with a formidable Annapurna of an idea to scale. In the first kind of text, the reader must supply his own mountain of reflection; in the second, the reader must provide her own sea of experience. Fiction is more like the first kind of writing; the writer's mountain is not so visible as it is in the personal essay. Readers must create their own "mountain of meaning." Academic pieces are more like the second. The reader must "work" to supply the concrete details from her own knowledge and experience if she is to grasp the writer's vision from the mountain. I want students to have experience with both kinds of reading, and to see this connection between the reading and writing processes.

I have been asked if using difficult "academic" texts to teach writing may be sending students a mixed message about the kind of writing we want them to produce. I don't think so. Freshmen are not yet skilled enough as readers to be able to see the complex ideas inherent in *any* good piece of writing. John Updike once noted "how docilely and utterly, the critic in one goes to sleep when a creative endeavour is afoot" (1987, 29). We don't want students' critics to go to sleep while we are trying to teach them how to read with an alert, questioning mind. When they cut their teeth on text that is thick with abstractions, students discover they really are capable of making connections and asking probing questions. Pieces like the following excerpt from Paulo Freire's "Banking Concept of Education" are not only difficult but daunting. Students' old habits of reading — decoding the words and summarizing the main point—won't make this text any more accessible:

> It follows logically from the banking notion of consciousness that the educator's role is to regulate the way the world "enters into" the students. His task is to organize a process which already occurs spontaneously, to "fill" the students by making deposits of information which he considers to constitute true knowledge. And since men "receive" the world as passive entities, education should make them more passive still and adapt them to the world. The educated man is the adapted man, because he is better "fit" for the world. (Quoted in Bartholomae and Petrosky 1987, 242)

To read this text, students must slow their reading rate and remake this text into their own language and experience before it will be comprehensible. Here, Liz explains how to read Freire's text and then shows why a reader who has "no thoughts of his own" would find this text incomprehensible:

> [Freire's] type of writing requires the reader to think more in-depth than most writing demands. The reader must go away and come back to the writing as often as necessary in order to bring his own information to it, such as personal experience. This will help in ultimately understanding the work. A person with a banking education would not be able to handle such material . . .because according to Freire, this type of person has no thoughts [of his own] and therefore no ability to think creatively. . . . Freire's style demands the reader bring his own collection of unique experiences to the reading. . . . A common theme can be understood by all even though the hardware [each person's unique experiences] used to excavate the meaning are different.

This kind of prose exists throughout the academy. As writing teachers, we can provide students with skills for accessing meaning and at the same time teach them ways to avoid writing such thick text themselves. Elizabeth Chiseri-Strater, working as a writing-across-the-curriculum consultant, found that professors assumed that students would not know how to write in the manner required by their discipline. However, they expected that students would know how to "read critically." They were surprised to find that many students could not.

To become better thinkers and writers, students need to experience the kind of reading that encourages them to hone their analytical skills, to conceptualize experience, to ask questions, to seek the subtle connections between the layers of text. The concrete, specific language (which "shows" and doesn't "tell") that we value so much in the personal essay is not always the best language to think with. This language may not work to talk about many kinds of complex ideas or to perform social analyses. Richard Ohmann (1988) makes this point very well:

> It is necessary to stay with the abstractions a while, penetrate them and the center of the contradictions they express, not throw them out in favor of a list of details. . . . The injunctions to use detail, be specific, be concrete . . .push the student always toward the language that most nearly recaptures the immediate experience and away from the language that might be used to transform it, and relate it to everything else. (355,360)

I think students can only *learn* to read "actively" by encountering a text that is not readily comprehended—but this does not have to be an academic essay. UNH instructor Carol Keyes uses a difficult poem to teach close, active reading. Poetry is ideal for introducing students to the process of reading because it is not easily grasped in a single reading, and yet a poem is a short enough text to be used as a class exercise. Keyes asks students to read through the poem "until you are satisfied or very frustrated." Students mark words and phrases that seem important and places where they see major shifts in the poem or that just appear difficult for some reason. Students keep a running commentary of how they read, write a concluding reaction to the poem, and then discuss their different "readings" in class.

Conceptually challenging texts are necessary for introducing active reading skills and perhaps for providing students with new frameworks as writers for examining their "sea of experience." However, these texts shouldn't be the only kinds that students read in Freshman English. Once students know what it means to read "with pen in hand," they will be more likely to look for the powerful ideas contained in all good writing, including their own texts. We would do well to remember what Aldous Huxley says about fiction:

> Dostoyevsky is six times as profound as Kierkegaard, because he writes fiction. In Kierkegaard you have Abstract Man going on and on — like Coleridge — why it's nothing compared with the really profound Fictional Man, who has always to keep these tremendous ideas alive in concrete form. (Plimpton 1990, 11)

What I Hope Students Learn About Reading over One Semester

1. *Reading and writing are related processes.* On the one hand, reading can widen the student's personal sea of experience; on the other, reading encourages students to climb to greater heights to view their own seas from new vantage points.

   To me, reading and writing were separate experiences that had little to do with each other. And to me, I was a writer. I didn't need to read everyone else's material — I wanted to create my own. . . . Just teach me to write. . . . Then I began to read . . . I was actually beginning to think about things I never thought about before — to think about things that I wanted to write about . . . and while writing, I would think of new ideas, feelings and avenues to explore.

   Kim

2. *People read differently. Active reading is not just an English skill.* A student told me that her used copy of our text had all the "important parts"

highlighted when she bought it. But when she read one of the essays in the text, she was sure the previous learner must have marked the "wrong things." She had just discovered that people read differently. The kinds of close reading and rereading skills we teach in Freshman English are transferable to students' other courses (and this is not a claim we can easily make with writing).

I can always remember my Psych 401 professor telling my class of 350 students the secret to studying. As a freshman I wanted to pay extra special attention and absorb it so as to do well in college. At this time I was very uncertain of my abilities. He said that the key was not to memorize, but to understand the material. He warned about the evil of the highlighter because it allowed the reader to "skim" the material for later memorization out of context. After these words of wisdom, I deemed the man in need of psychological help because what he was asking was not possible. I took out my highlighter and received a "C" for my effort. As I look back on it now, I could have had an "A" in that course had I known how to understand the text instead of memorize. I am curious to find out what my grade would be now if I took the class over and reread the text. Even more so, I wonder what the result would be after the third time of reading the text.

Sonia

3. *A pen in hand tends to engage the mind.* Gary Lindberg, literary scholar and a past director of Freshman English, used to say, "When the reading gets tough, readers turn into writers." Students need to see that they can stake their own claim to meaning. I show them examples of how I mark my text when I read, and I provide them with a list of the kinds of things they might look for in their reading: questions, confusions, strong emotional reactions, personal connections, connections to other texts. I encourage them to do more than highlight or underline by writing code words or symbols next to parts of the text that "speak" to them. I encourage different color pens for subsequent readings and I show them my "multicolored" texts.

I can no longer read a book without holding a pencil or a pen in one hand. All my books, school books and leisure books, are now filled with markings along the margins. . . . Four months ago I would have never thought of marking up my books. Today I am a far better reader for doing it. I read now to answer my own questions and to form my own opinions, whereas before I read to answer the professor's questions and to understand his interpretations first. . . . When I mark up the books I read for pleasure it helps me associate events and people of the books with things in my own life. Sometimes the books make more sense than what is really going on in the real world.

Connie

4. *Reading involves making connections.* I want students to use the text to "read" their own lives and situations and also to use their "situations" to read the text. Bartholomae and Petrosky (1987) call this process "framing." We can also use one text to help us "frame" or see another text in a new way. Framing helps students see how meaning is constructed by a specific reader in relation to the text. In class, I often have students read "companion pieces." They might compare Gloria Steinem's tribute to her mother, "Ruth's Song," with Wallace Stegner's "Letter—Much Too Late." Or we will read an excerpt from Richard Wright's (1945) autobiography in light of Richard Rodriguez's (1982) reflective piece on his educational experience. I make "framing" a part of students' written reading responses.

The characters in a book lead their own lives and I (as a reader) would stand back and observe. The words in the text did not bring the characters and me together, but only reinforced the idea of them being on paper, and not real people. I probably would have kept on reading like this if it weren't for Joyce Carol Oates's story "Theft." As I read along, the story of Marya was too difficult to leave on the paper. I saw too much of myself in her. It was through Marya I discovered "framing." How could I understand what was going on in an essay if I didn't care? Placing myself in a similar situation, searching for the common experience makes the essay important to you. It becomes part of your conscience.

Karen

5. *Awareness of the reading process reinforces what we want students to learn about the writing process.* When students experience active reading in conjunction with their own writing, a transference from one process to the other is more likely to occur. We can instruct students to consider the needs of their readers when they write, but when their own experience of being readers themselves confirms it, the learning is cemented.

Finding a focus in my reading and writing are two things that I thought would have been completely separate, but actually involve many of the same concepts: Understanding the material and involving yourself in it. . . . A focus is found in reading by re-reading and the way I find a focus in my writing is by writing and re-writing.

Sharon

As a reader, I like to sense a connection between the author and myself; so as a writer, I will use examples so readers can sense a connection between both of our ideas.

Felicia

Strategies I Use to Demystify the Reading Process

Over the years I have tried a number of techniques to develop students' active reading skills. I don't do all these things each semester.

1. *Reading journals.* I ask students to work through and examine their reactions to the texts they read by keeping informal reading journals. Journals are useful for creating dialogue between a student and an author, as well as between a student and the teacher. They work best if communication is constant and frequent. When I taught one section of Freshman English I could collect the ten- to twenty-page journals each student produced every two weeks and provide a generous response. When I began teaching more classes, I sought alternative methods (weekly letters or one- to two-page focused reading responses) that would still allow me to "dialogue" with each student, but would not exhaust me in the process. I introduce the concept of reading journals to my class by having students mark those places in a text we are reading that strike them as interesting for one reason or another. Students examine these initial personal and emotional reactions to the text by writing about them more extensively in their journal. As Kathy discovered, journal responses can help students become "thought developers."

> "I was a very good student. I was a very bad student." What did this mean? This was a thought provoker and in my response I needed to become a thought developer. Thinking I would try to answer my own question, I wrote . . ."What is a good student?"

I provide students with suggestions for the kinds of things they might respond to: ideas, confusions, questions, personal associations, craft, technique. Not all students will find it easy to use an exploratory writing style to follow through connections they make with their reading. Many students need to be taught to "play out their thoughts" in writing. I help them by responding in the margins, by questioning them and asking them to extend their thoughts. Students' journals gradually get better and more detailed with practice, but other ways of responding to reading (including discussion) may work better for some students.

I consider a good reading journal one that reveals the essayist's "habit" of making connections without the need for the essayist's polished form. Stephen Jay Gould (Shekerjian 1990) talks about the importance of making connections:

> My talent is making connections. That's why I am an essayist. . . . Can you see a pattern? I'm always trying to see a pattern in the forest and I'm tickled

I can do that. I can sit down on just about any subject and think of about twenty things that relate to it. . . . I could never understand why everybody just didn't do that. . . . Most people just don't see the connections. (5)

I want to see students make connections between the text and their own interests, ideas, and experiences. The journal should be tentative, questioning, exploratory. It should depict the process of *thinking* rather than the end product — thought.

2. *The double-entry journal.*

> I'm going to try to use the double-entry format more often after reading thought-provoking material to really find out what my views are. Using this journal method, a person can sort of force themselves into exploring new horizons of their own ideas on things they may otherwise never have thought about again.
>
> *Mick*

The double-entry journal encourages "dialectical thinking." It is one of the most versatile techniques I know for helping students become active readers. It has many uses: reading responses, taking notes for research papers, and reflecting on one's own drafts. The double-entry journal consists of two columns (or facing pages). One column contains the reader's observation about or reference to the text and the other column contains the reader's response and reactions. Andy uses a double-entry format to respond to an article on homophobia for his research project. In the left column, Andy writes down important facts. In the right column, he jots down how he thinks he might use the information and also notes his own feelings about relying on statistics.

"84% of people believe being gay is obscene and vulgar"	These statistics will be powerful "shockers" for the essay, yet I am not sure we want to use them as many readers and listeners (like myself) tend to tune out when statistics are cited. I hope to find some examples from life. . . .
"70% believe it is wrong even between consenting adults"	

When collecting information for research, students can record their impressions about the information they collect in the right column. They can say what this information might suggest in terms of their research question and how it connects to other information they have collected. Too many times when students collect information for research projects, they scribble facts willy-nilly. When they write their papers, they do not remember what they were thinking when they wrote the information down. Double-entry research journals are a way to begin connecting data and ideas. They make writing the paper much easier.

3. *Reading conferences.* I borrowed the idea of having reading conferences with my students from Gary Lindberg. I alternate reading conferences with writing conferences. One week we talk about their reading, the next week about their own writing. I have students keep a double-entry notebook on their readings. They bring these to conferences to share their insights and questions from their reading. They can respond to ideas in the text as well as to the technique and craft of the writer. Sometimes they read from their journal and other times we just talk. The main aim of the reading conference is for students to teach me about what they read and how they read. Reading conferences work particularly well when students select their own pieces to read each week (from our anthology as well as from outside readings). They can reread or rethink any piece and add comments to their journals any time during the semester. For the last conference of the semester, students read through their journal to see what they can discover about themselves as readers. I provide questions to help them notice patterns and changes in their reading:

How do you read? Did you stop to write in your journal as you went along or did you mainly write after you had finished reading?

What did you focus on in your reading? writing style? ideas of the author? story plot? personal connections?

Did you see any changes in the way you responded to the readings?

Did you change your thinking or elaborate on any of your first responses as a result of our conferences or reading groups?

These metareadings of themselves provide me with a great deal of information. At his last reading conference, I was finally able to learn why James had such difficulty keeping a reading journal most of the semester:

My mother always told me never to write in my books; they were for reading only. She also said reading was an escape. I was to read something instead of watching television, and because of this I wasn't use to . . . writing my reactions. The syllabus said, "Writing is a way for you to interact with the text." What? I thought. You interact with the text by forming images in your mind and using them to escape. Because of this . . .I never really got into the mind set of an active reader and it disrupted my reading and was uncomfortable.

4. *Small group discussions.*

I wanted to share all my wonderful ideas with the group so that everyone would say, "By golly, Kyle you know everything about this story, don't you?" WRONG!! What I discovered was that everyone else had different ideas and themes about the essay. Plus, their ideas made sense. In [Raymond] Carver's story "What We Talk About When We Talk About Love" I was convinced that Mel understood what the old guy felt when he was sitting in the hospital bed and couldn't see his wife. The group read me this quote. . . . To me, this [quotation] meant that Mel was upset and could relate to what the man must have felt. To my group, it meant that Mel just couldn't understand why the old man was so upset. . . . These group discussions helped me see these stories in new ways and caused me to look deeper the next time I read.

Kyle

Because I have redefined my purpose in Freshman English to emphasize reading and writing as learning tools, my classes are most often geared around talk about reading and writing. Learning is enhanced by community.

One way I build community is through reading groups. Reading groups work like small writing groups, but there is a difference. In writing groups, a writer asks other members of the group for feedback, but it is still her vision, her topic, her paper, her style. In contrast, reading groups are more of a collective: members work toward the same goal of understanding a common text. Reading groups provide students with a shared experience, language, and frame of reference for talking about both reading and writing. When students are encouraged to talk about their "readings" of the text without fear of being wrong, it shows them not only to what extent our individual background knowledge and experience determine what we "take" from a reading, but also how much everyone else gains from the sharing. In classes where students come from diverse backgrounds and interests, this sharing can be especially rich.

I use small groups to discuss readings in class because I think this format helps ensure that everyone will contribute to the discussion. In my class, reading groups consist of four or five students who meet every other week for the first two thirds of the semester to "workshop" the challenging pieces we read. When I first began using reading groups, one person from each group selected the reading and led the discussion for that session. I might have had five or six reading groups, each working on a different essay. Groups remained the same throughout the semester so that every member of the group had a chance to select an essay. Now I use reading groups in a slightly different way. I change the groups for each meeting because I want students to have the opportunity to work with as many people as possible. (This puts them in a better position to choose their groups for the collaborative research paper they do at the end of my course.) Sometimes I assign the texts for reading groups and sometimes I allow each group to select a reading to talk about. If all the groups are examining the same essay, I will follow the small-group sessions with a full-class discussion.

I want students to learn by working in groups that different readers focus on different aspects of the text depending on their knowledge, experience, and interest. We can each enrich our own sense and understanding of a text by sharing our "readings" with others. Because we talk and explain our ideas to other readers, these ideas become clearer in our own minds. So that groups won't mentally go back to their "training" and seek the "right reading," I emphasize that the goal of these reading groups is to uncover as many ways of looking at the text as possible. Students can then begin to examine which "readings" carry the most weight. Discussing ideas found in texts with each other is a process they can take away from my class and apply to learning (and enjoying) the material in any other course at the university.

Most small groups take a couple of minutes to settle in, and they may "go off task" during the course of the discussion. This doesn't worry me at all. These tangents not only help cement relationships among group members, but often provide good fodder for students' thinking and writing later. In my experience, groups eventually get back on topic — especially when a written response to the discussion is also required. When the groups meet, I circulate among them and I may join in if I think the group needs a boost or a new direction to consider. If the group is heartily engaged, I leave them alone. I usually incorporate these small-group discussions into the structure of their written reading responses or journals. I have students read the text and write their initial response (or journal entry) before coming to the reading group. After the group meets and discusses the text, students return to the text for a "second look." They may add to, confirm, elaborate on, or completely revise the ideas expressed in their first response.

Something that took me a while to learn and even longer to feel comfortable with is that when students are responsible for selecting their own readings and deciding what they wish to respond to in these readings, their insights will not be the same, and often not as elaborate, as mine. Sometimes I think we teachers have too strong a desire to enlighten students with all the insights we discovered in the text and they didn't. I constantly have to remind myself of my own philosophy: reading is a process. Students' first readings can be as shallow and skeletal as their first drafts. They just won't make all the connections that we do. But by talking and writing about reading, students do become better readers over the course of a semester.

The Reading Paper

One requirement of many Freshman English courses is that students do some kind of focused writing about a text, apart from their journal writing. Writing in response to reading gives students an opportunity to examine ideas and issues that originate beyond their personal experience. Students learn that they still must use what they know — their own experience — to make connections with the text. As one of my freshmen said, "How could I make sense of things if I did not give my version of the story a try?" In our program, the reading paper may either be a formal piece of writing or a number of shorter informal responses.

Formal Essay Based on Reading

The kind of reading essay most instructors in our department require is usually not the same thing as a literary analysis or critique, although some instructors may prefer papers that are more "text-based." What I call a text-based paper is one that focuses on the text, like Jay's response to Toni Cade Bombarra's "The Lesson" (1981).

> The issue I shall attend concerns the relationship between the narrator, Sylvia, and her instructor, Miss Moore. Miss Moore is a college educated woman who returns to the ghetto.... Her goal is to broaden the horizons and give hope as she sees it to this small group of inner-city black children. A very noble and sacrificing interest, but by her action and methods of teaching, she seems to want to agitate more than instruct. She continually provokes responses from the children, especially Sylvia, that force them to think of their position in society and how rotten it is. But ...I do feel she wants them to make a better life for themselves....

Using Reading in the Writing Classroom

Text-based papers pose specific questions about the situation occurring in the text. In contrast to text-based papers, I usually prefer what I would call a reader-based paper. This is in keeping with my course philosophy of reading and writing as meaning-making activities. Just as I emphasize the meaning writers derive from examining experience, I also emphasize the meaning individual readers construct from examining a text. What I try to encourage my students to do is to find an idea from one of the readings that they can use to illuminate (or frame) some issue in their own life. At the same time, I want students to use this issue to further clarify the ideas they see in the text. For example, George looked at the arguing couples in Raymond Carver's short story "What We Talk About When We Talk About Love" and focused on the role fighting plays in relationships. In his paper, he suggests that "fighting is as much a part of love as affection." He examines the relationship of his parents and his own relationship with his girlfriend to develop a theory that "when love is fresh and new, arguments are few and usually painlessly resolved." He finds support for this in Carver's text. But as relationships develop, he says, "love . . .can overcome one's own sense of individuality." His friends speak of "Jessica [his girlfriend] and George as if we are a single entity. . . . Arguing is a way of breaking away from that image by establishing my own point of view . . .to show her and myself that I am still autonomous to a point." George then uses this idea to "resee" the character of Mel in Carver's story.

It has taken me a long time to learn how to help students write effective reader-based papers, and I'm still learning. I receive many papers that are too general or merely reiterate an obvious or already established point. In this excerpt from his paper in response to Paulo Freire's "Banking Concept of Education," Sam uses a general example from his experience to illustrate the "truth" of Freire's banking theory of education. However, his experience does not help to clarify or elaborate the text (I have no idea if he understands the banking concept), nor does the text allow Sam to see his high school experience more fully.

> The way things were in high school (as I noticed), too many students just adapted to this "banking" concept. They accepted it as the status quo. It was, in fact, too prevalent. Although there were a few exceptions, it was mostly the same song and dance: You go to class, the teacher gives you the material, you take notes, then you memorize the important stuff and take a test.

Another frequent problem is that students will use the text to launch into their own story, but never return to the text. Lindsy does this when she first attempts to use Richard Rodriguez's autobiographical reflection,

Hunger of Memory (1982), to frame her own experience of being Albanian in America. Early in her paper she says,

> Growing up between two different cultures made me feel like a victim or like a ping pong ball being thrown from one culture to another. Like Rodriguez, I felt I was a "comic victim of two cultures."

But instead of exploring how both she and Rodriguez are "comic victims," she tells the story of her experiences and we do not hear about Rodriguez again.

However, when students have had the opportunity to develop their ideas about the readings through small group discussions, reading conferences, journals, or informal responses, they are more likely to eventually produce papers that work.

Focused Informal Reading Response

Many composition instructors require only short written responses to text. In these informal responses, emphasis is placed on honing, clarifying, and elaborating an idea rather than on producing a finished essay. Recently, I tried an idea I got from a paper written by Janet Bean-Thompson (1990), a former teaching assistant in our department. She suggested we ask students to focus on a specific passage that was particularly troubling or confusing to them in their reading-response papers. She found this encouraged a closer reading and helped students avoid writing about texts in superficial, generalized ways. Rather than have my students do a formal reading essay, I developed a set of questions for students to answer about a self-selected passage from their reading. Their responses are in three parts:

1. After students have read and "marked up" the essay, I ask them to choose a "chunk of text" or meaty passage that seems particularly troubling, confusing, or just "interesting" to them. They must respond to their passage in specific ways: (a) literally (What do you think is going on here?); (b) emotionally (What personal associations do you make?); (c) intellectually (What ideas or questions does this raise for you?); and (d) as a writer (What did you notice about the author's craft?). I also ask them to determine how the ideas in their passage connected to other specific passages and ideas in the rest of the text.

2. For the second part of the response, each person shares his or her passage, and reading of it, with the three other members of the reading

group. Afterward, for homework, students write a second response to their passage or respond to one of the other passages their group has discussed.

3. In the last part of the assignment, students read a second text, mark it up, and discuss in their same reading groups how the ideas of this piece helped clarify or enhance their understanding of the first piece. They follow this up by writing down concisely how the group discussion affected their reading.

My students do four of these responses during the semester. They learn four things: how to read closely, concentrating on specifics; what it's like for the reader to experience a written text on different levels (literally, emotionally, intellectually, and as writers themselves); how other readers and other readings may influence what a reader focuses on in a text; and how rereading and revision are necessary parts of the reading process.

Reading Themselves as Readers and Writers: Reflecting on Growth

> I learned how reading and writing are influenced by how I think and, at the same time, how my thinking is further shaped by what I read and write. I understand the process of learning now as the integration of all these things, not as the mere acquisition of facts.
>
> *Gina*

A course that emphasizes learning also builds in opportunities for students to reflect on themselves as readers and writers. Throughout the course, I encourage "metacognitive" reflection—in which students read themselves and their work to gauge their own development as readers and writers. The commentaries that accompany their weekly writing fall into this category. Students reflect on their progress at midterm and in their final piece of writing for the semester. They read their semester's efforts and describe themselves as readers, writers, learners, and thinkers. Most of the student quotes sprinkled throughout this chapter come from these final reader-writer reflections. I ask students to draw from the pieces we have read during the semester to frame what they say about themselves. For example, I might say:

> Like Rodriguez, I too have always "enjoyed the lonely, good company of books. . . ." But unlike Rodriguez I would not characterize myself as a scholarship boy.

They use examples from their own written work to support their findings. What I look for in these pieces is how specifically students can talk about their process of growth as literate individuals. In her end-of-semester reflection, Patty explains how she learned to connect the text she was reading with issues in her own life and how this process helped her writing:

> . . .One special connection [I made] was with "Theft." My initial reaction was that I had nothing in common with Marya. Then for some reason I picked a quote that dealt with failure as an indication of human qualities. Before I knew it, I was relating all my own experiences in high school. When I looked back and saw that I could connect my experiences with another's, this gave me more incentive to continue writing. Personally I view writing not as statements of fact, but rather as the writer's attempt to come to terms with something that he is learning or experiencing. Writing is learning, not teaching.

Patty's discovery of how readers connect to text allows her to critically examine her own writing for its effects on other readers:

> I've always been able to write description, [but] I almost never reflected on my descriptions. I just laid them out there in space for anyone to comment: "Nice verbs. Interesting metaphors. Refreshing adjectives. Over all, very effective." Effective in what sense? Sure, I'd create an atmosphere that was very realistic, but for what purpose? What I want to know is what you were thinking when you were there. . . . People just don't live in a world of scenery. They experience pain, joy, passion and thought. Without these in my essays, there is a void. The void makes it difficult for the reader to get close to me and what I want to express. What good is a paper if a reader can't relate and learn from it? I know now that the end result I want to achieve is for the reader to come away understanding his feelings and thoughts better and consequently learn more about himself.

What is interesting to me as a teacher is that Patty's actual papers do not begin to tell me all that she knows about reading and writing. However, this reflection assures me that a great deal of growth and learning has taken place over the semester.

Texts and Choice

In our department, instructors choose their own texts for their courses and often allow students an opportunity to select their own readings. A book that works well for one teacher may not work at all for another. My colleague Dot Kasik has had much success with Richard Rodriguez's autobiographical novel, *Hunger of Memory* (1982). She feels this book not only deals with many of the issues students are struggling with in their own lives, but also contains many good qualities they might emulate in their own reflective personal narratives. A few years ago, I assigned this book — and I was unsuccessful in helping my students connect to the ideas or the writing. And yet I find when I use a thirty-page excerpt from this book that deals with Rodriguez's examination of himself as a "scholarship boy" my students frequently produce some of their most riveting thinking of the semester! Every time I use the excerpt, I also have students consider other pieces on education. By examining a number of ideas on the same subject, students learn to construct and reconstruct their own theories. Because of the way I teach reading, I am more successful getting students to think about and synthesize ideas if I use related shorter readings than if I use one book-length piece. For this reason, I generally do not assign novels. Yet, other teachers discover that novels work best for them. In one sense, novels are a more accessible and familiar genre for most freshmen.

Just as many teachers allow students to choose their own topics for writing, many instructors sometimes let them choose what they read. How much choice depends on the instructor and the ways she uses reading in her class. "Guided" free choice works well when the instructor's emphasis is on reading as a way to study the craft of another writer or as a way to experiment with new techniques in writing. But in a course that aims to teach students how to read and respond to text, teachers are better qualified to select which texts will serve best, at least in the beginning of the course. Some texts work better than others for teaching the reading process.

My courses generally allow for some student choice, but not for everything we read. I select which pieces we read for the first part of the course because I want to teach students about the process of reading and I also want them to develop a sense of the essay. However, once they learn a way of reading, responding to, and talking about essays, I allow them to choose from our text. One way I do this is to ask each reading group to decide collaboratively what reading they will discuss. And for their last reading response of the semester, I give each student the choice of selecting a new piece from our text to write about or taking a second look at a piece they have already read. What students learn about reading develops over the semester, and many times they wish to use their heightened understanding to go back and consider a text we have read earlier. Geoff did this with "The Story Telling Animal" (Morton 1984). He said that when he first read the piece early in the semester, "it seemed she simply said 'People tell stories.' I read it again and it seemed like a different essay."

In the past, I have had students select articles, essays, and short pieces from magazines and newspapers each week to read and respond to in their journals. This not only generates new ideas for them to write about, it also shows them the places essays are found "in real life" and gets them into the library's periodical section.

Reading Myself as a Teacher of Reading and Writing

The texts we select for our courses, and what we ask students to notice and do with these texts, do more than suggest our philosophical approach to teaching and our goals as writing instructors; these things also reveal what we most value as readers and writers ourselves. For me, reading and writing are my primary ways of thinking and learning. Since reading and writing form the yin and yang of my literacy dialectic, I can no longer conceive of teaching one without the other in my Freshman English course. However, I realize that it was only after I had spent time concentrating on reading and writing as separate activities that I was able to discover how they fit together as meaning-making forms. Like Carrie, the student who never turned in a finished draft of her paper because it kept "changing and changing," my own text of Freshman English continues to evolve with each new reading of my students and each new drafting of the syllabus.

References

Ballenger, Bruce, and Barry Lane. 1989. *Discovering the Writer Within: 40 Days to More Imaginative Writing.* New York: Writer's Digest.

Bambarra, Toni Cade. 1981. "The Lesson." In *On Essays: A Reader for Writers,* edited by Paul H Connolly, 80-88. New York: Harper and Row.

Bartholomae, David, and Anthony Petrosky, eds. 1987. *Ways of Reading: An Anthology for Writers.* New York: St. Martin's.

Bean-Tompson, Janet. 1990. "An Approach to Critical Writing: Begin with Contradiction." In *Literature and Life: Making Connections in the Classroom.* Vol. 25 of *Classroom Practices in Teaching English,* edited by Patricia Phelan and The Committee on Classrooms, 175–81. Urbana, IL: National Council of Teachers of English.

Carver, Raymond. 1987. "What We Talk About When We Talk About Love." In *Ways of Reading: An Anthology for Writers,* 76–86. See Bartholomae and Petrosky 1987.

Haskell, Molly. 1989. Review of *Travels with Alice* by Calvin Trillin. *The New York Times Book Review,* October 22, 10.

Hugo, Richard. 1979. *The Triggering Town: Lectures on Poetry and Writing.* New York: Norton.

Knoblauch, C. H., and Lil Brannon. 1984. *Rhetorical Traditions and the Teaching of Writing.* Portsmouth, NH: Boynton/Cook.

Morton, Katherine. 1984. "The Story Telling Animal." *The New York Times Book Review,* December 23, 1–2.

Murray, Donald M. 1984. *Write to Learn.* New York: Holt, Rinehart and Winston.

Oates, Joyce Carol. 1987. "Theft." In *Ways of Reading: An Anthology for Writers,* 353-91. See Bartholomae and Petrosky 1987.

Ohmann, Richard. 1988. "Use Definite, Specific, Concrete Language." In *The Writing Teacher's Sourcebook,* edited by Gary Tate and Edward P. J. Corbett, 353–60. Second edition. New York: Oxford University Press.

Plimpton, George, ed. 1990. *The Writer's Chapbook: A Compendium of Fact, Opinion, Wit and Advice from the 20th Century's Preeminent Writers.* New York: Viking Penguin.

Rodriguez, Richard. 1982. *Hunger of Memory.* New York: Bantam.

Rubin, Donnalee. 1983. "Evaluating Freshman Writers: What Do Students *Really* Learn?" *College English* 45:4, 373–79.

Shekerjian, Denise. 1990. *Uncommon Genius: How Great Ideas are Born.* New York: Viking.

Stegner, Wallace. 1989. "Letter—Much Too Late." In *Family Portraits: Remembrances by Twenty Distinguished Writers,* edited by Carolyn Anthony, 237–50. New York: Doubleday.

Steinem, Gloria. 1987. "Ruth's Song (Because She Could Not Sing It)." In *Ways of Reading: An Anthology for Writers,* 472-87. See Bartholomae and Petrosky 1987.

Updike, John. 1987. "Tuning Out the Inner Critic." *New York Times Book Review,* July 21, 29.

Wright, Richard. 1945. *Black Boy: A Record of Childhood and Youth.* New York: Harper.

5

Teaching the
Research Paper

Bruce Ballenger

Some years ago, I had a student who was a marvelous writer. Jayne's first 401 essay, titled "The Sterile Cage," was a moving narrative about what it was like to spend several years as a child suspended in a stainless steel device designed to help her recover from a bone disorder. In our first conference, I told her I loved the paper and the voice she found in it.

Eight weeks later, when she handed me her research paper on child psychology, that wonderful voice was gone. The paper was dry, the prose wooden, and the writer seemingly missing in a swamp of facts. "What happened?" I asked. "Where was the writer who comes across with such power in your essays?"

"This is a *research paper*, dammit," she said. "It's supposed to be this way."

At that moment, it occurred to me for the first time that the research paper, a required paper I had often dreaded teaching, was really the most important assignment in my class. It challenged me to convince my students that everything they had learned until then about writing applied to the form they knew best and hated most. They believed essays were "creative writing," and research papers were a different beast altogether. Some believed that writing personal essays was an enjoyable vacation from the academic writing they were doomed to pursue when they left my class. The research paper, one of those things they were "doomed" to write in other classes, was a kind of payment I exacted for giving them the chance to be "creative" on other papers.

It never occurred to them that "academic" writing, exemplified by the research paper, could be "creative"; that is, it could be a paper in which the writer and the writing count. And it never occurred to them that the writing process they had developed while composing an essay about their grandfather's death could be applied to this more traditional and familiar form. It is crucial that we help them make these connections.

The research paper assignment is important for other reasons as well. For many students, it is the first time they work from an abundance of information. While personal essays often grow from draft to draft, the researcher collects a wealth of information *before* attempting the first draft. This experience of having on hand, for research assignments, more "stuff" than you can use forces student writers to tighter focuses and more purposeful writing. Freshmen also come to Freshman English with virtually no experience in the library. They are, in fact, intimidated by the place. If it does nothing else, this assignment gives students some valuable library skills. And finally, the research paper provides less introspective students with an alternative to the essay. Let's face it. Some of our students are uninterested in examining and reflecting on their lives, but they may be interested in exploring some aspect of the world around them. These students often find research papers much more comfortable.

Research Paper Versus Research Report

When you announce that a research paper is required, expect a groan. With a few exceptions, students initially dread the assignment. That attitude comes, in part, from their own mistaken assumptions about the nature of research, assumptions their instructors—in both high school *and* college—often seem to share. Because many teachers long ago despaired about getting much original or interesting work in research papers, they insisted on the one thing students should be able to get right: footnotes, bibliographies, formal structures, and other conventions. The result of this legacy is the privileging of form over content. Students quickly get the message that in this kind of writing what they think doesn't matter.

"Research was a certain number of pages with a certain number of quotes on a certain topic," one student wrote when asked about high school papers. "All of these 'measurements' were given to us before we started working. I found it very hard to learn much more than how to link quotes together from these papers." Another student wrote:

> You weren't expected to learn anything yourself with the high school research paper. The best ones seemed to be the ones that had the most information. I always tried to find the most sources as if somehow that would automatically make my paper better than the rest. . . . Everyone followed the same guidelines and format. So, it seemed that whoever found the most interesting facts won. . . . The subjects never gave me the desire to keep researching because I wasn't personally interested.

What many students call research papers are really research reports. In other words, students believe they must go out and collect as much information as possible on a topic and stitch it together into a quilt that reports on everything that's known about that topic—a recycled encyclopedia entry. They describe an assignment that sounds to me like those machines that pick up golf balls on driving ranges: scoop up as much scattered information as you can, throw it together, and then hand it to a teacher to take a whack at. The process usually involves heavy use of the *Encyclopedia Britannica* and the *Reader's Guide*, a large stack of five-by-seven note cards bound by a thick rubber band, and mindless hours in the library passing love notes until the night before the paper is due. Then it's the mad dash to write it. Students are not expected to build their papers around their own ideas about the topic. In many cases, they don't even get to choose their topic. Use of personal experience or observation is often forbidden, as is the pronoun *I*. When these formal papers are assigned in high school, students are sometimes told that this work will prepare them for college. Then when they dutifully write these papers in college, their instructors complain about how bad they are.

It's time we recognize that this approach to teaching research and research writing is a disaster. It alienates students from the genuine spirit of research, and it turns the research paper into a genre of writing that has little apparent connection to any of the other writing that goes on in the composition course. It produces students who are phobic about the library, certain that "facts" inevitably poison prose, and convinced that their ideas are irrelevant.

It's helpful to persuade them that the research paper we require in Freshman English bears little resemblance to a research report. We *do not* want a summary of what's known about their topics. What we *do* want is for them to *use the ideas of others to shape their own ideas* about their topic. What they think matters in the research paper as much as it does in the personal essay. Though their own experiences may be central to their research, they will be looking beyond them, to other sources of information, to find out what they want to know.

Absolutely key to the success of this assignment is challenging students to use their own curiosity to fuel the process. That means open topic choice. Weeks before we begin the research paper, I challenge students to begin thinking about what they've seen or experienced that raises questions research can help answer. I use lots of examples of topics that grew that way. One student summered on Cape Cod, and one rainy day her father invited her to tour local graveyards searching for the stone of an ancestor. She noticed the different gravestone designs, and the way they were grouped. She wondered, What accounts for those differences? She had a topic. Another student, coming out of an extremely abusive relationship with her boyfriend, wondered why she stuck with him so long. Her paper focused on how the abuser fosters dependency that's hard for a victim to shake. It was a powerful paper partly because of the revelations it provided the writer.

As with other writing, sometimes subjects lead to subjects. One of my students, walking past Thompson Hall (the oldest building on our campus) one day wondered about the building's history. As he started to research it, he encountered a news clip about a student strike at UNH in the spring of 1970. His paper became a critique of how the students and the administration handled the controversy.

For many students, this assignment will be the first time they are researching a topic they are genuinely curious about, and it often transforms the experience for them.

"This time I was able to really stay focused and realized that maybe I wasn't a great authority on my topic," a student told me, "but I'm writing to discover, not to impress people that I know everything."

Alternatives to the Formal Research Paper

I once did an in-service seminar for high school teachers on this approach to the research paper. When I passed out the paper on the gravestones, a paper that nicely wove a narrative of the writer's journey to Cape Cod graveyards with exposition on the meaning of the symbols on the stones, a lively argument ensued.

"This isn't a research paper," said one English Department head. "This is—I don't know what this is, but it's too informal, it lacks scholarly detachment, it lacks an introduction with a thesis, a body, a conclusion."

"I like it," said another teacher. "It's interesting, it's lively, and it's clear the writer did some first-rate research. She really seems to know her stuff."

We argued until time ran out.

Most of us here in the composition program weigh in on the side of the less formal research paper. As you'll see later, we all approach the scope of that paper differently, but most of us value the writer's personal experiences and observations if they're relevant, don't ban the word I, and don't decree what form the paper must take. Like any other piece of writing, the form the piece takes depends on the writer's subject and her purpose in writing about it. To further suggest a break with the more traditional research paper, many instructors here rename it the "research essay."

We don't abandon all the familiar conventions, however. Many of us insist that the writer build the paper around some controlling idea — or thesis — he develops about his topic, and that he establish his authority on the topic by skillfully borrowing the recognized authority of others. Outside sources will also be carefully documented by use of parenthetical citations. While many of those sources may be culled from the library, "live" sources — interviews — are encouraged. Ultimately, students have great latitude in how they approach the research paper.

I believe little is lost in not teaching the formal research paper. Many students never end up writing one anyway, and those who do, learn the formal conventions of the discipline from those better equipped to teach it: the faculty in the relevant field. With all the demands on Freshman English, we can't be expected to teach students how sociologists write scholarly papers. If anything, we should be working to convert faculty in other disciplines to the belief that good research doesn't have to mean bad writing.

What we gain in our approach is helping students overcome their alienation from the research process so they can approach papers in other classes with confidence not dread. We also introduce them, often for the first time, to the idea that through research, they can in fact become authorities who can interpret, posit, and analyze information; that what *they* think matters most of all.

Timing the Assignment

Most instructors assign the research paper in the last third of the course. Some put it off simply because they dread teaching it. Others want to emphasize other, more accessible forms of writing first.

My own class is organized around the nonfiction writer's four sources of information: memory, observation, interview, and research. It's a structure that seems natural to most students, who when given the choice quite instinctively gravitate first to memory and experience as a rich source of material. I also initially encourage the personal narrative because for many it provides topics about which they can feel like an authority, often for the first time. It's a confidence builder for the research paper.

Next I encourage students to pay attention to the world they live in right now, and through exercises and a "collage essay" (a series of anecdotes or sketches separated by line breaks that focus on some aspect of college life at UNH), I hope to hone their observation skills. Depending on their research topic, these skills can be quite useful. Another useful exercise is the news clip essay. I ask students to clip articles from the newspapers of their choice for two weeks, and bring in three that they find intriguing or that raise interesting questions. I then select the best twenty or thirty and reproduce them for the class, asking them each to choose one clipping as a launching place for a freewrite. They need to keep trying clippings until a short essay develops. Later, these often turn into research topics.

A profile (interviewing and writing about another student in the class) is the next assignment in the sequence, intended in part to give them interviewing practice. There are two kinds of interviews—those in which the interviewee is the subject, and those in which the interviewee is a *source* of information on a subject. The latter is, of course, more relevant to research writing, but profiles of both types give students confidence to seek out living sources for their research papers.

The profile is immediately followed by the research paper assignment, which may incorporate all four sources of information they've practiced in the preceding weeks: memory, observation, reading, and interviews.

It is a sequence of assignments that, I hope, encourages students first to look inward for material and then to begin looking outward at the world around them. The research paper is the culmination of this process because it's a look at the world in the widest sense; often the writer is examining topics that affect a lot of people and listening to what diverse voices have to say about these topics. I also hope that this sequence will encourage students to see research as potentially useful for any piece of writing, not exclusively for the research paper.

An alternative approach that some here use is to introduce library skills early in the course, simply as part of what Donald Murray calls "collecting." In much the same way that writing exercises help students collect specifics from memory, a library exercise helps students learn to collect information from libraries and reinforces the idea that research can be a part of any essay.

Whenever you choose to assign a research paper, make sure you help students see how it can build on what they learned from the writing that came before. Then you won't have students like Jayne who dust off their cookie cutter and stamp out another Research Paper, thinking that it can't possibly be creative.

A Five-Week Assignment Sequence

Though instructors here do different things with the research paper assignment, including group work, short research essays, and papers that research a specific problem (see "Alternative Assignments," p. 148), and devote less than five weeks to the work, the typical approach is an eight- to ten-page, documented paper, researched and written in just over a month. Other things go on in class during this time, but most other writing assignments unrelated to the research paper are on hold. It's a lot of time. But I see so much that's valuable coming from the research process that I'm willing to spend five weeks on it.

What follows is the week-by-week assignment sequence I use for teaching the research paper. It's not a recipe, of course. Adapt it to your own needs.

The First Week

Several weeks before I get started on the research paper assignment, I challenge my students to begin thinking about possible topics: What have you seen or experienced that raises questions research can help answer? Citing examples of papers by other students that grew from this question is crucial. Here's a journal exercise that might help students begin to explore their own curiosity.

Exercise 1: What Do I Want to Know?

For five minutes, brainstorm a list of things that you know something about, and that you might even consider yourself an authority on. Make the list as long as possible, and try to be specific.

Now for five minutes brainstorm a list of things you'd like to learn more about. Be as specific as possible. Don't worry if something appears on both lists.

Look at both lists. Circle *one* thing from either list that you want to take a closer look at. Now spend five minutes brainstorming a list of questions about that thing that you'd love to learn the answers to.

When the exercise works, students discover a wealth of questions about their circled subject that research can help them answer. Later, one of those questions may be the focus of their paper, but for now it's enough that they're starting to get curious about something. Next week they'll work more with it. I always tell them to discard a tentative topic anytime it stops sparking their curiosity. Other methods of generating interesting topics are

- Using a computerized index like *InfoTrac* at the library. Tell students to start with a general subject they're interested in ("AIDS") and then see how it's further divided ("AIDS—Educational Aspects"). Encourage them to keep narrowing their subject until they find an angle that piques their curiosity.

- Reading the newspaper. Consider asking students to clip newspaper articles that interest them and raise interesting research questions.

- Considering essays they've already written that might be further developed as research topics.

- Considering a topic related to a career they're contemplating.

- Looking close to home. What's happening on campus or in students' hometowns that suggests topics?

Most students come to us remarkably phobic about using the library. This week, students need to confront their library and research phobias in two ways: by talking about them in class and by being challenged to use the library with an exercise.

Devote some class time to talking about students' past experience with the research process. You might even begin by asking them to freewrite about their experience with libraries. Expect to hear lots of tales of long hours in the library hunting down missing books, or of boring research reports on boring assigned topics. Ask where students get the idea that research papers have to be lifeless things. Ask whether they've stepped into the college library yet and how they feel about spending the next five weeks there.

I use two handouts at this point. The first is a library exercise called "Befriending the Library." It's essentially a worksheet that students fill out and hand in at the end of the week. It takes about two hours, but when they're finished they'll have been exposed to all the major reference sources in the library. Many students say they didn't like doing the project but are glad they did.

There are several alternative ways to teach students to navigate the library. One I experimented with recently was individual meetings with a reference librarian; she walked them through the key computer stations and talked with them briefly about their topic ideas. There are also tours, guided by a library staff member or by a tape with earphones.

To reinforce the idea that research can be a part of any essay, I have also sent students on fact hunts during class. I put forty or so slips of paper in a box. On each is a request for some specific information; for instance, "You are writing an essay on lobster fishing; find out something about the biggest lobster ever caught." Each student takes a slip and is given thirty minutes to return with the information. Be forewarned, however, that some reference librarians are not keen on scavenger-hunt exercises.

The other handout I distribute this week challenges their assumption that all research writing is dead writing. I use Richard Conniff's article "Why God Created Flies" (1984). It's a wonderful research-based piece that explores the often disgusting habits of the common housefly. The prose is lively, and the writer has a strong voice and uses the information adeptly. Any research-based essay will do as long as it challenges students' assumptions about the ugliness of research writing. Consider choosing a model from essayists like John McPhee, Lewis Thomas, Joan Didion, David Quammen, Barbara Tuchman, or Barry Lopez—all of whom are wonderful writers who are also first-rate researchers. I ask students to write a one-page response paper, due the next week, that explores what devices the writer used to keep a research-based article interesting.

In our conference this week I urge them to talk about possible research topics, always challenging them to be driven by their own curiosity: "Are you *really* interested in that?" I used to be open to virtually any topic idea, as long as the students were motivated to explore it. I think it was a paper that tried to answer the question, Is Elvis dead? that finally turned me around. Now I prefer topics that might be more of an intellectual challenge, especially those that might lend themselves to use of scholarly sources (journals, interviews with experts, etc.) or that students find confusing in intriguing ways. Still, their enthusiasm is key. I also push them to consider topics that might lend themselves to "live" sources, to interviews or surveys.

I end the week with another exercise I call "The Myth of the Boring Topic." I ask students to put the most boring topic they can think of on a piece a paper and pass it to the person next to them, who now must try to come up with some interesting questions about it. For example, someone gave me *dolls* as a topic. I wondered what makes dolls like Barbie and Ken endure, and ones like the Cabbage Patch line flare and then disappear? Is play with dolls distinct by gender? Do dolls have therapeutic value? I was amazed how many interesting things I discovered I wanted to know about a topic that seemed dull. Your students may, too.

For next week, I ask them to come to the first class with a tentative topic.

The Second Week

Students need to get started researching their papers this week, especially now that they can navigate the library. But first, they need to narrow their focus.

Focus is something students struggle with in virtually every essay in Freshman English, but it becomes particularly crucial in the research paper. Too broad a focus means that the writer is swamped by information. A narrow focus, discovered early, means the research process is much more efficient—it allows them to pick five magazine articles from a list of forty on the general topic rather than look at them all—and it means they are much more likely to bring less obvious aspects of their subject to light. A photography metaphor works well here. I urge students to avoid being landscape photographers. They should try to find some part of the "landscape" of their topics and "zoom in" for a closer look.

All writing answers questions. That's especially true of research writing. The challenge in focusing is this: What question is the paper trying to answer?

You can try this focusing exercise to start the week.

Exercise 2: Finding the Question

Ask your students to bring a tentative topic and a felt marker to class. Give every student a large piece of newsprint (often available as remainder rolls from your local newspaper), and ask them each to tape it to the wall. On the newsprint ask them to follow these steps:

1. Write the title of your tentative topic on the top of the paper. Just a few words will do.
2. Take a few minutes and briefly state why you chose it.
3. Now spend five minutes or so and briefly list what you know about your topic already (for example, striking statistics or facts, extent of the problem, important people involved, schools of thought, common misconceptions, observations you've made).
4. Build a list of questions about your topic you'd love to learn the answers to through research. Make the list as long as you can. Spend a good fifteen or twenty minutes on this.

Now the students can help each other. Have them move around the room looking at the gallery of research topics and questions on the walls. Ask them to read each one and do two things: add a question they'd like answered about the topic, and check one question (it could be theirs) they find most interesting.

This exercise almost never fails to do several things. It impresses students with the range of interesting topics their peers have chosen. The list of questions helps them see multiple angles on their own topics. What they need to do is find *one question* that can be the focus of their paper. If you want to, you can push this exercise further by adding the following steps. Ask your students to:

5. Look over the list of questions on your newsprint, and circle one that you find most interesting and that might be a focus for your paper. Put that question at the top of a fresh sheet of paper.

6. Now build a new list of questions under that one. What else do you need to know to answer your focusing question? For example, suppose your focusing question is, Why do many college students abuse alcohol? To explore that focus, you might need to find out what the consumptive patterns among college students are. Do the problems differ from those of other groups? Do drinking patterns vary by gender? How frequently do college students seek treatment? What kind? Many of these questions may already appear on the list you and your classmates have generated. Pick out the relevant ones.

Encourage students to take this newsprint with them. If the exercise has helped, they will walk out of class with at least a tentative focus and a clearer direction for their research.

Library work will begin in earnest this week. Before it's over, set aside some in-class time to practice note-taking skills. It's a skill that has suffered from the wide availability of photocopy machines in every corner of the library. Why do any writing from a source when students can make a copy and bring it home, or check out the book? The answer is simple. By taking the time to write about their sources *as* they research, students are, in effect, starting to write the paper. I believe more strongly than ever that this prewriting is the best remedy for the dry, voiceless papers we often get. By paraphrasing, summarizing, and interpreting their sources in writing as they encounter them, students reassert their authority over the material. They make it their own.

The note-card method of note taking is described in many texts. I now believe that note cards are too small for the messy writing students should be doing as they're reading. An alternative is the double-entry journal. Tell students to divide each notebook page in half, and in the left column put quotes, summaries, or paraphrases from their sources, and in the right, free-write about what seems significant in what they've recorded. Try this yourself, and use it as an example.

139

Also try an in-class exercise on paraphrasing. Hand out a newspaper article (I use one on blue lobsters). Show them two sample paraphrases of part of the article, one of which is plagiarized. Ask them to guess which one it is, using the discussion to talk about how to avoid the problems in the plagiarized version. Next, ask them to summarize the article on newsprint on the wall, then choose an effective quote, and finally paraphrase another paragraph or two. Each step of the way, call the class's attention to students who do a good job with summaries, paraphrases, and quotes. Ask people to switch places and inspect their partners' paraphrase for potential problems with plagiarism. Discuss them as a class.

The response papers on "Why God Created Flies" (Coniff 1989) or a similar article can be the basis for an in-class discussion this week. It's an opportunity for you to help them make the connection between the essay writing they've done all semester and what they're about to do. You could explain it to them, but it's better if they do the work.

Write *essay* and *research paper* on the board, draw two lines that join the two expressions, and ask the class to help you make a list of qualities the two genres might share. This will work especially well after students have read "Flies" or some similar piece. Here's what you might come up with:

Essay   *Research Paper*

writer's voice can come through
specific information important
clear focus
built around some main theme or idea
personal experience or observations useful
can use "I"
strong lead, end
narrative can be element
"narrative of thought" (how writer came to
    understand what he or she understands now about
    subject)
writer defines own purpose
people on the page, use of quotes and dialogue
importance of unusual detail, surprising facts
goes beyond the obvious
awareness of readers: what do they want to know
    and when do they want to know it?
strong verbs
makes clear that the topic matters to writer and why
surprising comparisons
taps readers' own experience with subject, things
    they can "relate to"

If things are going well, you may notice that the students are now persuaded that they can do something different with this research paper. To help drive home the point, hand out a sample research paper in which a student incorporated some "creative" approach.

It's important to point out that there *are* several differences between this paper and their essays. It needs to be informative, authoritative, and well documented. Sources beyond the writer predominate. His or her personal experiences and observations are useful, when relevant, but probably won't take center stage as in the personal essay.

Conferences this week will not only help students narrow their focus, but get them started on a research strategy. Where will they start looking for information? Their library exercises should be helpful when you are talking about this. Next week in class, talk about research strategy in more detail.

The Third Week

This week students are immersed in the research. They should be choosing exactly what part of the landscape of their subject they want to look at most closely. Some may be changing their minds about their topic, discovering they're simply not curious enough to stay with it. That's fine. But others may claim that the narrow focus you encouraged them to pursue just isn't yielding enough information. Often the real problem is that they're looking only in the most obvious places, the references they know best from high school: the card catalog or popular periodical indexes like *Reader's Guide* or *InfoTrac*.

This week, challenge them to look under rocks before they give up on a narrow focus or topic. Hand out the inverted pyramid of sources found in Figure 5–1. Tell them that the farther down the pyramid they can work, the stronger their papers will be and the more likely they will find information that those relying on more general references might miss. Explain why an article about college drinking in the *Journal of Alcohol Studies* is more authoritative than one in *Time*, and why it's much more likely to yield more specific, sometimes surprising information.

Another metaphor might help here: Imagine that research is really an archaeological expedition. Once you decide where you want to dig (your focus), you don't give up until you've dug fairly deeply. Who knows what artifacts you might encounter? Also, suggest that your students might want to expand the site of the dig by searching some nonlibrary sources — including interviews, surveys, on-campus lectures, bookstores, TV and radio

Figure 5–1 *A pyramid of sources. From* The Curious Researcher, *by Bruce Ballenger (Needham Heights, MA: Allyn & Bacon, 1992). Used by permission.*

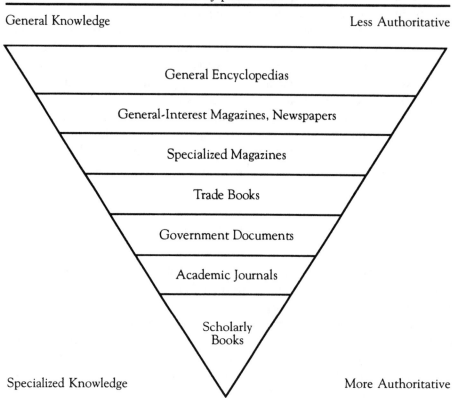

General Knowledge

Less Authoritative

General Encyclopedias

General-Interest Magazines, Newspapers

Specialized Magazines

Trade Books

Government Documents

Academic Journals

Scholarly Books

Specialized Knowledge

More Authoritative

programs, and so forth—as well as some unusual sources in the library, like the audiovisual or special collections.

Hand out a checklist of sources, with blanks that the students can use to fill in the titles of additional references they've consulted. Ask students to bring the checklist to your conference this week so you can discuss the ground they have covered.

Procrastination is the enemy of good research, and despite all these interim assignments, some students will need a push this week. I used to accomplish that by having students give me written progress reports on their research, but a much better way is to ask the students to make a short presentation to the class on what they've discovered so far about their topic. This reinforces the idea that, unlike other research papers they've written, this one is not written for an audience of one—an instructor who is an expert on the topic. Instead, the audience is the community of writers in the class—which includes the instructor—like every other essay they've written up until then.

Beginning this week, ask students to give a five-minute talk on their topic, a kind of "press conference," during which they highlight the more surprising, interesting, or puzzling things they've discovered so far. Ask them to make their presentation informal and engaging and to leave time for questions from the class.

This "press conference" is intended to be coercive, but it has a much more important impact on the students. They realize that they are becoming authorities on their topics. The effect is often visible: they begin talking tentatively about what they've learned, but as they start fielding questions, often answering them competently and confidently, the students come to life. They *do* know more than the rest of us about their topic. This can be a wonderful antidote to the helplessness or uncertainty many students feel when defending their own ideas against challenges from "experts" on their topic. Here, in essence, they become experts, too.

These presentations, which will begin in my class in the latter half of the week, will spill over into next week. Sometimes they take three full-class sessions, though I'm getting better at limiting each presentation to five minutes. It's a lot of time, but worth it.

Also this week, explain documentation conventions. I don't find this a very interesting thing to talk about, but the students are attentive. If you use a handbook, that can simplify this discussion considerably.

If you have conferences this week, keep pressing your students about what they want to focus on and encourage them to look in unlikely places for sources, especially the academic indexes. Now is the time to ask them what they think the point, or main idea, of their paper might be. If they still don't know, don't worry. Most won't. But it gets them thinking about it.

The Fourth Week

Some students will begin to feel ready to start writing this week. Others will still be in the thick of the research. Still others will abandon their topics for new ones.

Exercises and discussion this week should help them get started on the draft. Try beginning with this exercise, which is silly and fun and helps students understand what we mean by "writing voice," and what it feels like to adopt a voice unlike their own.

Exercise 3: The Dangers of Laryngitis

Assume that you're an upper-crust highbrow type with an interest in fine art and a highly refined class consciousness (that is, you think your class is classiest). A truly dreadful thing happened to you today as you were getting out of a taxicab—you stepped in an indiscreet pile of dog poo. Spend ten minutes composing a letter to a friend describing the incident.

Now assume you're the taxicab driver. Spend ten minutes composing a letter to a friend describing the same incident.

Ask for volunteers to read one or the other version out loud.

Students often lose their voices in research papers. It's understandable. Surrounded by the voices of many experts, and the often voiceless texts of their sources, students adopt the wooden, lifeless style they think is required to write with "facts." The often more natural voice in their essays disappears in the research paper, as it did with Jayne's. This exercise alerts students to the writing voice and to how easily it can be changed. The point is not to give them practice writing in the voice of someone totally unlike themselves, but to suggest that's often exactly what they assume they must do when they write research papers. Try asking them whether it felt weird to write in the voice of a rich snob or a taxicab driver. Ask whether they ever felt that way writing a research paper. Ask why they felt compelled to change their voices. Initiate a discussion of what determines writing voice (who the writer is, what the subject is, who the audience is). Tell students that the voice they find in their papers is a decision, not a mandate; it's a negotiation that involves who they're writing for, what they're writing about, why they're writing about it, and, most important, who they are. In fact, it may be appropriate to consider keeping the writing voice they found in their essays if it's appropriate for their research papers. Tell them at least not to make assumptions about what's the required voice for research writing.

Most texts on writing research papers emphasize defining a thesis statement fairly early in the research process. In some cases—say, a student is writing an argumentative paper in favor of legalizing marijuana—that's appropriate. But it's often bad advice. This approach to research emphasizes discovery; and how does the writer know what she thinks until she's explored the subject? Now is an appropriate time to try to nail down the controlling idea of the paper.

It's hard for students to know *what* to think when swamped with information and the many ideas of experts. At the end of this week, I encourage them to push their notes and their books aside for forty minutes and try this exercise to begin reestablishing their authority over the material.

Exercise 4: Looping Toward a Thesis

Quickly reread your notes and glance at your most important sources. Now clear off your desk. Begin a ten-minute freewrite in which you narrate how your thinking about this topic has developed since you began. What did you think when you started? Then what did you discover? Then what? What did you think then? Write fast for ten minutes. Time yourself.

Skip a few lines and freewrite for another ten minutes. This time focus on specific stories, anecdotes, people, case studies, observations, etc., that really stick with you when you reflect on what you've learned so far from your reading and interviews. Write with as much detail as you can.

Free write for another ten minutes, this time as a dialogue about your topic with someone you know. Begin with the question most commonly asked about your topic. Write this dialogue like a play, with you and your imagined partner each playing a part in the conversation. Try to sustain it for the full ten minutes.

Finally, spend five minutes composing a one- or two-sentence answer to this question about your topic: So what?

When this exercise works, several things happen. First, students begin to write, in their own words, about their topic — writing that can often be used in the paper. They also begin to formulate their own ideas about the topic, making sense of it for themselves, free from the chorus of experts they're surrounded by in their sources. They get control of the paper again. Then they can return to their sources more purposefully, using only what helps them develop their own ideas.

Discuss the results of this exercise in a conference or in class.

The Fifth Week

By the beginning of the next week, my students will hand in their papers. I view these papers as drafts. Students may revise them later *if* they choose to include them in their final portfolios. Otherwise they will not be part of their final grade. It's up to them. That may sound a bit odd. After all, the research paper is one of the few required papers in Freshman Composition; shouldn't students be required to hand it in for a grade? And if they know they're not being graded, will they do the work?

I've attempted all along to downgrade the research paper from a separate genre to simply another essay that relies instead on multiple sources of information. I think I reinforce that idea by allowing students to choose whether to include it in their final portfolios, like any other essay. They are incentives to do so, however. One of my criteria for grading portfolios is what I call *range*. Does the student demonstrate that ability to draw on more than one source of information to find out what he wants to know?

Students *do* work hard on this assignment as well, even though they know the paper may not be graded. They are researching something that really interests them, often for the first time, and for many that becomes reason enough to work hard on the project. Isn't that the motivation we're after, anyway?

In my many years of teaching them to approach their research paper this way, over 90 percent of the students chose to include their papers in their portfolios when given the choice.

Since beginnings have an enormous influence on how a draft develops — they establish its tone, its focus, and the writer's relationship to the subject — try a "leads" exercise early in the week.

Exercise 5: Flashlights into the Story

Ask your students to bring in the lead — or first one or two paragraphs — of their paper, even if they haven't written the rest. Ask each student to take a piece of newsprint, tape it to the wall, and write the title of the paper (if it has one) and the first sentence of the lead. Go around the room reading first sentences, asking people to think about which first sentences make them want to read on, and which don't.

Now have them write the rest of their lead on the newsprint. Since they won't finish simultaneously, urge them to walk around the room looking at the gallery of leads others have written. Ask students to pay attention to interesting leads and different ways of beginning.

Finally, have them pair up, and instruct them: Look at what's on your partner's newsprint, and on a separate piece of paper do the following with regard to your partner's lead and what it suggests about the rest of the paper:

- On the basis of the lead, predict what the paper will be about, what its focus will be.

- If you can, make a list of questions raised by the beginning that you hope the paper will answer.

- Describe the tone of the paper in a few words.

Discuss in class.

This exercise can inspire students to consider imaginative ways to open their research papers that not only engage their readers, but accurately frame what the purpose of the paper is going to be. In a 1977 talk at UNH, nonfiction writer John McPhee described leads as "flashlights that shine down into the story," illuminating an aspect of the subject and establishing a direction for the entire piece. By considering whether their lead does or does not help readers predict where the paper is going, writers can see if they're on the right track.

A variation on this exercise is to ask students to write multiple leads — each one a paragraph or two long — for their research paper. Ask them to try different ways in, including a scene-setting lead, an anecdotal lead, a background lead, a descriptive lead, a profile lead, a lead that begins with dialogue, and so forth. Have them bring these leads to class (say, four or five different ones) and pass them around, having each student check the one he or she finds most intriguing.

As students begin writing their papers, it's a particularly good time to bring some inspiring examples of other student papers to class, especially inventive ones. Sample papers might illustrate, for example, visual devices that help make the paper more readable, including subheadings or subtitles, blocked quotations, diagrams, photographs, or bulleted lists. They also might suggest some unusual ways of organizing the material. If you think it's useful, point out how a paper might be one of the following arrangements or a mixture of them:

- Question to answer
- Cause to effect, or effect to cause
- Chronology
- Problem to solution
- Comparison and contrast
- Known to unknown, simple to complex
- Specific to general, or general to specific

Be prepared this week to field questions about citation conventions. Bringing an *MLA Handbook for Writers of Research Papers* to class is a good idea. Issue warnings about a few common problems with research papers, including "floating quotes" — quotations that simply appear in a paragraph and are attributed to no person or publication — and an excessive reliance on a single source.

In your conferences try to nail students down on their main point or thesis.

Follow-Up

If your students bring their drafts to class, consider doing an in-class editing exercise. Begin by giving them several paragraphs of manuscript that need editing. I use several pages from William Zinsser's *On Writing Well* (1985, 10–11) in which he reproduces three or four paragraphs of edited manuscript for the book, complete with his handwritten editing marks. I retype the paragraphs *without* the editing and ask students to do what he did, cutting as many words as they can—eliminating redundancy and clutter—without sacrificing Zinsser's meaning. Then I give them the edited version as it appears in the book so they can compare their editing with his. After they hack away at a professional writer's draft, I ask them to choose a random page of their research paper and do the same thing, cutting at least seven words. It's not hard, since research papers are notoriously full of clutter like "due to the fact that" and "in my personal opinion."

Another useful follow-up exercise is Peter Elbow's cut-and-paste revision, a technique particularly well suited to a long research paper because it often generates new ideas about organization. Simply ask students to bring a copy (photocopied on one side of the page only) of their draft, scissors, and tape to class. Then instruct them to cut it up, paragraph by paragraph, shuffle the pieces, and then go through the pile trying to find the "core" paragraph. That's probably the one with the thesis statement. Ask the students to set the core paragraph aside, and make two new piles of the remaining paragraphs: those that are relevant to the core, and those that don't seem to be. Then have them play with the order of the relevant pieces, looking for gaps and taping together any new order that seems promising. Your students may be slightly appalled that their carefully written papers are cut to pieces. But it teaches them a healthy disrespect for a draft.

Finally, you might also have the class discuss how these papers were different from any they've written before. Point out how important it is, when given a paper assignment in any course, to query the professor about his or her expectations and format requirements. Warn them that the less formal paper they've just completed may not be appropriate for all their classes. Tell them, though, that they might be surprised how many instructors appreciate reading an interesting and informative research paper.

Alternative Assignments

All good writers—academic or not—instinctively know how to cast a wide net to find out what they want to know. My central purpose with this assignment is to help student writers develop that instinct, so by the end of the course they will plan to use personal experience, observation, interviews, and research in *any* essay they write, if it serves their purpose. Later, in upper-level courses, they'll learn more formal conventions of academic discourse from those more qualified to teach them. They have, however, practiced skills that will be useful if they are asked to write more formally, such as finding library references, taking notes, and purposefully studying outside sources. More important, they've been introduced to the genuine spirit of research.

Many instructors here share that purpose, but with a different emphasis. For example, Tamara Niedzolkowski is one of several instructors who assign collaborative research projects. She explains,

> I assign [them] for two reasons. First, I believe the collaborative effort more closely resembles research projects you do in the "real" world. Unless you are a newspaper reporter or [an] academic, most jobs (science, business, advertising, etc.) will require a team effort when it comes to research. . . . I [also] find that people write better papers when their individual information discovery is enhanced by discussion with other people working on a related topic.

Tamara gets students working in "topic groups," and encourages each member of the group to find his or her own angle on it. For example, one group on the history of the Seacoast had members research the Isles of Shoals, granite and stone architecture in New Hampshire, and how the city of Portsmouth got started. Everyone writes his own eight- to ten-page research paper, but they collaborate on a class presentation and on an introduction and a conclusion to their collected work.

Donna Qualley and Barbara Tindall also teach collaborative research essays. They say:

> Collaboration puts emphasis on the research process. In traditional research papers, students want to reach closure as quickly as possible, so that little time is spent working with the information, or more importantly, working out the writer's relationship to the information. When many writers create a single paper, they need to negotiate the task, the teacher, the information, one another, and their own history as writers.

Donna and Barbara organize students into groups of two or three, then challenge each group to come up with a compelling topic through negotiation. Then the students begin the research, sharing what they find, discussing — and often arguing about — its significance, and working toward a focus. Even the resulting paper is collaboratively written. Perhaps most important, Barbara and Donna ask students to keep a double-entry journal in which they document and reflect on the process of working together. One student wrote about her experience with this approach:

> When you're writing a paper with another person, you force yourself to ask a lot of questions. Then you force yourself to ask more questions when you write in your journal. The gift of being able to ask why is essential to writing. The "why" is the most important question in life and writing is simply a reflection of that.

Ken Macrorie (1988) suggests a paper that is essentially a narrative of the students' experience learning about their topic. He encourages students to define a research question that is not only relevant to them, but may even be practical. One student wrote a paper on what to look for in a 35-millimeter camera because she got some birthday money to go out and buy one. Another student wrote about what to look for from a real estate agent. Another asked, "Could I be a fire fighter?" The papers rely heavily on "live" sources, or interviews, rather than library work. The papers are stories of the quest to find out what the writer wants to know, often ending with a "What I Learned" section.

All of these approaches reflect each instructor's sense of what's important about research writing in Freshman English. Tamara wants students to experience collaboration on a project, in part because it mirrors research in the workplace. Donna and Barbara hope students will use each other to critically explore a subject and their relationship to it. Macrorie wants them to enjoy the hunt for information. I want them to see how the writing and the writer matter, even in the research paper, and how natural research can be to all prose writing. When designing your assignment, decide what you think is important. Consider how much time you want to devote to it and how it can build on the things you hope to teach about writing.

Your own enthusiasm for the assignment may matter most of all. Our students are used to grim teachers teaching tired formulas for research papers. But after forty years in which students have learned a formal, mechanistic approach to the research paper, the genre is finally being transformed into a piece of writing integrally connected to the other work our students produce. They'll like the change. And so will you.

References

Coniff, Richard. 1989. "Why God Created Flies." *Audubon Magazine*, July, 82–85.

Macrorie, Kenneth. 1988. *The I-Search Paper: Revised Edition of Searching Writing.* Portsmouth, NH: Boynton/Cook.

Zinnser, William. 1985. *On Writing Well.* Third edition. New York: Harper.

6

Editing
The Last Step
in the Process

Jane Harrigan

Steve gazed at me steadily, daring me to scream. I was tempted. For weeks our conferences had followed the same pattern: I would praise the content of his papers, we would explore ideas for a while, and then I would point out that readers were going to have trouble understanding his terrific thoughts unless he made an effort to learn punctuation. I'd explain one rule about commas and ask him to apply it to a few of his sentences. He'd do it correctly. Then the next week he'd be back, bearing a new paper whose strong ideas gasped for breath in an unpunctuated sea.

On this particular day, I was fresh out of new approaches; I felt, to use my students' favorite word, *clueless.* "You know, Steve," I began, with absolutely no idea where I was going, "a person who says he wants to write but doesn't care where he puts the commas is like . . ."

Steve looked up alertly. " . . .like a carpenter who doesn't care where he pounds the nails?"

Yes. Exactly. Thanks, Steve.

If you listened only to people unfamiliar with writing-process teaching, you'd think its primary accomplishment so far had been to produce a generation of carpenters who don't care where they pound the nails. Helping students feel free to write is all well and good, these critics say, but when do the students learn to write *correctly*? Isn't the "touchy-feely" process method responsible for the fact that so many young writers don't know, or don't care about, spelling and grammar?

We who champion the process method can insist staunchly that these critics are wrong, that freedom of expression is its own reward, that students' mechanics are no worse today than they ever were. Deep down, however, I think we know better. Everywhere we turn in the world we encounter writing that is unclear, redundant, sloppy, and just plain bad. Whether or not the process method is the problem, shouldn't it be part of the solution? Can we legitimately call ourselves teachers of the writing process if we don't teach the last step in that process—editing the writing to conform to standard grammar and style?

You'll notice that I'm asking a lot of questions. That's the way I think; I'm a journalist. I'm also an editor, and I'm not apologizing on either count. Good writing is good writing, and the lessons I learned writing and editing millions of words for newspapers have served me well in teaching all sorts of writing courses. I loved being an editor. I think it's right up there with writing as the most fascinating life imaginable, and I have no idea how such a wonderful field got such a horrible reputation.

Now one of my major missions in life is to turn the reputation of editing around. Because I can't seem to shut up about that mission, and because I teach editing and am writing a book on editing, people tend to seek me out when they have questions on the subject. I don't know all the answers, but I always learn something by taking a stab at the questions.

What Is Editing, Anyway?

If you teach writing, you are an editor. When you sit with students in conferences, listening as they feel their way through a piece and nudging them toward new realizations, you are editing. When you sit alone reading a student's work (or your own) and tearing out your hair trying to figure out what it needs, you are editing.

Editing is a way of seeing. As good editors read a piece, they see not only what's there, but what's not there and could be. Editing is part of the writing process, not its opposite. It is the last sentry between writer and readers. Most of us talk in composition courses about the difference between writing for yourself and writing for readers. That discussion is a good way to introduce the idea of editing. We can tell students that unless they're writing a journal for their own eyes only, they are writing to be read. And there's only one way for writers to ensure that readers understand what they're saying: They must express their ideas in commonly accepted words and patterns of words.

Commonly accepted, it's important to note, does not mean *common.* Somehow, some practitioners of the writing process have come to equate *correct* writing with *dull* writing. That's crazy. In reality, it's incorrect writing that's dull; bad writing is bad in a very finite and predictable number of ways. Good writing, on the other hand, expands our view of the possible. Once writers learn to use the language correctly, there's no limit to where it can take them.

Sue Wheeler calls editing the last glance in the mirror to pick off the lint. To belabor her analogy for students: You wouldn't just throw on any old clothes in any old manner if you were going out to meet someone you wanted to impress. Even if you thought it was stupid that people are judged by the way they look, chances are you'd give in and spend some time on your appearance. Ideas, too, are judged by their appearance, and what forms that appearance are words. A great idea expressed in messy words loses its impact as surely as a gorgeous sweater worn inside out and upside down.

Wait a Minute. What's All This Philosophy? Aren't Editors Just Those Ogres in Eyeshades Who Slash at Your Story with Bloodred Ink?

No, those are *bad* editors. Actually, they're bad *copy* editors. Copyediting— editing for spelling, grammar, style, and accuracy –is just one kind of editing, but it seems to be the kind most people think of first. I like to give students a sense of the full range of editing before we start talking about how the word applies to their work. Most students will acknowledge, at least grudgingly, that they're likely to need good communications skills after college. What many don't realize, however, is that reading and writing, besides being wonderful fun in their own right, are job skills. If a person can become a truly expert writer, a truly insightful reader, he or she can make a living at it. Thousands of people do. I like to encourage students to figure out where those people work: at magazines, newspapers, book publishers, universities, hospitals, nonprofit organizations, government offices, ad agencies, public relations firms, and businesses of every type. Wherever words are used, word experts are valued.

Writers' work is obvious; we see their bylines atop neat columns of type. But what do editors do? Sometimes I ask my students to choose a place where editors work (they usually pick a magazine), and together we make a list of what editors do there. The list gets longer and longer: decide what subjects the publication will cover and how; assign stories, photos, charts, and illustrations; enforce deadlines; work with writers on focus, organization, length, tone, and flow of stories; solve any legal or ethical problems a piece raises; try to determine and meet readers' needs; lay out pages and write headlines; and on and on.

We talk about the people called assigning editors, who work with writers at every stage from idea to finished manuscript. With the students assuming their rightful role as writers, we make lists of what a good editor can do to help, and what a bad editor can do to hurt. We talk about the editing profession's new emphasis on "coaching," or guiding the writer toward his or her own discoveries about a piece — at which point someone is sure to shout, "Hey! That sounds like conferences!" There's a good lesson in that: Conferences are editing; therefore, editing is nothing to be afraid of.

Finally we talk about copy editors, who begin work after the writer and assigning editor have finished with the story. Again I stress that copy editing is not the only kind of editing. Good editors edit for focus, order, tone, and the million other hard-to-pin-down characteristics of good writing. In this book, others have addressed those issues as part of the revision process. My role is to deal with copy editing, or examining writing word by word. When I ask a class what copy editors do, someone is sure to intone solemnly, "Copy editors fix grammar."

Oh No, Not Grammar. Shouldn't We Try to Avoid That Word?

Why? Why is it that master composition teachers can fearlessly face a roomful of spring-fevered freshmen, yet panic at the mention of the word *grammar*? Grammar is nothing more than a system, a way of linking words into patterns that will convey the same meaning — the writer's own unique meaning — to each person who reads or hears them. Trying to teach writing without mentioning grammar is like trying to teach music without mentioning scales.

But What If I Don't Know Grammar?

You do know it. If someone is paying you to teach writing, you must be a good writer, and you can't be a good writer unless you understand grammar.

That doesn't mean you can conjugate a verb in twelve tenses and rattle off the difference between a gerund and a participle without looking it up. It simply means that you have a feel for language, for what works and what doesn't, and that you have some idea of why.

One of the best "you do *so* know grammar" exercises I've heard comes from Pat Sullivan. She makes up a sentence in a nonsense language and writes it on the board. Then she asks the students to figure out what part of speech each of the words is. Let's say the sentence is *Wkh jluo uhdg wkh erm.* Just by looking at it, the students can figure out that *wkh* is probably an article, like *the*, and thus that *jluo* and *erm* are nouns. If that's so, then *uhdg* is probably a verb, and so on. In this way, students are reintroduced to grammar as a familiar system, rather than as a set of arbitrary rules imposed by androids from Neptune — or, worse, as some foul-tasting medicine that only an irrational being (read, a teacher) would force them to swallow.

When it comes to the language, I'm a hardliner. If you're afraid of grammar, I have only three words of advice: Get over it. Find a user-friendly handbook (*The Bedford Handbook* by Diana Hacker [1991] works well for me) and start flipping through it. Chances are, just about everything you see will look at least vaguely familiar, and most of it will make perfect sense. The few things that don't, you can read up on and understand in a matter of minutes. If you're a zealous grammarphobe, you probably won't believe me until you've actually picked up the handbook. But I'd be willing to wager large sums that half an hour after you do, you'll be standing there scratching your head and saying, "Geesh! What's the big deal about *this?!*"

Maybe. But Even If I Can Convince Myself That Word-by-Word Editing Is Important, How Do I Convince My Students?

First, accept a lesson I learned the hard way: There's no use getting angry. Most students who reach college without a firm grasp of the English language really are not to blame. They honestly have never learned grammar, at least in part because each teacher who guided them through the writing process in elementary and high school thought that *next* year's teacher would be the one who would finally reach the end of the process, who would encourage students to look at their writing word by word. But no teacher ever did. As a result, some students are not only unaware of basic, useful rules of grammar — what a run-on sentence is, for example, or how to use an apostrophe—but they also truly believe *grammar doesn't matter.* That attitude, even more than lack of knowledge, forms the challenge for composition teachers.

Some students tell me that their previous writing teachers have scoffed at grammar, waved it away as nit-picking that betrays the higher purpose of the writing process. (One students recalls her high school English teacher decreeing that grammar books belonged "in your locker under the tunafish sandwich.") Other students say they've made a simple deduction: none of their writing teachers ever mentioned grammar; therefore, it must not important. They were, of course, only too happy to deduce this.

So There's the Question Again: How Do We Change Their Views?

There are lots of ways, including one big practical one: You can tell students that out there in the "real world," people are judged on results, not intentions. Wonderful ideas might as well be worthless if no one can understand them. More to the point, in these hard economic times, when hundreds of people compete for each job, employers don't have to settle for someone whose communication skills look iffy. My students are usually impressed by this simple truth: If you apply for a job by sending a cover letter that contains even a single typo or grammatical error, there's a good chance that letter will immediately earn you a place—on the recycling pile. Meanwhile, more and more employers have started giving spelling and grammar tests to job applicants. They don't want any employee, whatever the person's job is, to write a letter or make a presentation that will embarrass the company.

When we're talking about jobs in this way, I like to show students a classified advertisement that a Massachusetts magazine publisher ran in the *Boston Globe* when it was looking for an editor a few years ago. The twist is that the ad was full of errors; applicants had to edit it and send it in with their résumé. The woman who created the ad told me later that it had succeeded wonderfully. First, because it required work, the ad limited the number of applicants. Second, and more important, the ad provided a screening device for the company. Some of the errors in the ad may be more obscure than you'd necessarily want to take up with a freshman class. (You might want to make up your own ad, containing the types of errors you often see in students' papers.) Still, when students see the real ad, many of them "get into" the idea that the ad was actually published and could actually have helped them get a job. (In fact, a senior in my editing class did end up getting the job—but that's another story!) The ad follows. A copy of it, edited, appears as Figure 6–1.

> Please pick up your red pen before reading this ad. Ready? Networking Management, a business/trade magazine which serves the telecommunications industry is looking to hire a detail oriented editorial professional with with 3-years experience in copy editing and writing. Familiarity with PCs and word processing is essential, basic understanding of the typesetting, layout and production process is preferred. With a degree in Journalism or a related field, it's also important that you are a quick learner who can juggle many projects on deadline. You will perform substantive copyediting on feature articles, co-ordinate and write the magazines' New Products section, and do some newswriting. Occassional attendence of trade shows and press conferences will also be part of your job.

Figure 6–1 *The edited version of the classified ad a publishing company ran to test candidates for editing jobs.*

(a) The correct use of *which* and *that* plagues even experienced writers and is probably nothing you'd want to discuss in a freshman class. *Which* begins a non-essential clause, one that requires a comma. *That* begins an essential clause and is not preceded by a comma. The woman who created this ad said she used the *that/which* confusion to screen applicants. Changing *which* to *that* in the sentence is correct (the clause is essential), as is rewriting the sentence as shown.

(b) When a descriptive phrase follows a name, most writers remember the first comma, but many forget the second.

(c) *With a degree in journalism or a related field* is a dangling modifier. The word after the comma should be the word being modified.

Jane Harrigan

Hey! Editing the Ad Was Sort of Fun!
Does That Mean Something's Wrong with Me?

Nope. I get this reaction all the time from students in my editing class. They sidle into my office when they think no one's looking, glance around nervously, and almost whisper, "I kind of like this stuff. Do you think I'm really weird?" The first few times this happened, I was surprised — not surprised that the students liked editing, but surprised that they associated it so strongly with nerds carrying pencils in plastic pocket protectors. These days I'm less surprised, but I do try to talk more in class about how fascinating the language can be, how much fun I had (and still have) as an editor, how satisfying it is to work with words until they convey exactly the message the writer wants to convey.

Editing is not negative; it is much more than a simple error patrol. Still, it's true that the last step of the writing process, more than the others, involves rules. The irony is that although some writing instructors find this reality troublesome (Rules? Won't that mean emphasizing conformity over content, criticism over creativity?), many students find the rules of language reassuring. At last, they say, something definite! Something that's either right or wrong! (Of course, even grammar isn't that clear-cut, but they don't have to know that right away.)

Whenever I teach a writing course, I'm reminded anew of a strange truth: Most students' ability to critique other people's writing develops far faster than their ability to critique their own. You can use that knowledge to incorporate editing into a class. Try giving students a set of copyediting marks (one version is included as Figure 6–2) and turning them loose on some writing that belongs to no one in the class. The student newspaper is usually fertile territory, provided your students don't write for it. You'll probably find that they're able to spot all kinds of grammatical errors, including ones they make constantly themselves.

An expansion of this idea involves what my students call "clip sheets," sheets of paragraphs I've clipped from published writing. I tell them that the assignment is easy because they don't have to read a whole story, just a few paragraphs. I tell them that the paragraphs may contain one or more errors, or none — although, come to think of it, I don't think I've ever included an error-free paragraph. The students' assignment is to find the problem, explain what it is (subject and verb don't agree, for example), and solve it. (You'll find a sample clip sheet in Figure 6–3, the answers in Figure 6–4.)

Of course, giving too many such assignments can create editing monsters, red-pen-wielding pouncers out for miscreants' blood. But that's a

158

Figure 6–2 *Copyediting marks. Since copyediting marks vary, it helps to have everyone in the class use the same ones.*

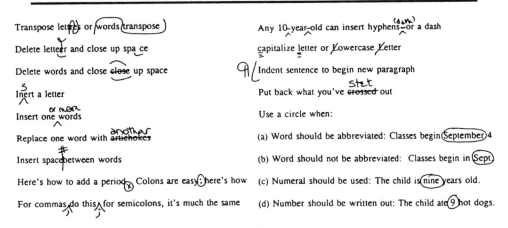

small threat compared with the danger of producing writers who don't see errors at all. At any rate, monsterish tendencies develop slowly; it's easy to head them off at the pass through constant reminders that errors are not the point. Precision is. That's what's so satisfying about introducing editing through a stranger's work. Students quickly see not only errors but their *effects:* Errors distract readers from the writer's message, or in some cases deliver a message the writer didn't intend at all. From there, it's only a short leap to apply that lesson to their own writing.

My Class Is a Long Way from Leaping.
How do I Start with Something More Basic?

Okay. Let's take the idea that unless a writer follows the standard rules of grammar, readers might not know what the heck he or she is talking about. To get at that concept, I like to work backward from "problem" sentences. Usually I take the sentences directly from students' papers, though I change the details so that the writer's identity won't be obvious. Working from real writing allows me to address common problems students are having—and besides, no teacher could invent sentences as strange as the ones students write every day! The goal is to let the students figure out the rules, and the reasons for the rules, themselves. Once they've realized that they, as readers, truly might not understand a sentence unless it's grammatically correct, the idea of aiming for correctness in their own writing makes a lot more sense.

Figure 6–3 *A sample of clippings from the print media. Each item may contain one or more errors, or none.*

1

Dear Abby: I am a 25-year-old female flight attendant who, while on vacation in Los Angeles, went to dinner with some friends. After being seated at the restaurant, the cocktail waitress came by and asked if we wanted something from the bar.

2

3

Fatal Shootings Of Children Prompts Call For Gun Law

4

Even in the midst of remodeling, the Fraser's found time for entertaining. In fact, just before they tackled the major renovations on the second floor, in the midst of one dreary February, the couple decided to treat their friends to a real beach party.

5

. I could hear when his cat jumped off his kitchen counter. The fights the guy had with women no amount of pillows on my head could drown out. Sometimes he and the women threw crockery at each other, and shards rained down on me through holes in my ceiling.

6

The young professionals also tend to live in condominiums or apartment complexes, where they let the managers worry about shoveling the grass and mowing the lawn.

7

DANVILLE, Vt. — Residents of Danville, a rural northeastern Vermont town of 1,705, have rallied behind a Polish family threatened by deportation and is trying to gain them political asylum.

8

160

He reached the pond where the water slid over the beaver dam. He saw the dog right away, its head bobbing up and down as it sunk beneath the water and struggled to breath. It had broken through not far from the dam and between 40 and 60 feet from shore.

9

" IF ALL THE WORLD'S A STAGE, HOW COME THERE'S SO MANY UNEMPLOYED CARPENTERS ? "

10

WHO'S HALF GLASS OF ORANGE SODA IS THAT?

IT'S MINE, DAD.

11

In the case of a person who has been referred to her from out of town, Gallagher typically interviews the person over the phone, asking about the person's personal life, about how many children they have, about interests and tastes.

12

There's no blood, Butler said, because the pigs have been properly slaughtered. "When you kill a pig, always cut off it's nose," he noted. It lets the blood drain out.

13

Day One of the new bottleneck on Route 1 southbound in Charlestown proceeded far smoother than expected yesterday, but officials were bracing for the first test during morning rush-hour traffic today.

14

EXCUSE ME, I'VE MISSED A FEW LECTURES, CAN YOU TELL ME WHEN THE NEXT EXAM IS?

UHHHM, TODAY.

FEW, I THOUGHT IT WAS LAST FRIDAY!

NO, THAT WAS WHEN THE 10 PAGE PAPER WAS DUE!

OH.....DO YOU THINK HE'LL EXCEPT IT LATE?

WELL......HE SAID SOMETHING LIKE, I'LL EXCEPT A LATE PAPER WHEN HELL FREEZES OVER.

15

For example, consider this sentence: "Sue asked Katy whether she had met her new roommate yet." A class dialogue involving the sentence (using *student* to mean various students, and leaving out the many interim answers) might go this way:

Teacher: Is this a good sentence?

Student: It looks okay at first, but then I can't tell *who* was supposed to meet *whose* roommate.

Teacher: Okay. Now, what exactly is it that makes the sentence confusing?

Student: You can't tell which person the writer meant by *she* and *her*.

Teacher: What parts of speech are *she* and *her?*

Student: Pronouns.

(Teacher might want to ask for other examples of pronouns and for other examples of possessive pronouns like her.*)*

Teacher: What do pronouns do?

Student: They "stand in" for nouns in a sentence.

Teacher: Why do you think somebody invented pronouns in the first place?

Student: Because it would look pretty boring if you kept saying the same word or name over and over. That's like how little kids write.

Teacher: What do you call the noun the pronoun replaces?

(It's worth asking this question. You may find that students who know grammatical terms like antecedent *are students who are having trouble with the course; they just can't seem to find anything interesting to write about. That may be because they learned writing the old-fashioned, brimstone-and-rulebook way. But the flip side is that they do know grammar. And sometimes, just finding out that they know something other people don't know gives them confidence to apply to their writing.)*

Teacher: So, if you look at what's confusing about that sentence, what rule about pronouns could you form?

Student: When you use a pronoun, you have to make clear what noun it refers to. Now that I look at it, the *she* in the sentence is clear. It's got to be Katy, since Sue wouldn't ask about herself. But the *her* could be either one of them.

Figure 6–4 *Answers to the clip sheet in Figure 6–3.*

1. Wrong word. Should *have*, not should *of*. Because of the contraction *should've* many students think *of* is correct.

2. *After being seated at the restaurant* is a dangling modifier. Literally, the sentence says the waitress was seated. Either change the sentence so that the word being modified follows the comma (*After being seated, we were greeted by the waitress*), or rewrite in some other way: *After we had sat down, the waitress came by.*

3. *Your's* should be *yours*. Possessive pronouns do not take apostrophes.

4. Subject/verb disagreement. Shootings *prompt*.

5. Incorrect possessive. *Frasers* should be plural, not possessive. If you were talking about their home, it would be the *Frasers'*.

6. Wrong word. *Number* of pillows, not *amount*. *Amount* is for things that cannot be counted: a *number* of glasses, an *amount* of water.

7. Nonsense! Doing *what* to the grass?

8. Subject/verb disagreement. Residents *are* trying to gain them asylum.

9. Two errors. (a) Wrong past tense: *sank*, not *sunk*. (b) Wrong word. *Breathe* is a verb; *breath* is a noun.

10. Incorrect contraction. How come there *are* so many unemployed carpenters? (Note: This might provide a good chance to discuss the passivity and general flabbiness of the *there is/was* construction.)

11. Wrong word. *Whose* is the possessive pronoun. *Who's* is a contraction for *who is*. (*Who's that knocking on my door?*)

12. Pronoun/antecedent disagreement. *They*, which is plural, refers to *person*, which is singular. You could replace *they have* with *he or she has*. But to streamline the sentence, it might be best just to make everything plural: *When clients are referred from out of town, Gallagher usually interviews them over the phone, asking about their lives, their children, their interests and tastes.*

13. Two *it* problems. *Its nose* should use a possessive (no apostrophe), not a contraction. The *it* that begins the final sentence has no antecedent. You could replace *it* with a more specific subject, such as *this procedure*, or you could rewrite the sentence: "When you kill a pig, always cut off its nose" to let the blood drain out, he said.

14. Adjective/adverb confusion. Proceeded far *more smoothly*.

15. Lots of errors (and also good fodder for discussing how high a standard comics should or should not be held to). Frame 1: Run-ons. *Excuse me. I've missed a few lectures. Can you tell me when the next exam is?* Frame 2: *Few* should be *Phew*. *10-page* should be hyphenated (compound modifier). Frame 3: *Except* should be *accept* in both instances.

Then you could talk about ways to make the sentence clear ("Sue asked whether Katy's new roommate had arrived yet" is one possibility), which could lead you to point out that there are lots of ways to get it right and only a few ways to get it wrong. (Again, I try to convey that editing expands rather than contracts possibilities.) Or maybe the discussion of possessive pronouns could lead to another common snafu: confusion of *its* and *it's*. You might point out that no one would put an apostrophe in *his* or *hers*, and that *its* is the same kind of word. Or you might ask students to reveal the trick they use to remember which of the two has an apostrophe. (I've learned some great tricks from students—for example, that you can tell *effect* from *affect* because *affect* starts with an *a*, like *action*.)

Or maybe, just to test out the new rule the students have devised, you could create another sentence with an unclear pronoun; for instance: "On the radio it said our professors might go on strike." (That one's a little more complicated, since the pronoun doesn't refer to any word in the sentence. The students would have to recognize the need to add something, such as "the newscaster said," or to ask the writer what he or she meant.) Or you could use a sentence like "Each student is responsible for their own assignment" to nudge students toward recognizing singular and plural pronouns and working out a rule on agreement. That could lead to . . . but you get the idea.

Doesn't All This Take Forever?
What Else Can I Do in Class?

Actually, it takes a lot less time to have these discussions in class than it's taken me to write about them. Even in my editing course, however, I rarely spend a whole class talking about grammar; if I try, I catch more people looking at the clock than at me. Instead, we take up one or two points per class, often based on something a student has asked about or something that everyone has seen. Should that beer advertisement talk about "less calories" or "fewer calories"? And how about those signs in the supermarket checkout lines that say "7 Items Or Less"? Questions like these can lead to some good discussions, even arguments, over how precise one needs to be in speech or casual writing, as opposed to writing for a class or for publication.

If you really want to make a commitment to grammar, try the five-minute usage lesson. Make a list of common and fairly simple grammatical problems, one for each person in the class. Set up a schedule that assigns each problem to a date, and write each problem and its date on a separate card. Drop the cards into a box and have each student pick one at random. Then tell your students that on the date listed on their card, they will make a brief presentation to the class on the point in question. (It helps if you've already designated an official class reference book, such as *The Bedford Handbook*.) They will need to explain the word or concept and then give the class some sample sentences to try.

After everyone has finished groaning "I got the hardest one," most of them plunge into the assignment with a vengeance. They make handouts, come up with bizarre tricks for remembering their lesson, and just generally start acting like people who know what they're talking about. Almost invariably, they'll tell you that as soon as they've done a usage lesson, they start seeing the problem everywhere and driving their friends crazy with grammar corrections.

One day one of my editing students illustrated the difference between *compose* and *comprise* (probably not something you need to do in Freshman English) with a huge bag of M&Ms™. The M&Ms composed the bag; the bag comprised the M&Ms. At the end of the semester, the other students agreed that they remembered this usage lesson more clearly than the others because when it was over, they ate the props. Ever since, I've added one more assignment to the usage lesson: The person giving the lesson has to bring food for the class. And if they want to, students can follow their usage lesson with a news question and a general knowledge question (à la *Jeopardy*) for the class. I've learned a lot of strange stuff this way. (Did you know that it's good luck to find a full-length Indian on the wrapper of your Tootsie Pop™?)

If you're thinking of doing the usage lessons and need ideas, take a look at the list that Bob Connors and Andrea Lunsford include in *The St. Martin's Handbook* (1989). By analyzing more than twenty thousand freshman and sophomore essays from around the country, they determined the twenty most common errors.

1. Missing comma after an introductory clause or phrase
2. Vague pronoun reference
3. Missing comma in a compound sentence (two independent clauses connected by a conjunction)
4. Wrong word
5. Missing comma(s) with a nonessential element
6. Wrong or missing verb ending
7. Wrong or missing preposition

8. Comma splice (two independent clauses connected only by a comma)

9. Missing or misplaced apostrophe in a possessive

10. Unnecessary shift in tense

11. Unnecessary shift in pronoun

12. Sentence fragment

13. Wrong tense or verb form

14. Lack of agreement between subject and verb

15. Missing comma in a series

16. Lack of agreement between pronoun and antecedent

17. Unnecessary comma(s) with an essential element

18. Fused sentence (two independent clauses connected without punctuation)

19. Dangling or misplaced modifier

20. *Its/it's* confusion

I Don't Think My List Would Look Quite Like That

Mine either. For one thing, I'd put subject/verb disagreement in the top five. But the list is a good place to start, either for making your own list or for assigning student-run usage lessons. If you decide to try the usage lessons, remember to review the day's grammar point before you go to class — just in case the student in charge misses the boat or invents sentences that confuse everyone. Even if you prepare carefully, chances are you will eventually be faced with a grammar question you can't answer.

This happens to me all the time. The only response I know of is to say, "I'm not sure. I think the answer is X, but I'll look it up and let you know for sure next time." I used to feel terrible about these incidents until I started noticing a trend in my end-of-semester evaluations. Over and over, students would say that they appreciated hearing a teacher say she didn't know something but would find out especially for them. In fact, just remembering to look up the answer earns you lots of credit. Everyone else, including the person who asked the question, has usually forgotten all about it.

Needless to say, you can also use the "top twenty errors" list above, or one like it, to create your own sentences for helping students deduce rules (such as the "roommate" sentence on page 162). One set of sentences I adapted from student papers is included as Figure 6–5. The semester I developed this handout, I made it a practice to turn on my computer whenever I read papers at home, typing in student sentences that illustrated common problems. Later it was simple to use those screenfuls of gibberish to make a worksheet of sentences illustrating the most widespread grammar glitches. As I recall, I had fun using the worksheet to do a sort of relay race in class. I wrote each sentence on the board, then stood there holding the chalk until someone "rescued" me by taking it and fixing some errors. Then someone else would "rescue" that person to correct any errors that remained, and so on until everyone agreed that the sentence was perfect.

Occasionally someone would go beyond perfect, "fixing" things that weren't really wrong simply because the "editor" didn't like the style, or altering the meaning of a sentence by making a seemingly innocuous change. Those, too, were learning experiences. The class could talk about getting carried away with grammar zeal, and I could deliver one of the most important rules of editing: The rules are no substitute for thought.

Figure 6–5 *An in-class correction exercise using sentences adapted from student papers.*

1. During lunch every one has the same thing on there minds, whats going on tonight, there has to be a party.

2. "Its to cold in here" I think to myself, "our's is definately the coldest cabin".

3. I felt alright, I laid there and looked at the stars.

4. After getting off the phone with my friend, my mother came upstairs. She could not of come at a worst time.

5. Since I beat my brother up the stairs meant I had the choice of which bedroom to choose.

6. We use to go there often, eventhough the hill seemed like it was getting steeper every time.

7. Ignoring the clouds I concentrated on my thoughts. "Mind if I hang around?", my friend asked. "Your bothering me I replied.

8. The memory of holidays and family gatherings are recalled. Each one in the family played their parts well.

9. He new he had to go. Because if he didn't, he'd be in alot of trouble.

10. We were scared but, didn't move. The bears were busy eating the vegetation and they didn't seem interested in us at all.

Jane Harrigan

I Like the Game Idea. How Else Can You Keep This Stuff from Being Deadly Dull?

Look for the humor. For example, humor is especially easy to find when you're talking about dangling or misplaced modifiers. Once students have finished laughing at a sentence like "Floating in the water, I saw the ship," or "When stewed, I love tomatoes," it doesn't take them long to realize they wouldn't be so amused if they had written the sentence and meant it seriously.

Humor also works well to convey a message that's essential to making students care: Every word—in fact, every letter, space, and punctuation mark—counts. Because I clip errors from everything I read, I have a collection of all sorts of strange stuff that's very convincing on this score. Consider, for example, the community organization that urged people to take part in a painting party by telling them to "bring paint and rollers and drop clothes and join the fun." Students like the way one extra *e* turned a call for help into an invitation to an orgy. They like the silliness of the newspaper that mistakenly labeled its advice column "Dead Abby," or the one that ran a tux-shop advertisement for the "After Sex Bridal Collection"— a wild typo for "After Six."

Books full of crazy headline errors can also help you convey grammatical information in a humorous way. (*Columbia Journalism Review* has published two of them: *Squad Helps Dog Bite Victim* [1980] and *Red Tape Holds Up New Bridge* [1987]). Let students talk about what's wrong with "Squad Helps Dog Bite Victim" and how to fix it. I can't think of a better way to lead them to the idea that compound modifiers (dog-bite victim) require hyphens. Once they've seen what the lack of punctuation can do, it's much easier for students to believe that every mark on paper counts, that they must make sure every mark says *exactly* what they mean.

Of course, an example doesn't have to be funny to convey the message. I often mention a column in which a friend of mine wrote this sentence: "He was stunned with outrage." Somehow, either through a computer glitch or an editor's error, the sentence was printed in the newspaper this way: "He was stunned without rage"—a pretty strong example of how even a space can make a huge difference.

If you have a lot of students partial to run-ons (comma splices), here's an example in which using a comma instead of a period makes a paragraph say the opposite of what the writer meant:

> Our teacher told us that many teenagers refuse to designate a driver
> before a party because that would be acknowledging that they expect to

get drunk. "It's too bad," the teacher said, "a designated driver can save your life."

Ask the students whether they notice anything strange about that paragraph. Eventually someone will realize exactly what the teacher is quoted as saying: "It's too bad a designated driver can save your life." Changing the comma after "said" to a period restores the meaning.

How About Some Other Exercises?

1. *The grammar game.* Make a list of basic grammar terms, phrasing them as questions. (Some sample questions are included as Figure 6–6.) Put each student's name on a card or slip of paper, and mix up the cards or papers. Divide the class into groups of three or four. Tell everyone that you know this is silly, but you don't mind looking foolish for a good cause.

   The rules: You ask a question. Each group has a set time (thirty seconds is usually enough) to confer and come up with an answer. Then you pick one name from the pile. That student, helped by his or her group, has fifteen seconds to answer. If the group can't do it, pick another card. Be sure to ask the question *before* you pick the name, or else only one group will bother conferring on the answer.

   The game often has the happy effect of showing students how much they already know. Take, for example, the question "What do adverbs modify?" Everyone names verbs right away, then takes a while to come up with the other two answers: adjectives and other adverbs. When I ask for a case where an adverb modifies an adjective, everyone usually looks at me blankly. If, after I've chosen two names, no one can answer, I call a time-out in the game and ask everyone to think of something they say all the time. Invariably, in the silence, a smile slowly spreads across one student's face just before he or she shouts out, "Totally awesome!"

2. *The punctuation assignment from hell.* This one, as you might imagine, was named by my students. You'll appreciate the name as well; the thing is hell to correct. I've tried variations of this exercise in several classes, and although it puts me on the receiving end of some killer looks the week the students are working on it, they invariably concede at the end of the semester that it was the most useful torture I forced them to endure. The exercise lends itself to just about any grammatical points you want to

Figure 6–6 *Sample questions (and answers) for "the grammar game."*

1. What are the eight parts of speech? (*noun, verb, adjective, adverb, pronoun, preposition, conjunction, interjection*)

2. Make up a sentence that uses all eight. (*Ouch! These creepy mosquitoes move so quickly that you can't see or escape from them.*)

3. What are the three words called articles? (*a, an, the*)

4. If articles are not one of the eight parts of speech, what part of speech are they? (*adjectives*)

5. What do adjectives modify? (*nouns or pronouns*) You could also ask, What questions do adjectives answer? (*which? how many? what kind?*)

6. Make up a sentence in which an adjective modifies a pronoun. (*The teacher always picks on poor me.*)

7. What do adverbs modify? (*verbs, adjectives, other adverbs*)

8. What's a sentence in which an adverb modifies an adjective? (*This class is totally awesome.*)

9. What's a sentence in which an adverb modifies another adverb? (*He runs awfully fast* — or, in New England, *wicked fast.*)

10. Many words can be used as more than one part of speech. If I say, "I want *that* office," what part of speech is *that*? (*adjective*)

11. What part of speech in this sentence: *That* is my office. (*pronoun*)

12. What part of speech in this sentence: I don't take school *that* seriously. (*adverb*)

13. What part of speech in this sentence: I hope *that* you already know this stuff. (*conjunction*)

14. Verb tenses have to do with what? (*time*)

15. What are the three simple tenses? (*past, present, future*)

16. Every verb is in one of two voices. What are they? (*active and passive*)

17. Make up a sentence with a passive verb. (*I was told by my mother never to talk to strangers.*) Now rewrite it to make the verb active. (*My mother told me never to talk to strangers.*) Note: Be sure students undertand the difference between *passive* verbs and *past-tense* verbs.

focus on but seems to work especially well with punctuation or even just commas (the bane of many young writers' existence).

The exercise is simple. It works only if you've designated a single grammar handbook for the class and everyone owns one. (If they've avoided buying it, the exercise will send them to the bookstore.) First, invent — or adapt from other handbooks or steal from students' papers — four or five sentences containing punctuation errors the class makes often. (I usually gum up the sentences with lots of nonpunctuation errors as well.) The directions and some sample sentences are included as Figure 6–7, an answer sheet as Figure 6–8. The basic idea is that students must not only correct the errors but also explain every punctuation mark they put in or take out by referring to a specific rule in the handbook.

By the time they get to college, most students have at least a vague idea where to put commas. But because many of them don't know *why* they put them where they do, they're left feeling uncertain. They think of punctuation as a mysterious potion understood only by an initiated few. This exercise, though hardly a paragon of creativity, seems to assure them once and for all that there's a reason for everything. After spending a "weekend from hell" looking up every tiny point, they finally know, for example, why some sentences need commas before conjunctions and others don't. (If this is the first time they've heard of dependent versus independent clauses, fine. At least now they have a reason to learn the difference.) The exercise shows them that punctuation involves no mystery, just consistent rules. The usual response, after the moaning, is a huge sigh of relief.

Correcting this exercise is difficult because of all the permutations the answers can take. Students can get the punctuation right but the explanation wrong, or the punctuation wrong but the explanation right, or use correct punctuation but neglect to explain it. Usually I just put a minus-one, circled, by each thing each person gets wrong, either on the original sentences or on the explanation sheet. Then I total the minuses and plot out the scores to assign A's, B's, etc. But there's one more step. When I hand the assignments back, I tell the students they must return to punctuation hell one more time. Their next assignment is to correct everything they got wrong the first time, and to explain *why* each new answer is correct.

I grade this second try on a strict percentage: If they got twenty things wrong the first time and miss four of the corrections, they'll get 80 percent (sixteen out of twenty). I tell them it should be the easiest A

Figure 6–7 *Sample sentences for "the punctuation assignment from hell."*

Instructions: This assignment has two parts. (a) Copy edit the sentences on both sides of this page, using the usual marks and reference books. (b) Then, on a separate sheet, type **an explanation for each punctuation mark you put in or took out.** Find the explanation in the handbook. Resist the temptation to guess; this assignment will keep coming back to you until you get all the explanations right. Might as well bite the bullet and learn the reasons.

1. I have three brothers. My oldest brother who is in the marines once said "you can take a man out of uniform; but you cant take the uniform out of the man. Noone knew quiet what he meant but, it sounded good.

2. The pay for social work is low, eventhough the job is physically, and emotionally draining. She knew that but she still choose to get a master's in social work, it was the only field she felt comfortable with. She didn't realize she had other options such as, teaching or she could attend business school.

3. "It was a long exhausting solitery ordeal she said after sailing alone around the globe but its made a new person of me. She admitted though that she wished every day that she was home.

4. Yesterday, a woman, who lived in China for a year, spoke to our class about what she learned there. She was suprised to learn for example that some of the beaches were comparable to the Florida Keys.

5. Breaking up the party, the students were questioned by the dean. "What's going on here" he thundered, "you've broken the rules, therefore you're suspended".

they'll every earn: They already know something's wrong, and they can work together or ask anyone they want for help with the corrections. In fact, freshmen might benefit from doing the correcting stage of the assignment in groups. By pooling their knowledge, they'll each realize that they know something about this grammar business. Meanwhile, the wide variety of remedies the group proposes will drive home the lesson that there's more than one "right" way to express any thought.

3. *Student-generated exercises.* Have each student create a page of bad writing containing every problem, grammatical or otherwise, that he or she can think of. All of them should prepare answer sheets for their pages as well. Then they can swap "bad pages" with another student, and each can edit the other's. Afterward, have them compare answer sheets until they've agreed on the best way to address each problem. Hang onto these sheets; students invent some great examples that you can use in other classes.

As much as you can, let the students drive the editing component of your course. How much help do they need? How much of the nitty-gritty can they stand? Which issues (the large, shared ones) can be addressed in class, and which should you save for individual conferences? Part of the fun is inventing new exercises to suit each class's unique needs. If, for example, you have a class that loves clichés, have the students dictate to you all the clichés they can think of. (At first you can prompt them: "Stiff as a . . ."). Write the clichés on the board. Then have everyone choose a few and turn them around. "Running around like a chicken with its head cut off," for example, might become, "Running around like a robot with a system error" or, "Running around like a windup soldier gone AWOL." "Old as the hills" might become, "Old as a Christmas fruitcake" or, "Old as my father's jokes." (Students are a heck of a lot better at this than I am!)

What Role Does Word-by-Word Editing Play in Conferences?

I always talk about grammar in my conferences. I don't know how to avoid it; it's essential in deciding whether the writer has delivered his or her message in the best possible way. That's not to say that students leave my office thinking we just had a conference about grammar. On average, we probably talk about grammar for three minutes in a fifteen-minute confer-

Figure 6–8 *Answers to the first two sample sentences in Figure 6–7.*
(Answers include other points in addition to punctuation.)

---

1. I have three brothers. My oldest brother⊙who is in the marines⊙once said⊙"you can take a man out of uniform⊙but you cant take the uniform out of the man." Noone knew quite what he meant⊙but⊙it sounded good.

(a) Because the person has three brothers, *who is in the Marines* is not essential to distinguish which brother did the talking. When a phrase or clause is not essential, put commas around it. (A trick learned from my students: The commas are like handles for lifting the clause out; the sentence can get along without it.)

(b) Always a comma before a complete-sentence quote.

(c) Comma required after *uniform* because *but* separates two independent clauses (each can stand alone). Use a semicolon to connect closely related sentences only when a conjunction is *not* used. (Most freshmen are better off ignoring semicolons altogether.)

(d) Put an apostrophe in a contraction at the point where something is left out (in this case, the *o* from *not*).

(e) When you start a quote, don't forget to show where it ends.

(f) A conjunction that separates two independent clauses requires a comma. The comma goes before, not after, the conjunction. (This is a favorite student error.)

2. The pay for social work is low⊙even though the job is physically⊙and emotionally draining. She knew that⊙but she still choose to get a master's in social work⊙it was the only field she felt comfortable with. She didn't realize she had other options⊙such as⊙teaching or she could attend business school.

(a) No comma required before a concluding adverb clause that's essential to the sentence.

(b) Either *even though*, two words, or *although*.

(c) No reason for this comma. If you want to set off *and emotionally* for drama (pretty iffy in this case), put commas both before and after it.

(d) Comma needed before *but* because each part of sentence has subject and verb.

(e) Run-on or comma splice: two full sentences stuck together with only a comma. Either change comma to period or semicolon, or eliminate comma and add subordinating conjunction such as *because*.

(f) The comma goes before, not after, a non-essential phrase beginning with *such as*.

(g) Parallelism: parallel ideas should be expressed in the same grammatical form. You could make both *-ing* verbs: *teaching or attending business school.* Or you could rewrite the sentence: *She didn't realize that she could teach, go to business school, or try many other options.*

ence. Sometimes I tell students in advance that the last five minutes of their conferences that week — after we've done all the good, positive content-editing stuff — will be reserved for on-the-spot editing. There's something about watching a person mark up your writing right before your eyes that conveys the importance of language better than dried ink marks on a page ever could (especially since I've come to doubt that most students actually *look* at the marks we make on their pages). I don't pounce gleefully on errors with a red pen. I just sort of casually say, "Hmmm- . . .here's a run-on sentence" or, "How do you spell this word?" as I circle passages in pencil.

Speaking of marking up, I've developed a system that works for me; I have no idea how common it is. I never make marks on the first page of a student's writing. That way, when students come to conferences, I can get them talking about their writing on their own, without written clues to what I think (and without the distraction of hunting for those written clues). On the pages after the first, I simply underline or circle any word or passage I'd like to talk about, for reasons of either content or mechanics. At the end of the paper I make a quick list of the issues those lines and circles indicated, in case I need to refresh my memory.

Perhaps I should backtrack here and point out something I do in every student's first conference of the semester. For all I know, every other writing instructor on the planet does it, too. But, like all of us, I always think I made the good stuff up. I tell students that conferences are their time, to be used in any way they choose. They can ask any questions they want, discuss any topics they want, say anything at all — except for three forbidden words: "I don't know." Those three words cannot be uttered in my office. You won't need those words, I tell them, because I'm not going to ask you about Einstein's theory of relativity. I'm going to ask only about your writing, and on that you're the world's foremost authority. You *do* know, so don't hide behind that three-word smokescreen.

So far, my One and Only Conference Rule has worked wonderfully. Occasionally students will slip and say, "I don't know," but they always catch themselves and hazard a guess. (More often, they'll come out with something that sounds like "I don't kn-oops!") The "you do *so* know" rule is extremely handy when it comes to looking at the language issues raised by students' writing. After we've conferred about the big stuff (topic, approach, focus, organization, liveliness), I start paging through the paper and picking out passages I've marked. If the issue is grammatical, I'll often point and ask, "Why do you think I underlined that?"

"I don't kn-oops!" comes the answer, followed by several theories. Though a few of the early guesses tend to be pretty fanciful, most students quickly make a crucial realization: While it may at first appear that they've perpetrated four thousand grammatical errors in a piece, they have in fact made only two or three, over and over. Just pointing and repeating, "What's this one?" and, "How could you fix it?" conveys the message that such errors are easy to spot and easy to fix. After the same problem has arisen two or three times, most students, even in their embarrassment, find some satisfaction in being able to identify the next instance, and its remedy, so quickly. And, of course, if you encounter grammatical points the student honestly knows nothing about, a conference is a great place for a quick, nonintimidating lesson.

At the end of a conference, I ask students to recap what we just talked about; I like to know what they're taking with them. Sometimes I'll simply ask, "So what'd we just say?" Other times I'll be more specific: "So what three things can you get from this piece that you can apply to your next one?" I've always done this with content issues, but in recent years I've started doing it with the fine points of language as well.

I call this the "grammar prescription," and I'm so weird that I actually write an ℞ at the top of the student's paper. Then I ask the student either to develop her own prescription and write it after the ℞, or dictate it to me. ("No more run-on sentences," she might say. "Read up on commas. Don't start so many sentences with *And*.") Because the student is creating the prescription herself (with strategic nudges from me, of course), she is much likelier to remember at least part of it. And if the same problem crops up again, I can always say, "Hmmm . . .wasn't this part of your prescription last week?"

So, Do You Talk about Editing All the Time?

Not really. As with everything, there's a time and a place for broaching the subject—and lots of times and places not to. In a conference, big issues come first. If a paper has no focus or is deadly dull, there's no use belaboring its lack of apostrophes. On the other hand, you can use editing to show where dullness comes from. The other day I asked a student to circle the verbs on the first page of her story. Until then, she hadn't been able to figure out why the piece was so boring. When she looked at the circled verbs and saw that every one of them was *is* or *are*, she knew.

Editing

When you encounter a student whose internal critic is so strong as to be more accurately called a censor, you may want to delay all talk of editing for a while. Generally, you can engage students in discussion of language in a way that won't cause them to freeze, but an occasional student who's already blocked will fixate on the fear of grammar failure and give up entirely. Finally, of course, you'll want to lay off the grammar talk when a student produces a piece of writing on a subject that's clearly causing him or her emotional trauma. Commas look pretty trivial by comparison.

Aside from those relatively rare instances, though, I guess I *do* talk about editing all the time — in class, in conference, in life. When I look at the exercises in other chapters of this book, I see ways to adapt them to include a grammar component, and every semester I test out new ideas for coming at editing from another angle. Not long ago, frustrated by a class in which no one's writing seemed to *flow*, I hit upon the scheme of taking a beautifully written paragraph and breaking it down into raw information, stated in the most boring and repetitive sentence structures. I showed the students the dull passage, got their responses, then showed them the well-written passage that sprang from exactly the same information. We looked at the way the writer had combined thoughts gracefully, selecting the words, hearing the sounds, feeling the rhythms. A few light bulbs went on. I gave the students a second choppy, boring passage and asked them to combine the ideas in a way that flowed. As they left class, I handed them the "real" passage. Many of their own were just as good.

I haven't perfected this exercise yet, but I like it. I like it because it gets at what is, for me, the heart of the writing process. Sometimes I think everything I try to tell students comes down to this: Good writing creates magic, but it is not created *by* magic. It's created by writers doing hard, picky work. First comes the idea; then come the words. When we talk about editing in class, what we're really saying is that words have their own satisfactions, and those satisfactions do not in any way detract from the excitement of ideas.

One of these days when I look at a piece of writing with my students, I should just say it, say the words that lie behind anything else I try to convey. Look at that sentence, I'll say. Look at the effect it has on you. That's not an accident; the writer *made* it happen. The writer did it by choosing just the right first word, second word, third word, by fitting them together just so, searching out precisely the tone and the sound and the feeling he wanted to convey. Look at that sentence. Isn't it something?

References

Connors, Robert, and Andrea Lunsford. 1989. *The St. Martin's Handbook.* New York: St. Martin's.

Hacker, Diana. 1991. *The Bedford Handbook for Writers.* Boston: Bedford Books/St. Martin's.

Red Tape Holds Up New Bridge. 1987. Compiled and edited by *Columbia Journalism Review.* New York: Perigee Books/Putnam.

Squad Helps Dog Bite Victim. 1980. Compiled and edited by *Columbia Journalism Review.* Garden City, NY: Dolphin Books/Doubleday.

... as Acts of ... esponse, and ... lection

... Chiseri-Strater

... is a *process*. And it's a process that reflects Longoi... ...ctices, not just end-of-term procedures. Student feedback during my ... of teaching writing has greatly reshaped my thinking about evaluation to the extent that my grading process now mirrors the same practices I stress in my writing classroom: critical reading, constructive response, and reflective thought. But I didn't always approach evaluation this way.

When I started teaching Freshman English, grading made me feel so vulnerable and confused that my attitude was one of avoidance. Since I didn't quite know what I was doing and had no idea how to get better at it, I left grading until the last minute, closed my office door, and privately muddled through. Pat Belanoff has recently described this solitary response: "Most of us would just rather not talk about [grading] at all; it's the dirty thing we have to do in the dark of our own offices" (1991, 61). I rationalized my insecurities about evaluation by convincing myself that students valued their learning over their grades. Wrong! Far more than being upset over getting a poor grade in Freshman English, students resent not understanding the grading process being used. If they end up with a C when they felt that all along they had been doing above-average work—a belief most likely reinforced by my positive feedback in conferences and on papers—they

179

become angry. And rightly so. Students feel manipulated and co-opted by teachers who refuse to reveal their grading process or who cover their own anxieties by suggesting that grades are not an important part of the course.

When students express their feelings towards grades, what they say is startling in its honesty and directness: grades *are* important to students; moreover, they have a twelve-year history of dealing with them that is not easy to erase. In an essay called "Problems With Writing," a first-year student discusses how grades affect her writing, how grades, in fact, shape her writing:

> When I am given a writing assignment, a series of mixed emotions race through my mind. At first, providing that the topic is at least somewhat interesting, and most are, I am excited at the possibilities I might create. Then I assess my grade necessity. Do I need an A or am I doing well enough that any grade I receive will not hurt my overall mark? I don't know why that consideration comes into my head because I personally don't believe in grades. Most of the time the one letter evaluation never reflects how much I actually took from the class. In the case of English papers, on occasion a piece that took hours of frustration, aggravation, and intense thought has been returned to my hands with scarcely a comment and a low grade at the end of the page.

Both students and teachers, then, have troubles about grades and the influence of grades on our teaching and learning practices.

When I emerged from the "muddling" phase and admitted to myself that I didn't know what I was doing, my next response was to seek outside help from authorities by searching for published grading guidelines. Many grading criterion sheets were available since this was roughly the period when such assessment scales were in favor around the country. While grading scales were easy enough to locate and duplicate (one example is shown in Figure 7–1), in trying to apply them to my students' work, I found that there was not all that much relationship between the discrete parts of such scales and my assessment of my students' writing. Many instructors rely on published assessment scales early in their teaching careers to give them some overall sense of standards for writing. While I still find such guides useful for initiating class discussions about evaluation, objective scales are no longer part of my grading process. I'm now convinced that objective grading scales foster an overreliance on external standards of authority, prevent teachers from figuring out their own attitudes and procedures for evaluation, and mask the many interesting pedagogical issues involved in the assessment process.

Probably the activity that helped me most in developing my own attitudes and procedures for evaluation was sharing student papers in weekly Freshman English staff meetings. Starting with Don Murray's directorship,

Figure 7–1 *The Diederich Scale.*

1—Poor   2—Weak   3—Average   4—Good   5—Excellent

Reader _____

Quality and development of ideas	1 2 3 4 5
Organization, relevance, movement	1 2 3 4 5

_____ × 5 = _____
Subtotal

Style, flavor, individuality	1 2 3 4 5
Wording and phrasing	1 2 3 4 5

_____ × 3 = _____
Subtotal

Grammar, sentence structure	1 2 3 4 5
Punctuation	1 2 3 4 5
Spelling	1 2 3 4 5
Manuscript form, legibility	1 2 3 4 5

_____ × 1 = _____
Subtotal
Total grade: _____ %

writing instructors brought problem student papers to weekly meetings, and in small groups, we discussed how we would respond to the papers and then how we would grade them. Just distinguishing between the two phases of response and assessment was helpful to me. I noticed while working in these groups that I often agreed with other instructors' responses to the student writing but seldom agreed with the actual assigned grade. Student papers that we discussed would run the whole range of A to D in staff members' evaluations. Instead of finding that mixed response confusing, I began to understand the extent to which grading was subjective even for trained teachers of writing and, in addition, I realized how important it was for me to reflect on my own evaluation process, on how I read, responded to, and evaluated student work.

Elizabeth Chiseri-Strater

What We Evaluate: Learning to Read and Respond

One of the most difficult things to unravel about evaluation is to decide what it is that we are actually assessing: the student, the paper, or her writing process. Over time I began to realize that I cared almost as much about students' understanding of their writing processes as I cared about actual textual changes in their writing. And because my writing classes and intensive conferencing methods afford such intimacy with my students, I also know that I care about the students apart from their texts or metacognitive awarenesses. This web of the personal, the textual, and the developmental took much practice to untangle, but I now accept that all of these issues affect my response to and evaluation of students' work.

I can also acknowledge how intimately evaluation is tied to response. When I read student writing, I respond with my own values toward what makes writing good. As Chris Anson puts it, "What a teacher says about a student's writing is saturated with her beliefs, values, and models of learning" (1989, 354). It is tempting to suggest that response is an act apart from evaluation; that is, to think we are able to respond as subjective readers to student writing throughout the semester and then act as objective evaluators of it at the end. Such a division, however, feels impossible.

I did find it possible, though, to identify which of my responses to students' texts are evaluative and which ones offer support. For example, I learned how to avoid mixing responses with negative evaluations (e.g., This part of your essay worked well for me *but....*) I am able to frame my responses so that they steer clear of evaluation by indicating the places where I find myself most engaged as a reader and locating the parts of papers where I have further questions by writing such comments as, I was wondering if . . . or, In this section I am confused by . . . or, Is this what you meant by . . . ?

Colleague Lisa Sisco has suggested that our goal in responding to student writing should be to turn the teacher-student relationship into a "reader-writer" relationship by explaining to students how we *read*. I agree with Lisa that as teachers we should share our reading processes with our students, but I feel that even then we cannot fully extricate ourselves from the evaluative stance. What seems to work best for me is to recognize and understand this tangled web of evaluation and response as we approach our students' writing.

Here's an example of a male freshman writer who presented me with many faces of this response/evaluation conflict in a rather exaggerated way. To provide some context: Eric had already written two fairly standard sports papers for my freshman writing class, one about being a caddie and another about being a sports fan. When he handed me this particularly interesting new paper titled "House of Pain," I anticipated that he had found a topic in which he could discover something new rather than report on something known. The paper, about his father's abuse of his mother, is full of potential for learning about writing and learning about himself. In reviewing this paper, I will show how my own responses to Eric's text were mixed with my evaluations.

First, I had already read Eric as a student in some ways. At each class and conference he showed up in an interesting assortment of purposefully matched sports clothing: A Pirates cap with a Steelers T-shirt and a pair of shorts with a Penguins emblem. I could not ignore these outfits and used them in a friendly way to establish rapport. In addition to reading him personally, I read his attitude toward my course. The fact that Eric brought me new papers each week was also something I could not ignore, since my course stressed revision. While I had offered him some suggestions for rethinking his papers, I am sure Eric sensed my lack of interest in his sports topics and at the same time I sensed that he was fairly satisfied with them. So when Eric brought me this potentially risky paper on wife abuse, which he was both willing and eager to discuss as being a topic of personal and public value, I was relieved and verified as his teacher: Here was a draft we could work with together. Even though I always tell students that the text is theirs, that the decisions to change, revise, or abandon material are theirs, I am clearly more enthusiastic about some topics than others. And students read that message very clearly.

I felt not only that I could help Eric personally to write himself to some place of understanding about his mother's abuse by his father but also that in helping him I would begin to understand the male perspective on this important political/social issue and thereby potentially contribute to change. This change excited and interested me, and I would be dishonest if I did not admit that this possibility engaged me far more than trying to find new meaning in his sports narratives. As I worked with Eric on the multiple drafts of both his narrative and eventually his researched essay on wife abuse, I was eager to help him revise, rethink, and research this issue. Had Eric refused to work further on this paper, in fact, I might have become somewhat angry, although I would probably have rationalized that he wasn't developmentally "ready" to approach the topic yet. I offer this analysis to make it clear that response and evaluation are wedded even at the topic level.

Certainly response and evaluation are intertwined for me at the textual level. For example, Eric's paper began with an eight-stanza MTV video song by Faster Pussycat, which he then refers to throughout. When I first read Eric's paper, my response was that he should get rid of all references to the video and song and start the paper with the authority of his own personal experience. In preparation for our conference I wrote on the edge of his paper, "I'm not sure you really need this video reference or that it adds all that much.... " Now I can see that in writing this comment, I devalued the use of the video song as the lead for his paper even though Eric clearly explained its importance within the body of the paper as being the thing that freed him to write about this topic at all: "House of Pain is one of my favorite songs because it lets me secretly speak of what has happened, something my mother asked me never to do." Had Eric started his paper with a poem of some merit, would I have insisted that he get rid of it or would I have encouraged him to foreground it? These are some of the questions that surrounded my reading of Eric's paper. I'll share here the first page of Eric's paper, accompanied by my responses and evaluations, which were never seen by Eric but remain in my head as I reflect on how I responded to the paper.

Text	Responses
"House of Pain" "I'm not trying to fake it ain't the one to blame No there's no one home in the house of pain.... " Faster Pussycat	I like this title very much. These lyrics make me understand the gap between me and my students. These lyrics evoke no meaning. Would that be true of Dylan lyrics or the Beatles? Now that I see that the title is not original with Eric but borrowed, I like it less.
A series of memories ran through my mind. Not pleasant ones, but those of fights between my parents. These memories were stirred by a video on MTV about a young couple that gets divorced and the kid wonders where his father has disappeared to. The specific scene that sparks the memories is when the two parents are arguing and the husband slaps his spouse, meanwhile the child is standing idly by. The video is House of Pain by Faster Pussycat.	Here he's connecting the eight stanzas of song with his own experiences. Too much telling in this first paragraph. I'm not sure that he really needs any of this introductory material. I want him to dive into the actual experience and use his own voice rather than someone called Faster Pussycat. I recognize my preference for getting right into a paper rather than lead-ing up to it. Besides being my own preference, I might also acknowledge that such leads are valued by English teachers over those in other disciplines.

The first big fight to my knowledge occurred in the summer of '77 when I was six years old. It was at Honeybrook Campground—we went camping every summer for two weeks back then. On this infamous trip was my immediate family: my brother (age five at the time), my mother, my father and myself. The event occured on our seventh and last day there while we were packing for our next destination: Keystone Campground. I do not remember what sparked the fight but it is safe to guess that my father was complaining about my mother's packing. From there it just escalated.

Here Eric is *telling* all about this incident rather than showing it. He's aware that he isn't sure when this domestic violence actually started since he says "to my knowledge" and "back then," which imply that things started at some point that he can't recall. His use of the word "infamous" also seems ironic here. The actual event he records here seems like the place to begin his paper in full descriptive detail.

Will my suggestions about writing this paper be helpful to his sorting out of this paper? I need to be sensitive to his needs when talking to him. I wonder how he felt watching all this violence—the male is supposed to protect his mother. Working with this paper is going to be rough going for me since I feel pretty strongly about the topic already, but this is so much more interesting than his sports papers.

While reexamining my work with Eric on this paper, I realize the extent to which my "response" cannot be detached from my "evaluation" of him, his issues, his text, and his world. As a writing teacher, I have become over time more reflective about my own responses, more critical of my evaluations, and more careful about my grading procedures. This careful analysis of my reading habits prompted me to move away from teacher evaluation by bringing students themselves into the assessment process.

Bringing Students into the Evaluation Process

The first step toward engaging students in the evaluation process, but one that can make an enormous difference, is to have them draw up their own list of criteria for what makes writing good. Even first-year composition students, I've found, have already internalized standards about good writing from their private reading and their exposure to literature. The lists they create together of what constitutes good writing most often replicate the criteria of the writing workshop guidelines. Good writing, they agree, must have focus, organization, clarity, voice, detail, etc. After they have developed these guidelines together, I have students work in groups to categorize and prioritize their lists. I push them to decide whether or not honesty in writing really comes before clarity or whether mechanics are more important or less important than focus. Students then read a range of papers collected from previous semesters for this purpose, apply their newly created criteria to these samples of student writing, and finally grade them. When they assign grades to peer writing, agreement about the quality of writing usually clusters at two ends of the scale: the best and the worst. But all that in-between writing from the B to D levels (which is most similar to the papers they would write themselves) is much trickier for them to evaluate. By participating in this exercise of applying newly developed evaluation criteria to peer work, students begin to argue about particular stylistic preferences, rules of grammar, and features of writing, such as whether writers can begin a sentence with *but* or whether *I* is appropriate in a college paper. While the lack of clear rules makes students uncomfortable because they want the evaluation of their essays to be as neat as that of objective tests and they want the responsibility for assigning grades to lie entirely in the hands of the teacher, this activity produces important dialogue. This talk about assessment allows students to see their own responses to writing as subjective rather than objective, and because everyone brings somewhat different standards and criteria into the writing class, students also begin to understand evaluation as an intersubjective process. Moreover, this evaluation exercise helps promote the idea that the writing class is a community that's responsible for developing its own norms of operation within the larger discourse communities in the university.

Many instructors have adapted this exercise of drawing up class guidelines for evaluation. My colleague Dot Kasik and her class generated the guidelines shown in Figure 7–2. Kasik suggests that another value of this exercise for beginning writers is that it creates a "vocabulary" for students to use to talk about writing. Some students, she points out, have never heard terms like focus, lead, or voice in their high school English classes, and this exercise helps students start to understand the language of the writing class. And once students have generated their own criteria, they can then use their guidelines to assess their essays, to work in peer groups, and to prepare for their conferences. "Since the student has had a hand in its production, [the guideline] carries more validity, is less threatening, and is far more authoritative," Kasik says of her student-generated grading criteria. Once students

Figure 7–2 *Peer guidelines for evaluation.*

Peer Guidelines for Evaluation

CONTENT
Are the ideas provocative?
Is there a reason for this essay? What's the "So What?"
Where is the "eye" of the story (what point of view is it written from)?
Are there gaps in understanding that the reader can't bridge?
Is the topic sufficiently researched?
Has the reader sufficiently posited and analyzed?
Is information that needed summarizing from more complex sources clear?

STRUCTURE AND ORGANIZATION
Is the lead interesting?
Are the major points clear?
Is the conclusion appropriate and satisfying?
Is the focus clearly defined?
How does the "eye of the story" affect the focus?

STYLE/VOICE
Is the language consistent with the story content?
Is the language consistent throughout?
Is the writing exciting enough to support the topic?
Who is the author: Can you "see" her/him?
Are characters fully described?
Are there lifelike details in the story?
Is their conversation when necessary? Is it realistic?
Should more description be added?

MECHANICS
Check: commas
        quotation marks
        complete sentences: no fragments, no run-ons
        misspelled words
        parallel constructions in all series
        dangling modifiers
        misused words
        paragraph divisions
For research papers:
        properly annotated citations and bibliography

are brought into the process of evaluation, their involvement in self-assessment also becomes stronger.

Becoming Your Own Best Critic: The Role of Self-Assessment in Freshman English

The last act of writing must be to become one's own reader. It is, I suppose, a schizophrenic process, to begin passionately and to end critically, to begin hot and end cold: and more important to be passion-hot and critic-cold at the same time.

John Ciardi (Murray 1968, 234)

Self-assessment is encouraged in Freshman English by inviting students to participate in a process of shared responsibility and collaborative evaluation throughout the entire course. Self-assessment takes place in Freshman English in many different ways that have already been mentioned in this book. Self-critique, for example, is very much part of the conference for which students are asked to prepare by writing evaluations of their papers. Such written critiques — often based on class-generated guidelines— encourage students to take responsibility for their work by rereading it before conferences. Self-assessment is also part of the reading and rereading processes discussed in Donna Qualley's chapter on the connections between reading and writing. Acts of self-reflection help students develop a more critical stance on their own work by developing what Donald Murray has described as "the writer's other self" (1968, 243).

Peer-group work also affords students some practice in giving and receiving feedback and in playing the roles of critic, editor, coach, and tutor. Many instructors ask that students write about the feedback on their papers they receive in peer groups. This way students have another opportunity to use the process of writing for the purpose of reflecting on and evaluating their own writing. These circles of peer and teacher responses push students away from relying on teacher evaluation and toward becoming their own best critics. Many writing teachers have developed self-evaluation guides, which are submitted with each paper (see the example in Figure 7–3).

Taking Stock: Starting with Self-Assessment

Freshman writing instructor Dianne McAnaney begins the self-evaluation process on day one of her writing course with a short exercise that requires students to take stock of themselves as writers. In survey format, her students respond to a series of questions about their writing histories and habits: What is the ideal environment for you as a writer? Describe your own writing process. What is the adjective that best describes you as a writer? Students then use the answers to these questions to frame short writing histories, the first essay that they bring to their conferences. What students don't know is that on the last day of class, Dianne will return these essays and ask students to reread them as frames for writing a final in-class essay about the changes they have undergone as writers in her course.

Students' initial essays report common attitudes about writing, such as "I have no particular writing style" or "When I know my writing will have

Figure 7–3 *Guide for self-evaluation.*

Self-Evaluation

This evaluation should be attached to the back of your paper. Each section requires a grade and an explanation of the grade.

1. FOCUS: (Does the paper have a focus? Does it stick to the focus? Does it make a point? Does it answer the "Why" questions?)

2. INTRODUCTION: (Does the introduction capture the reader's interest? Is it indicative of what follows?)

3. EXAMPLES AND DESCRIPTION: (Does the paper back up ideas with examples? Does it show events, people, and places instead of telling about them?)

4. MECHANICS: (Does the paper have errors of spelling? Grammar? Are there too many typos?)

5. OVERALL GRADE AND COMMENTS:

an audience, I put less feeling into my work." Yet their later essays reveal a new appreciation of and confidence in their writing abilities. Such transformations in the attitudes of freshman writers — from self-effacement to self-assurance — explain why writing instructors emphasize self-assessment in their courses: it validates much of what we are teaching and furnishes a way of formalizing reflective practices in our classrooms.

Timeline for Grading: What to Grade, When to Grade

An informal survey among our Freshman English staff revealed that while grading practices vary among instructors, there is some agreement on the principles of evaluation. One common but unstated rule is that no instructor grades every paper. Rather, the majority of instructors grade a compilation of student papers at least twice — at midterm and at the end of the semester. Some instructors also grade specific assignments such as the research essays, reading essays, or collaborative projects, and still others grade journals, peer critiques, and process accounts. As a staff we tend to assign grades only to final drafts while all other grades remain tentative, since there is always an opportunity to revise until the end of the course. Another common agreement about grading is that a paper submitted and graded at midterm may be substantially revised and resubmitted at the end of the term. This practice of reevaluation encourages the revision valued by most staff members.

When I grade student papers at midterm, I give an in-depth written response to each student on one or two of his or her revised papers. Earlier in my teaching experience, I would mark up each paper, making comments about grammar, syntax, and spelling along with comments about focus, voice, and detail (see the example in Figure 7–4). Under that standard grading procedure, I did not really distinguish among my many responses, and for that reason it was difficult for my student to decide which comments were more important than others. Some students appreciated this kind of close commentary while others resented it. Beth reacted in writing to one of my short marginal responses on her midterm paper:

> ... on the second draft of my paper there is an inked line and the words "I like this part." As the writer I wonder: Which part? Which words? Why? What does "like" mean? How does it fit with the rest of the work? Do you like it so much that you will grieve if I take it out during revision? What is wrong with the rest of the page? Why only that part? Do you understand what I am trying to say with these words? How are you interpreting them?

Figure 7–4 *Example of a teacher-marked student paper.*

This lead sentence has good ideas --I think maybe the subject (voice) and the modifiers are too far apart.

Black Ribbon *wonderful title*

The (voice) on the other end of the line sounded vacant and
hollow, trying to be detached from something that was far *too* to near
to avoid. Stevie's mother said that he never made it out of the
emergency room. His body decided that it was too much work trying
to live and surrendered. She hung up. *Did you feel cut off?* I walked away from the
phone. I felt *nice word* obligated to cry. My friend is *was* dead, I owe it to
him to bawl my eyes out. I tried to push the tears out. They
wouldn't come. It's not that I was afraid to show my emotion, I
just didn't know what they were. It seemed that tears were right
for the occasion but at the same time were totally out of place. *of what?* *you + all other riders?*
All I could do was think. It's the risk we all take whenever we
point the front wheel of the motorcycle down the quarter mile
tarmac strip. One minor screwup and we're road meat, sliding *great phrase -- just right*
down the track on our leather suit and a prayer. Sometimes we get
up and walk away, other times we don't. The thrill, the money, the
challenge overpowers the very real threat of destruction. There
is nothing quite like the feeling of man-and-machine versus man-
and machine in the ultimate test of speed: drag racing. (Its) the *What does this mean?* *It's = It is*
g-forces of acceleration trying to separate arms from torso and
push eyes through the back of the head. *Vivid Image* (Its) the sight of the
bikes rearing up on the wheelie bars and carrying the front wheel *good phrase*
a foot off the ground as they race side-by-side down the track.
who- you and stevie?
We've had some close calls in the past but last night was hell. *you + stevie?*

nice quick sentence

Do you feel guilty that you're STILL alive,

wonderful sentence

what's a G-force?

There's a tense problem here... write it all faster all present tense

191

Since teachers' written comments often promote such inquiries, I prefer now to write more global comments to each student on my computer and leave the draft alone (though if a student asks for a close response to her work, I will provide that on one or two pages of her draft). My current procedure involves dividing my evaluation into categories and trying to be very specific. Here is a sample response, framed as a letter to Scott about his midterm paper, "Black Ribbon," which he had submitted for grading.

Dear Scott,

"Black Ribbon" is a very powerful paper, filled with strong realistic images and vivid language. As you continue to work on this paper for your final portfolio—and I encourage you to do so—you may want to consider some of the following suggestions.

Style/Voice: You use language with precision for the most part, and much of the authority of this paper comes from your inclusion of specific biking terms such as "road meat" and "wheelie bars." As a writer you come across as someone who both knows and cares about this biking world. Sometimes, however, your language is sentimental, and this detracts from the overall impact of the paper. The lead, for example, uses the words "vacant and hollow," which seem trite next to some of your other specific phrases. The last line in the first paragraph also feels strained: "We've had some close calls in the past but last night was hell." As you work through this draft you may want to do some more editing, distinguishing between fresh, lively use of language and tired, overused phrases.

Content: Your story about your relationship with Stevie and how you felt after his accident carries the universal theme of grief and death. It's content that we all care about. I am a bit confused over your actual feelings toward bike racing after Stevie dies. It seems as if you are withdrawing because of fear and grief, but I'm not quite clear when I finish what conclusions you've come to about Steve's meaningless death. From your perspective, what attitude about his death do you want your reader to adopt? Some of your details support a kind of existential attitude about this death—the candy bar wrappers in the breeze and the background music—but your conversation with your mother about Stevie's death makes me feel your overall ambivalence. As you revise, you need to think about the focus of this piece. If your focus is ambivalence, then let the reader really feel that all the way through.

Structure/Organization: You are presenting miniscenes and then reflecting on them for the reader. That works well for me most of the time. I did get confused during the flashback scene and wondered if this wasn't just a technical problem. Fiddle with that part a bit more, and see if you can take us back in time more smoothly. The narrative line of celebrating Stevie's death with the painting of roses on the motorcycles seems less well developed than the actual scene of the accident. You may want to

192

think about the proportions of this paper and how much space you want to allow for each scene. The way you decide to cut and shape this piece depends, of course, on the point of view you want your reader to take on Stevie's death and on biking in general.

Readability (Mechanics): There is so much tension and good detail here that the paper moves quickly and drives me to want to read it. At first I was slowed down by all the biking language, and then I became used to it. Some other students wrote in their critiques of your paper that they were confused by too much technical detail. When you revise, make sure that you use technical language only when it helps move your meaning forward. You may want to think about your ending and see how you can get out of this powerful narrative without being too moralistic but, at the same time, leaving us with some sort of message, some kind of reflective "so what."

Overall: The challenge of revising this piece is to keep up with the fine work you have put in motion and not just diddle around at the word level. Try moving scenes around. Do radical surgery on your sentences. Shape the final scene so that it assumes the proportion you want it to. Make us know how you feel about biking now that you've lost a friend to it. This paper is an A paper at midterm, Scott, but I'll expect major changes if you include it in your final portfolio. I'm impressed with the commitment you have to rendering this painful experience fully for other readers.

Elizabeth

I compose my response at the computer while I read and think about a student's writing. Since I'm already familiar with my students' work, this evaluative response doesn't take long to draft. To me, it's important to offer detailed feedback at midterm, when my students still have enough time left for it to be useful in their revision process. After grading midterm portfolios or papers in this manner, I follow up with an evaluation conference in which the student and I discuss the grade and set goals for the rest of the semester. The oral conversation that follows the written evaluation gives students an opportunity to challenge my grading of their work.

If I was unable to provide this kind of extensive written feedback, I would either hold an evaluation conference with each student or provide more limited feedback, using the peer-generated guidelines to shape my responses. These more abbreviated responses would emphasize what I think is working best in the draft and the key things the student should consider in revising the paper. A shorter version of Scott's letter might be written on a form and would look like this:

Content: Strongest part of your paper as it stands now. As you revise, try to clarify your focus. If your focus is your ambivalent feelings about Stevie's death, then let the reader feel that ambivalence throughout the paper.

Structure: Some of the flashback scenes feel confusing to me. Fiddle around with these sections to see if they can become smoother.

Readability/Mechanics: Some students felt there was too much technical biking language. Think about where it is most appropriate to use these terms.

Overall: Keep reworking this paper, shaping scenes, honing your line-by-line writing. Try to avoid being too moralistic. Right now this is an A paper, but I will expect continued changes if you submit it in your final portfolio.

At midterm, I try to offer as much response as possible since I have found that many freshmen have problems with calculating their grades. Perhaps students anticipate that because of the smaller class size and the collaborative nature of the course, their grades will be higher. Midterm is a good checkpoint for both the students and the instructors to stop and assess their progress in the course and to make expectations clear for the end of the term.

Midterm Self-Assessment

Most instructors wait until midterm to ask students to do some formal evaluating of themselves as writers. After seven weeks of college writing instruction, students are asked to reflect on what they have learned about their writing up to that point. This is the ideal time to hand over a great deal of responsibility to students, to ask them not just to assess their own writing but also to rate their good-faith participation in class, conferences, and peer-group work.

Students compose these midterm self-assessments in the form of a letter, in which they introduce, describe, and evaluate their collected writing as well as their progress and performance in my course. I tell students that since I read these introductory letters first, they should be written as persuasive essays. I urge students to be specific and to quote from their own writing. Here's the beginning of Joanna's midterm letter to me:

Dear Elizabeth,

This midterm portfolio is a reflection of myself as a writer and thinker. Included are my various voices and styles of writing as well as some papers reflecting on my values and ideals for writing. Each paper says something about who I am as an individual writer and who I am as part of this writing community. I would like you to think of my portfolio as pieces of a mirror: Each paper refracts parts of myself in different ways. . . .

Joanna's letter continues to discuss in detail each paper she has submitted, explaining why her two most successful papers are included and why she's left out others. In her midterm writing, Joanna includes one freewriting to show what she describes as her "most personal voice." She submits a process paper on an assignment because, she says, "the process of learning is integral to writing. It's not enough just to write something. I need to learn from the process as well." She includes an argumentative paper for formal evaluation because she says that this paper shows her "ability to deal with opinions outside of myself." Joanna's midterm letter, like much of my students' reflective writing, is much stronger than her submitted work. While I cannot grade Joanna on her self-assessment alone, I can fold that growing ability to be critical about her work into her midterm grade.

Not all students are as easily able to reflect on their learning processes at midterm. Some students submit writing that shows a minimal effort, and their accompanying letters also reveal a lack of understanding about either revision or reflective thought. The midterm letter of the average student writer might include such unsupported and global statements as these:

> This is an array of papers submitted for midterm evaluation. The first paper in my portfolio tells the reader something about the person who wrote it. The second paper in my portfolio is included because it has lots of personal feelings in it. The third portfolio piece shows how I am able to write leads.

My own responses to these vague statements will attempt to push the student toward considering *what* the reader will learn about the student and his writing skills by reading a particular paper and *why* a paper with "personal feelings" in it might be important to submit. While I do receive some standard midterm self-assessments, I always am challenged by those students whose ability to reflect on their learning exceeds their actual writing competence.

Midterm self-evaluation takes many forms among the writing staff, but whatever the format, all midterm evaluations are shaped by teachers' desires to get students to assume more responsibility and accountability for their work. UNH instructor Michelle Payne's midterm self-evaluation, for example, is a collaborative process, which takes place in a conference. Michelle and her students prepare for this conference by answering a series of questions about class participation, improvement in writing, understanding of their writing processes, and overall commitment to the course. Both the instructor and student assign a global rating (average, below, and above) to this written self-assessment and then confer about their responses. Because such careful student participation in the assessment process is built into the Freshman English course, students' final grades will be easy for both the instructor and student to anticipate.

End of the Line: Final Self-Evaluation Projects

... the growth of students' ability to exercise good judgment is harder to measure than the growth of their store of knowledge. It may even be impossible to measure.... (Gage 1986, 23)

Self-evaluation continues throughout the writing course and becomes a major part of the end-of-term evaluation as well. When I ask students to repeat the evaluation letter at the end of the semester, I find them better at it than they were at midterm. They have more to say because they've written more, and they have more to say because they've had more practice at being self-reflective and critical of their work. These final letters are a pleasure to read, mirroring the overall development of skills and attitudes about writing that many students achieve and affirming my own goals as a teacher for the course.

One important use for this final letter is to help me evaluate my own teaching by assessing which parts of my curriculum have been most helpful for my students and which assignments need rethinking. If, for example, few students include their researched essay as a final portfolio piece, I might reconsider how I go about teaching that essay the following semester. Reading through these letters makes me see not only that students do find new ways to talk about themselves as writers and learners, but also that as a teacher I am given new ways of thinking about my writing classroom.

The strongest recurring theme that emerged from my most recent set of freshman letters was that of "confidence"—many of my students stressed what Tina says: "I am feeling more and more confident each day that I continue to write." While I agree with John Gage that there is no "accurate" measure for self-critical growth in writing, students' thinking regarding their own development in confidence and in reflective "habits of thought" does serve as a yardstick for me as a teacher of writing.

Instructor Barbara Tindall's final self-assessment is based on another section from John Gage's essay, in which he suggests that "students improve as thinkers in small undetectable increments of change, brought about by the level of challenges they face..." (23). Barbara asks her students to identify five changes in their experience that have resulted from challenges encountered in her course. To describe these transformations, Barbara tells her students that they must "look closely," which requires detailed and specific analysis of their own writing abilities and habits. Finally, Barbara asks her students to gauge how these changes in attitudes and abilities might prove useful beyond the writing classroom.

Don Jones, another UNH instructor, has designed a final self-assessment project based on an assignment in Belanoff and Elbow (1989) for which students create a case study of themselves as writers. For this project, Don asks students to frame a letter, written either to incoming freshmen or to him, that considers (1) their writing abilities and processes before and during his course, (2) how their assumptions about writing have been affected (or not) by the freshman writing course, and (3) an analysis of a few pieces of their own writing in detail to show changes or development in both skills and attitudes. Students have written strong papers for this assignment, ones that Don tends to place in his "save" file. For example, in Lisa's letter to Don, she stresses the changes in her attitude about herself as a writer:

> I can honestly say that my attitude towards writing has changed drastically. I can also see changes in my actual writing, but those changes are not as apparent to me as those I have observed in my attitude toward writing. Before English 401 I thought of a writer as a person who wrote books for a profession. Writers were these people who had great skills, got paid to write, and what they wrote affected society. I saw writers as a step above me. Now I will give my definition of a writer since I've taken English 401: a person who writes.

One reason Lisa evolved in her attitude about writers and writing was an interview she conducted with her own mother as part of the course. She discusses this experience in her letter to Don:

> I was truly shown that anyone can be considered a writer when I did my interview paper on my mother where I say that "I have always seen her as the person who will love me no matter what I do, a parental figure who tells me what I should have done instead of what I did do. . . . After talking to my mother, I see that *she* is a writer too."

Lisa also draws from some of the course readings to show how her attitudes about writing have changed:

> Some of the qualities [of] a writer were introduced to me in William Stafford's essay, "A Way of Writing" [1990]. The first quality is that a writer must be willing to fail. If a writer is not willing to fail when he/she writes, then how will they know when they succeed? If he/she has never failed, they have nothing to compare success to. I experienced this when I was revising. I took my descriptive essay—which I had the urge to tuck away and deny that I [had] ever written—and decided to accept that the piece

was not one of my better papers and work with it. In the end, I saw my efforts as a success.

As a writer, Lisa shows how she has learned to take responsibility for her own ideas in writing and not lean on the authority of others. She states,

> Instead of looking towards a teacher to justify what I wanted to write, I justify it by the fact that it occurs to me.... That is not to say that a writer should be closed to the suggestions by others, but the writer should be happy with the final outcome. I have learned to write more for myself rather than a teacher in this course.

Assessment letters like this one afford students an opportunity to pause and reflect on what they have actually achieved in the short span of a writing course. Lisa's changes in her Freshman English course show that she is "at ease" with writing and feels that her own ideas are "justification" enough for a writing topic. Having such an understanding of her own needs and processes as a writer should serve her well when she writes for other audiences in different disciplines as well as when she writes for other purposes throughout her lifetime. Lisa's English course has fortified her to see that she is a writer and that her ideas matter.

Final Grades: Portfolios

My process of grading is best reflected in the changes I've made from using writing folders to instituting literacy portfolios in my freshman writing classes. When I began teaching Freshman English, students revised from twenty to twenty-five pages of their weekly writing and submitted these revised pieces in a folder for part of their final grade. While other evaluation considerations were and still are part of that grade — class and conference attendance, weekly writing exercises, class participation, the research paper, and reading journals — the writing folder accounted for 60 to 70 percent of the course grade. When I began teaching, I saw the writing folder mainly as a student's "collected" works and the evaluation of that folder as my function.

The major difference between the writing folder and the portfolio in Freshman English is a change of focus on who does the evaluating: I no longer view the teacher as the sole judge of student writing. I've added another layer: student assessment of their own work. This change is mainly seen in the portfolio letters, which provide guided accounts of students' learning processes and progress throughout the writing course. I now take into consideration students' metacognitive awareness of their writing processes and of their development during the semester as readers, writers, and critics; I invite them to write about their own growth. While I cannot assign a grade to this developmental aspect of the course, I know I value students' understanding in assembling, evaluating, and reflecting on their writing portfolios.

It was not until I closely read students' reflective letters that it occurred to me that students themselves should decide the principles around which they would assemble their portfolios. If a student wanted her portfolio to display improvement in revision, then revision might be the overriding portfolio theme; or if a student really wanted to show a range of genres attempted, then he might include in the portfolio certain unfinished pieces in particular genres that didn't work as well as some that did. When I finally let go of "quantity" (number of pages) requirements and allowed students to describe the "quality" of their writing and learning in Freshman English from their own perspectives, I was surprised and encouraged by the content and arrangement of their portfolios and by the reflective letters that analyzed their learning and growth.

The first time I tried this more open portfolio concept, I allowed it to count as the only grade in the course. There are two main reasons for my retreating from this approach. One is that educators have been so quick to use portfolios for assessment purposes that there hasn't been enough exploration of alternative options for them. The other is that students scramble too much at the end of the term to improve their portfolios when it's the only grade assigned—I now prefer steady work to be submitted and revised throughout the course (in "Opening the Closed Portfolio" [1992] I give a close account of what I learned from this experiment with open portfolios).

My written response to students' final portfolios is much more abbreviated than at midterm, since by then I am out of the feedback loop that leads to final assessment. My experience with extensive end-of-term comments is that they go unread; students at this point are mainly interested in their grades, not in ways of improving their work. Therefore, I write a short letter (one page, two abbreviated paragraphs) to each student emphasizing one strength I feel he or she has shown in the portfolio and at least one area to continue to work on. The portfolio in my course still constitutes over half of the entire grade (70 percent), but I feel as if I am now taking into account students' self-assessment and critical understandings of writing when I assign final grades.

Other instructors have different guidelines and weighting procedures for final portfolios. Sixty percent of the final grade for instructor Bruce Ballenger is based on twenty pages of portfolio writing while the other 40 percent comes from class participation and graded assignments. There are four things that Bruce looks for in grading the final portfolios: ideas, range, design, and language. In his portfolio instructions, Bruce advises his students to revise everything submitted and to pay particular attention to mechanics and spelling, areas that he has not previously graded. Explicit guidelines, like Bruce's, for assembling and submitting portfolios are helpful to students and instructors alike.

All instructors make it clear from the outset that while Freshman English is primarily a writing course, many other factors are included in the final course assessment. One type of student who fares poorly in my Freshman English course comes in with well-developed writing skills and assumes that she can rest on this expertise for the entire course. Unless a student demonstrates a willingness to participate in the writing community by meeting deadlines, risking some new approaches to revision, being a responsible peer-group member, and reflecting on her own learning, she will not earn a grade higher than C, no matter what the initial quality of her writing. I make it clear from the start that Freshman English is designed to introduce students to ways of thinking, reading, and writing within the academy and that growth in critical abilities and steady improvement in skills are what I evaluate in the course, not innate talent.

Assigning Grades: In the Final Analysis

Grading student work in my introductory writing course is no longer the fumbling procedure of my first years of teaching. Now that I've invited students into the evaluation process by emphasizing self-assessment and self-reflection, grading includes not only my subjective responses to student texts but students' evaluations of those texts as well. Bringing students into the evaluation process has helped to develop in them more tutored abilities at reading, responding, and reflecting on writing.

Yet, in the final analysis, I am the one who assigns the grades. And when I first take home that thick pile of student portfolios, I always wonder if I will really get through them all. Practically speaking, I first grade the portfolios of those who have had the most trouble with my course; I save for last what I perceive to be my best portfolios (I am always really surprised). I prefer to spread my grading evenly over a week's time, reading a specific number of portfolios each day, but many instructors undertake marathon grading sessions, often finishing over fifty portfolios in two days.

Evaluation as Acts of Reading, Response, and Reflection

In evaluating final portfolios, I look for surprises and changes, for over-all improvement in the quality of students' revisions, and for a range of writing that displays several styles or genres. Finally, I consider students' over-all growth in the course, and I make that assessment by examining their own reflections on their strengths and weaknesses in their portfolio letter. My outstanding portfolios now seem even better than when I used only writing folders, which included neither self-assessments nor reflections. Each semester some students get totally immersed in putting together a portfolio that not only will satisfy my course requirements but will show other aspects of their writing or literacies as well. Many devote a great deal of time and energy to revising every paper for their final portfolio, creating decorative covers, and organizing the contents carefully for their readers. Such students view the portfolio as more than an assessment tool; they see it as a mirror of who they are as literate readers, writers, and thinkers. The idea of a portfolio that displays multiple facets of students' literacies is one that many students understand as being far more valuable than taking an exit exam or averaging individually graded papers. Portfolios hold great potential for students and teachers alike, since we all have much to learn from them as we continue to try out different portfolio practices.

My evaluation procedures have evolved through what Donald Schön (1983) has called "reflection-in-action," whereby teachers learn to inquire rigorously into their own practices and institute change. Just as students' writing evolves through practice, teachers' evaluating skills improve over time. When we sit down to grade our students' work, we are, in part, grading ourselves. The process of evaluation invites us to reflect on what we have learned about ourselves, our classroom practices, and our students. We ask ourselves questions about the quality of our teaching during the semester. What did our students seem to learn? What parts of our students' writing portfolios best reflect overall writing improvement? Why did some students fail? What did our students have to say about the value to themselves of their own writing? What are the types of writing that students valued least, and for what reasons? What ideas for changes in classroom curriculum emerge from reading our students' portfolios?

Evaluation is a process. We get better at it as we go along. Instead of dreading it, avoiding it, or muddling through it, I've come to see this part of teaching writing as an opportunity to revise. As my teaching changes, so does my evaluation process. I have not got it quite right yet. Maybe that shows more growth than if I had.

References

Anson, Chris. 1989. "Response Styles and Ways of Knowing." In *Writing and Response: Theory, Practice and Research*, edited by Chris Anson, 332–66. Urbana, IL.: National Council of Teachers of English.

Belanoff, Pat. 1991. "The Myths of Assessment." *Journal of Basic Writing* 10(1):54–66.

Belanoff, Pat, and Peter Elbow. 1989. *A Community of Writers: A Workshop Course in Writing.* New York: Random House.

Chiseri-Strater, Elizabeth. 1992. "College Sophomores Reopen the Closed Portfolio." In *Portfolio Portraits*, edited by Donald Graves and Bonnie Sunstein, 61–72. Portsmouth, NH: Heinemann.

Gage, John. 1986. "Why Write." In *The Teaching of Writing: Eighty-Fifth National Society for the Study of Education*, edited by Anthony Petrosky and David Bartholomae. Chicago: The University of Chicago Press.

Murray, Donald. 1968. *A Writer Teaches Writing.* Boston: Houghton Mifflin.

Schön, Donald. 1983. *The Reflective Practitioner: How Professionals Think in Action.* New York: Basic Books.

Stafford, William. 1990. "A Way of Writing." In *To Compose*, edited by Thomas Newkirk, 17–20. Portsmouth, NH: Heinemann.

Zemelman, Steven, and Harvey Daniels. 1988. *A Community of Writers: Teaching Writing in the Junior and Senior High School.* Portsmouth, NH: Heinemann.

Recommended Reading

Work in the field of composition has grown exponentially in the past decade. No one can follow it all anymore. Any list of recommended reading, therefore, rests equally on ignorance and personal preference. With that disclaimer, listed below are books and articles that can serve as a starting point for teachers interested in composition teaching and scholarship.

Anson, Chris, ed. 1989. *Writing and Response: Theory, Practice and Research.* Urbana, IL: National Council of Teachers of English. An outstanding collection of essays devoted to theoretical and practical issues involved in reading student texts.

Ballenger, Bruce, and Barry Lane. 1989. *Discovering the Writer Within: 40 Days to More Imaginative Writing.* Cincinatti, OH: Writer's Digest. This book is filled with exercises designed to foster risk taking and imaginative writing and has been very useful in our program.

Bartholomae, David, and Anthony Petrosky, eds. *Facts, Artifacts, and Counterfacts: Theory and Method for a Reading and Writing Course.* Portsmouth, NH: Boynton/Cook. Presents in thorough detail the rationale and method for a reading/writing course for college students unfamiliar with academic discourse. Based on work at the University of Pittsburgh, this book has influenced a number of composition courses.

Britton, James. 1980. "Shaping at the Point of Utterance." In *Prospect and Retrospect: Selected Essays of James Britton,* edited by Gordon Pradl, 139–45. Portsmouth, NH: Boynton/Cook, 1982. A classic essay on the composing process by one of the most humane and penetrating scholars in the field.

Brooke, Robert. 1987. "Underlife and Writing Instruction." *College Composition and Communication* 38:141–53. Brooke, drawing on the work of Erving Goffman, looks at the kinds of resistance that teachers face from students. The essay helps us understand the way institutions push individuals to resist the roles they are expected to take.

Chiseri-Strater, Elizabeth. 1990. *Academic Literacies: The Public and Private Discourse of University Students*. Portsmouth, NH: Boynton/Cook. An ethnographic study that shows the various literacy demands that universities place on students. A fine example of case study research.

Coles, Robert. 1990. *The Call of Stories: Stories and the Moral Imagination*. Boston: Houghton Mifflin. An eloquent account of the ways in which stories can affect people's lives, and an antidote for the pretentiousness of much current work in critical theory.

Elbow, Peter. 1973. *Writing Without Teachers*. New York: Oxford University Press. This book, one of the most influential ever written on composition, introduced the widely used practices of freewriting and peer response groups.

Emig, Janet. 1983. *The Web of Meaning: Essays on Writing, Teaching, Learning, and Thinking*. Edited by Dixie Goswami and Maureen Butler. Portsmouth, NH: Boynton/Cook. A collection of very influential essays that helped establish the theoretical underpinnings of writing process work.

Fulwiler, Toby, ed. 1987. *The Journal Book*. Portsmouth, NH: Boynton/Cook. A collection of articles that show very specifically how informal journal writing can help students across the curriculum. Filled with examples and teaching ideas.

Graves, Richard L., ed. 1990. *Rhetoric ana Composition: A Sourcebook for Teachers and Writers*. Third edition. Portsmouth, NH: Boynton/Cook. A wide-ranging collection of some of the most important current work in the field, drawing heavily from *College Composition and Communication* and *College English*.

Knoblauch, C. H., and Lil Brannon. 1984. *Rhetorical Traditions and the Teaching of Writing*. Portsmouth, NH: Boynton/Cook. A vigorous and controversial book that contains excellent chapters on responding to writing.

Murray, Donald. 1984. *A Writer Teaches Writing*. Second edition. Boston: Houghton Mifflin. A complete rewrite of the 1968 edition, this version is especially good on Murray's theory of responsive teaching.

Newkirk, Thomas, ed. 1990. *To Compose: Teaching Writing in High School and College*. Second edition. Portsmouth, NH: Heinemann. This collection includes important essays on the writing process by Linda Flower, Sondra Perl, and Donald Murray. Also including case studies and essays on teaching, it is more focused on classroom teaching than the Graves collection.

Peterson, Linda. 1991. "Gender and the Autobiographical Essay: Research Perspectives, Pedagogical Practices." *College Composition and Communication* 42:170–83. This study finds clear gender differences in students' performances in the autobiographical writing so often required in freshman writing courses.

Rule, Rebecca, and Susan Wheeler. 1992. *Creating the Story: Guides for Writers.* Portsmouth, NH: Heinemann. A series of practical exercises that will help demystify the craft of fiction writing—and that can help nonfiction writers as well.

Rose, Mike. 1989. *Lives on the Boundary.* New York: Penguin. A moving account of students living on the margins of schools and universities. Drawing on his own struggles on the margins, Rose shows the kind of teaching that is needed—and why universities often fail to provide it.

Shaughnessy, Mina. 1977. *Errors and Expectations: A Guide for the Teacher of Basic Writing.* New York: Oxford University Press. A major study of the errors that underprepared students make in college. Shaughnessy shows that these errors are the logical products of intelligent people unfamiliar with the conventions of written language.

Stafford, William. 1978. *Writing the Australian Crawl.* Ann Arbor: University of Michigan Press. A poet describes his processes of writing in such a way that it all seems possible.

Tobin, Lad. 1993. *Writing Relationships: What Really Happens in the Composition Class.* Portsmouth, NH: Boynton/Cook. According to Tobin, scholars and practitioners have not talked openly about the personal relationships—the tension, resistance, competition, confusion of roles—that exist in the composition classroom. With his own classroom as laboratory, Tobin candidly begins this discussion.

Zinnser, William. 1990. *On Writing Well: An Informal Guide to Writing Nonfiction.* Fourth edition. New York: HarperCollins. One of the most engaging guides to writing I know, filled with wonderful examples from the best practitioners of nonfiction—and from Zinnser himself.

Contributors

Bruce Ballenger has taught writing nine years at UNH, where he is now earning his doctorate. His books include *The Lobster Almanac* (Globe Pequot Press), *Discovering the Writer Within* (Writer's Digest), and *The Curious Researcher* (Allyn & Bacon), a text on writing the college research paper. His essays have appeared in the *Boston Globe*, the *Hartford Courant*, *The Christian Science Monitor*, and other newspapers and magazines.

Elizabeth Chiseri-Strater is an assistant professor of English at the University of Illinois–Chicago. She has published essays on a variety of literacy issues, most recently on portfolios and the evaluation of writing. Her book *Academic Literacies: The Public and Private Discourse of University Students* was published by Heinemann–Boynton/Cook in 1991.

Jane Harrigan is an associate professor and the director of the journalism program at UNH. She has written an editing textbook, *The Editorial Eye*, published in 1993 by St. Martin's Press. Her book *Read All About It!* traces one day's operations at the *Boston Globe*. She previously worked as an Associated Press reporter and was the managing editor of the *Concord Monitor*, a daily newspaper in New Hampshire.

Thomas Newkirk is a professor of English at UNH, where he teaches in the Freshman English program that for four years he directed. He is also the director of the New Hampshire Writing Program, a summer institute for public school teachers. He has published work on a wide range of topics ranging from beginning literacy to the writing process of college students. His most recent publication is *Listening In: What Children Say About Books (and other things)*, published by Heinemann.

Donna Qualley, a former composition instructor, is currently a doctoral candidate in reading and writing instruction at the University of New Hampshire. She teaches Freshman English, conducts in-service courses and workshops for teachers, teaches in the English department's Summer Studies

Contributors

Program, and waitresses at the local lobster restaurant. She is currently coediting *Writing and Reading (in) the Academy* with Patricia Sullivan.

Rebecca Rule taught at UNH off and on from 1978, when she was a teaching assistant, until 1991, when she retired at age thirty-seven to write full-time. In 1992, she published two books: a collection of short stories, *Wood Heat*, from Nightshade Press of Troy, Maine, and *Creating the Story: Guides for Writers*, cowritten with Susan Wheeler, from Heinemann. Her work has appeared in *Yankee*, *The Christian Science Monitor*, *Country Living*, and literary magazines. She received the 1992 Emerging Writer Award from the New Hampshire Writers and Publishers Project and is books editor for the *Concord Monitor*.

Patricia Sullivan is an assistant professor at UNH, where she teaches American Literature, Popular Culture, and Modern Poetry in addition to her work in the writing program and the doctoral program in composition and literature. Her research has focused on the way in which graduate students are taught (or not taught) the conventions of academic scholarship, and she has also explored the relationship between critical theory and composition teaching and research. She has recently coedited *Methods and Methodologies in Composition Research*, published by SIU Press, and she is completing an edited collection on writing in the academy.

Susan Wheeler is the coauthor of *Creating the Story: Guides for Writers*, which she wrote with Rebecca Rule. Her fiction has appeared in *The North American Review*, *Willow Springs*, *The Bradford Review*, *The Lyndon Review*, and other literary magazines. She teaches in the English department of the University of New Hampshire and at the Molasses Pond Summer Writers Workshop in Maine.

Also available from Heinemann-Boynton/Cook. . .

■■

Writing Relationships
What Really Happens in the Composition Class
Lad Tobin, Boston College

In the ideal composition class of the 1990s, everything seems to go smoothly: all learning is happily collaborative, all authority is successfully decentered, and all students are part of a conflict-free community of writers. No student is ever bored or boring, angry or provocative, and no teacher ever responds in ways that are self-serving, subjective, or idiosyncratic. Since most books and articles on the teaching of writing describe the ideal as if it were the norm, many teachers feel embarrassed by what does or doesn't happen in their own classrooms -- and envious of what they believe is happening down the hall.

Writing Relationships goes beyond the idealized talk about what should happen in "process" teaching to examine what really does happen in the day-to-day interactions of one classroom: competition and cooperation, peer pressure and identification, resistance and sexual tension. This book is about how interpersonal relationships -- between teacher and student, student and student, and teacher and teacher -- shape the ways that teachers read and grade their students' writing and the ways students respond, or don't respond, to their teacher's suggestions.

Through narratives and case studies, the author demonstrates that much of the tension, confusion, and anxiety associated with a process approach is inevitable and, in part, desirable. But this book is more than a series of failure stories: the author gives teachers specific and useful ideas and strategies for * reading student essays * responding to student writing * leading a discussion of an essay * running a writing workshop * grading * setting up peer and co-authoring groups * conferencing * and publishing in the field.

Writing Relationships is a useful resource for college composition instructors and -- since the interpersonal tensions described in the book operate in similar ways with younger students -- for secondary and middle school teachers as well. Though written primarily for practitioners, the book's solid grounding in psychoanalytic, feminist, and literary theory will also interest scholars in the field. Combining autobiography, classroom research, critical theory, and pedagogical methods, *Writing Relationships* is a rare academic book -- useful, readable, and entertaining.

Boynton/Cook   0-86709-322-6   Paper

■■

Thirteen Weeks

A Guide to Teaching College Writing

Irvin Y. Hashimoto, Whitman College

The title, *Thirteen Weeks,* refers with ironic intent to the typical first semester college writing course and the fanciful belief and expectation that students who are non-writers -- through no fault of their own -- can become writers if they take the thirteen-week cure. Hashimoto takes the position that what's expected ought to be done, but that the usual teaching approaches hinder rather than help getting anything useful done at all.

Thirteen Weeks is not a ''how-to'' book or a book promoting some new notion of ''composition theory.'' It's a book about teaching and thinking about teaching: How do we decide what to do in class? How do we evaluate, weigh, prioritize everybody else's advice? How do we begin to think about classroom lessons that are more than lectures, talks, sharings, gropings, and predictable mainstream exhortations, like ''Simplify, simplify, simplify'' or ''Know who you're writing for'' or ''Prewrite!'' or ''Show, don't tell?''

The book contains discussions of priorities, assignment-making, evaluation, and mechanics, and it includes sample lessons, assignments, and even a syllabus; but the author is more interested in getting teachers to do things for themselves, to develop their own methods and materials, to push aside, question, modify, trim, and evaluate traditional, expected, accepted, and conventional wisdom. He wants them to discover what else is out there to do, test their own limitations as teachers and resuscitators, and explore what it means to be ''academic'' in the best sense of the word.

Boynton/Cook   0-86709-261-0   Paper